MISSIONARY THEOLOGY:
Foundations in Development

Edmond J. Dunn

Foreword by
Richard P. McBrien

University Press
of America™

Library of Congress Catalog Card Number: 80-67259

"I put no value on my life if only I can finish my race and complete the
service to which I have been assigned by the Lord Jesus, bearing witness to
the Gospel of God's grace."

Acts of the Apostles 20, 24

Dedicated to my brother, Paul,
who, in his own special way,
has truly been a missionary of
the Good News.

ACKNOWLEDGEMENTS

I offer a special note of thanks to my bishop, Gerald O'Keefe, of Davenport, who has supported me throughout this project. I thank my professors, Richard P. McBrien, Max L. Stackhouse, Gabriel J. Fackre, and the late Gerald R. Cragg, whose critical scrutiny helped me clarify my own theological position. I am grateful to the Rector, faculty and staff of Pope John XXIII National Seminary and especially my dear friend, Walter Flaherty, all of whom offered me hospitality and help without reservation. I appreciate the assistance given me by the administration of St. Ambrose College, Davenport, Iowa, the untiring work of my typist, Janet Minor, and the invaluable help given me by Mary Jo McDonald in the final days of preparation. I thank Frank Wessling of the Davenport Catholic Messenger for his critical reading of the text, and finally, I thank Teresita Hernandez whose encouragement and suggestions have urged me on to what I hope is a successful conclusion of this mission.

Grateful acknowledgement is made to the following publishers for permission to use material under their copyright.

American Press, Inc.: THE DOCUMENTS OF VATICAN II, Abbott-Gallagher edition. Copyright ©1966. Reprinted with permission of American Press, Inc., New York.

Basic Books: PYRAMIDS OF SACRIFICE by Peter Berger. Copyright ©1974. Reprinted by permission of Basic Books, New York.

Beacon Press: ETHICS AND THE URBAN ETHOS by Max Stackhouse. Copyright ©1972. Reprinted by permission of Beacon Press, Boston.

Doubleday & Company, Inc.: ON BEING A CHRISTIAN by Hans Kung. Copyright ©1976. Reprinted by permission of Doubleday & Company, Inc., New York.

Harper & Row: TOMORROW'S CHILD by Rubem Alves. Copyright ©1972. Reprinted with permission of Harper & Row, Publishers, Inc., New York.

Used by permission of Orbis Books, Maryknoll, New York:
THE COMMUNITY CALLED CHURCH by Juan Luis Segundo. Copyright ©1973.
THE LIBERATION OF THEOLOGY by Juan Luis Segundo. Copyright ©1976.
THEOLOGY FOR A NOMAD CHURCH by Hugo Assmann. Copyright ©1976.
THE THEOLOGY OF LIBERATION by Gustavo Gutierrez. Copyright ©1973.

Oxford University Press, Inc., SOCIAL CHANGE AND HISTORY by Robert Nisbet. Copyright ©1969. Reprinted by permission of Oxford University Press, Inc., New York.

Used by permission of The Seabury Press, New York:
GOD OF THE OPPRESSED by James H. Cone. Copyright ©1975 by the Seabury Press, Inc.

"Liberation Movements in Theology" by Gustavo Gutierrez from JESUS CHRIST AND HUMAN FREEDOM, Concilium Vol. 93 edited by Edward Schillebeeckx and Bas Van Iersel. Copyright ©1974 by McGraw-Hill Inc., and Stichting Concilium.

"Capitalism-Socialism: A Theological Crux" by Juan Luis Segundo from THE MYSTICAL AND POLITICAL DIMENSION OF THE CHRISTIAN FAITH edited by Claude Geffre and Gustavo Gutierrez, Concilium Vol. 96. Copyright ©1974 by Herder and Herder Inc. and Stichting Concilium.

TABLE OF CONTENTS

PART THREE: REFORMULATION AND ITS IMPLICATIONS

CHAPTER SIX

xi

F O R E W O R D

Edmond Dunn is not simply raking over old
ground in this foundational work. On the contrary,
he moves the discussion of mission theology forward and thereby makes a discernible contribution
to contemporary ecclesiology.

Pursuing a solidly systematic course, Dunn
recognizes that our understanding of mission is
always a function of our understanding of the
Church itself and of the ways in which God commun-
icates with the world, both through the Church and
apart from it. He argues that a theological shift
has occurred in our time which requires a reformulation of the traditional concept of mission. The
Church is no longer perceived as an end in itself.
The Church and the Kingdom of God are not the
same. Christians must acknowledge, and learn from,
the saving presence and action of God outside the
borders of their own communities of faith (the
"signs of the times"). Accordingly, the success or
failure of missionary outreach must be measured by
standards other than increases in membership
alone.

But there have been political, economic, social, and cultural developments as well. The emergence of the Third World churches clearly parallels the emergence of Third World nations. Consequently, the theological method employed in this
study is one of correlation: the Christian message
and fact are read always in light of, and in relation to, the various nontheological elements which
are a constitutive part of the present missionary
situation, and these are, in turn, interpreted
ecclesiologically.

Although some readers will undoubtedly resist
Edmond Dunn's decision to give so central a place
to the concept of development, rather than liberation, they owe it to the author to hear him out

and to give the same careful consideration to his arguments as he has to theirs.

This is no regressively conservative work. Drawing upon his own substantial experience as a Papal Volunteer in Peru and as a theologian educated in an unusual ecumenical context (his doctorate was earned in a program jointly sponsored and administered by Catholic Boston College and Protestant Andover-Newton Theological School), he lays a foundation for a missionary theology that is at once personal and political, liberating and responsible, self-critical and hopeful.

Richard P. McBrien
University of Notre Dame

INTRODUCTION

A crisis has developed in the missionary endeavor of the Christian Church. Formerly, a church's very strength and vigor were determined by the extent of its missionary program. Today the questions arise, "Why missionaries?" "What are they supposed to do?" Or, simply, "Why missions?" Missionary theory has become a "quaestio disputa." This is evident in the ambiguity of the relevant discussions and documents of the World Council of Churches as well as in the struggle over the missionary document at Vatican II. The crisis is further underlined by the inability of the Synod of Bishops, during the 1974 meeting in Rome, to come to an agreement on the direction and scope of evangelization and its relation to human liberation and development. Many missionaries who have dedicated their lives to work in the "foreign mission field" feel that they have been betrayed by certain contemporary theologians and church leaders.

It is clear that theological reasons do not account entirely for the crisis of missions. Political and economic shifts, social and cultural developments have had a deep impact on the missionary situation. The era of colonialism, which was also the time of the Church's great missionary expansion, has for the most part come to an end. But political independence has not necessarily brought socioeconomic and cultural emancipation. Rising expectations, frustated by what the developing nations see as neo-colonialism, are often accompanied by anti-Western and anti-Church sentiments and movements. Even within the churches in these young nations, the emergence of local leadership has challenged excessive outside interference. There is, at the same time a growing awareness of the oneness of the human family, of an interdependence among nations and peoples, especially on the global questions of food, population, ecology and energy. Moreover, rapid trans-

portation and communication, along with what some
have called the "dechristianization" of the West,
make "foreign missions" or "overseas missions"
almost a meaningless label.

The primary thrust of the present study is
theological or, more specifically, ecclesiological. The theological reasons for the crisis in
the missionary endeavor of the Church will be
examined. Then a theological and ecclesiological
base for refocusing the Church's missionary activity toward full participation in the integral
development of persons and peoples of the world
will be outlined. At the same time, the "nontheological" factors mentioned above are taken into
consideration. The theological method to be employed here, basically the method of correlation,
allows and even demands that due consideration be
given the nontheological factors that contribute
to the present situation of missions.

On the one hand, it will be argued that the
underlying crisis of the missionary endeavor of
the Church is theological. It stems from an inadequate understanding of some of the basic tenets
of fundamental theology as displayed in both traditional and modern formulations of missionary
theology. A critique of these formulations will
clear the ground for a reconstructed theology of
missions. On the other hand, in light of the present situation, it will be argued that this reconstructed theology of missions can best be
expressed under the aegis of development. The
increasing gap between rich and poor nations, the
realization that technology does not necessarily
bring with it humanization, and the growing awareness among men and women everywhere that they
should share the responsibility for shaping the
world, make it imperative for the Church to focus
its missionary endeavors on integral human
development.

Although the term development has fallen out of popular favor recently, especially among the advocates of liberation theology, a case will be made for its continued use. Once freed from a narrow, exclusive identification with economic growth, the term development becomes the most comprehensive and "ecumenical" term to designate the whole range of changes that must take place in individuals, institutions and societies as they move toward a condition regarded as more fully human. The term development does not in itself specify in particular instances by what means or at what pace this change may take place. In other words, it is less specific yet more rational than a theory of revolution, and more comprehensive than a theory of technological progress or modernization.

The term development, as it will be employed here, is closely related to the concept of humanization. Development has been chosen rather than humanization, however, because the former is so deeply ingrained in the vocabulary of international discussion at all levels and lends itself well to broad dialogue. Development cannot be limited to economic and technological advancement, but neither can these factors be realistically ignored. Although humanization is the ultimate goal of development, it does not carry with it the pragmatic connotations of development.

Liberationists are correct in insisting that the term development, in contrast to liberation, is not immediately identifiable with one of the great biblical themes. But it does lend itself to theological elaboration. Christian men and women dedicated to the overall development project glimpse in their efforts a participation in God's work of creating and re-creating, of forming and re-forming the earth and its people. They presume to perceive "something more" in their work for integral human development--signs of God's saving presence, God's revelation.

Finally, in their attempt to establish a more just, equitable and peaceful world, they sense elements of lasting value. Caught up in faith and hope with the promise of a coming Kingdom, they struggle to understand the relationship of the present and the past with what is to come. Consciously claiming that they have been "called out" to continue the work of Jesus Christ, Christians attempt to locate their community and its mission in relationship to the present world with its need for integral, saving development and the future Kingdom.

Development, therefore, does have a relationship to the theological concepts of revelation, eschatology and ecclesiology, and yet it still serves as a broadly accepted term in nontheological discussion. It can, therefore, provide a bridge for dialogue and cooperation between the Church and the rest of the world.

In assessing the theoretical reasons for the crisis in missions, the following process will be followed: The historical background and theological underpinnings which prepared the Church for "the great era of missions" will be sketched in broad outline and then contrasted with the present situation and the important "theological shift" that has taken place in Christian theology. This "theological shift" affects the entire theological enterprise because it involves the very basic tenets of revelation and eschatology, which in turn affect ecclesiology.

In the question of revelation, this shift is characterized by a move from what might be called a type of biblical or doctrinal "positivism" to a position which emphasizes the availability of God to everyone within the range of every-day human experience. The eschatological shift involves seeing the present conditioned and illuminated by the future Kingdom of God.

Following from this shift in the interpretation of revelation and eschatology, ecclesiology
is cast in a new light. Formerly the perspective
was "church centered," that is, the Church, often
identified with the Kingdom of God, was conceived
as the ordinary or sole means of salvation. Now
the Church is conceived to be, among other things,
a prophetic people, a servant community called to
announce, embody and facilitate the coming of
God's Kingdom. It is in light of the "theological shift" and the present situation that an outline for a reconstructed missionary theology as a
theology of development will be presented.

It will be argued that the missionary challenge today can be understood in a new and enlightened way through a reinterpretation and,
indeed, a restatement of the traditional threefold
mission of the Church. Kerygma will be formulated
in a more dialogic manner, koinonia from a more
demonstrative orientation, and diakonia more as
development.

All three aspects of the mission of the Church
will be treated. Dialogue will focus especially
on the relationship of this community that pro-
fesses the Lordship of Jesus to other world religions and ideologies. Demonstration will insist
on a definition of Church which emphasizes the
communal celebration of this faith in word and
sacrament and the church's abiding call to the reform of its own institutions. This internal life
of the community must not only demonstrate to
those outside the meaning and value of the Kingdom
which it claims to signify, but serve as a source
of strength for the external, prophetic demonstration which the community is called upon to make.

Special emphasis, however, will be given to
the diaconal or servant aspect of the Church's
mission under the term development. The urgency
in the world today to bridge the gap between the

so-called developed and developing nations deems this emphasis necessary. Approaching the concept of development from an ecclesial-diaconal perspective gives it a firm theological basis and establishes it as an integral dimension of the Church's mission. In other words, the main goal of the missionary endeavor in earlier times was to gather and maintain within the Church as great a number of people as possible in order to "save their souls." Diaconal work or human development was justified only from the point of view of "pre-evangelization:" "Feed them so you can preach to them; teach them to read so they can find salvation in the biblical word." Now the focus must be shifted to the integral development of persons and peoples. This involves, as a part of the eschatological shift mentioned earlier, a reinterpretation of the concept of salvation.

In spite of this emphasis, the Church's mission of evangelization is not invalidated. Indeed, the theology of integral human development includes the liberating message and witness of Jesus. Founded upon its commitment to make the Good News of Jesus Christ available to all, and anxious to be a sign of hope for others, the Church is confident that through dialogue and demonstration some will see that their true vocation lies within the sacramental community and will join in the Church's eschatological mission of announcing, embodying and facilitating the coming Kingdom.

An attempt will be made to show that development, as an integral aspect of the mission of the Church, must be at the same time personal and political, liberating and responsible, self-critical and hopeful. A missionary theology as a theology of development must critically assess and embrace, and yet not be absorbed by, such current movements as political theology, the theology of revolution and liberation theology.

The manner of critically assessing these contemporary theologies will be as follows: After establishing a definition of theology in light of the theological shift discussed above, it will be shown that many who have attempted to formulate the theology of the Church's witness and role in the world, whether this formulation comes under the designation of politics, liberation or revolution, display a certain methodological naivete. Critical review of their works reveals that many modern theologians who appear to be liberal, in so many ways, make uncritical assertions or presumptions on the level of fundamental theology and thereby become ambiguous in the specifically theological character of their work. This is especially true in their understanding of that most basic element in any theology--revelation.

To be more specific, among the so-called theologians of revolution and liberation such as Shaull, Alves, Segundo, Gutierrez, Laurentin, and Cone, there is, to a greater or lesser degree, an understanding of revelation which can be termed "positivistic." As these theologians work out their theological positions, revelation becomes a mere presupposition, taken for granted as having been given, and posited in some source such as the Bible or the official doctrine of the Church. Revelation is contained in these "sources" and available for examination as if it were as concrete and verifiable as a contemporary documentary. On the other hand, some writers on liberation have moved beyond or relativized the traditional Christian understanding of revelation to the point that, by their own admission, they no longer express themselves from within the Christian Church.

Many of these same theologians, while critical of any theology of development or political theology because of its supposed ideological bias, precisely because of their own questionable eschatological stance, slip from theology into ideology. According to some, the Kingdom can be established here on earth through human effort. For others, the revolutionary fervor has waned and a certain passivity has set in.

Political theology, which has arisen primarily in Germany in reaction to the "privatization" of faith and the existential understanding of eschatological salvation, has much to contribute to a theology of development. The work of Metz and Moltmann, especially, will be referred to in focusing our development theology. And yet, by itself, this political theology is hindered by an identification with a theology of politics by some, and with the charge of being abstract, theoretical and uncommitted by others. Moreover, it is based on an analysis of the "post-industrial" West, and more specifically the German situation, and therefore is somewhat parochial in the eyes of Third World theologians. Like liberation theology, it is strongly biblical in its vocabulary and does not lend itself readily to broad ecumenical dialogue with non-Christians and non-believers.

Once these various theologies have been examined critically on the basis of revelation and eschatology, the outline for a missionary theology as a theology of development will be constructed, pointing out the specific contribution which the Church can and should make to the broader task of world development. Finally, the ecclesial structures necessary to facilitate such a reformulated missionary rationale will be suggested.

CHAPTER ONE

COLONIALISM AND MISSIONARY ACTIVITY

THE AGE OF EXPANSION: ITS ROOT AND REASONS

It is impossible to understand the current crisis in the missionary activity of the Church without considering the question of colonialism, or, as many today would prefer to call it, imperialism. Colonial domination came about as the result of the expansion of Western Europe. During the sixteenth century, the great age of discovery, Europe burst its bonds and began to impose its military, political and economic powers upon the whole inhabited world. For the Christian Church, this expansion opened new horizons of missionary activity in a dramatic way, enkindling the desire to bring the true Gospel to heretofore unknown peoples. There was even speculation that contact could be made with unknown Christian churches which were believed to be in existence in those far-off lands. A world-wide alliance of Christians was envisioned that would be able to break the menacing power of Islam.[1]

The missionary surge took place, it should be remembered during an era when "Europe was the faith and the faith was Europe." Although there were serious internal divisions, "Christian Europe" still represented a limited and fairly well-defined part of the inhabited world. In spite of divisions caused by the Reformation and the wars of religion which followed, Christian values and legitimation were claimed by diverse political factions. At least from a broad sociological point of view, Europe was a self-contained entity, barely conscious of the existence of the rest of the world.[2] It is true that there was the constant pressure of Islam on it borders, and yet even this

9

provided a barrier against contact with the other great religions of the East.

During this age of discovery and expansion, the Church sent forth missionaries steeped in European culture that was Christian and a Christianity that was intimately bound to European culture. This new surge of missionary activity was, as Lesslie Newbigin says, "...part of that explosion of human spirit which has carried the debris of Western Christendom into every corner of the world to shake the ancient structures of society and create new forms of thought, of personal and family life, of commerce and statecraft."[3]

The interrelationship between colonialism and expanded missionary activity can be approached from two points of view. The first, which I have designated the "accompanist" perspective, suggests that it was on the wings of colonialism that the Christian message spread to the ends of the earth. Christian missionaries merely accompanied the explorers, merchants, imperialists. The second approach, which I have called the "matrix" perspective, would insist that Christianity itself was not the mere accompanist of colonial expansion but indeed its very matrix. We shall look first at the "accompanist" perspective.

1. Christian Missionaries: The "Accompanists" of Colonialism

Portugal and Spain, with their control of sea routes, took the lead in early explorations. Portugal began with probes along the west coast of Africa. Soon its ships rounded the tip of Africa and sailed east to Asia. The Spaniards went to Central and South America; the Portuguese to Brazil. Later the English, French and Dutch went to North America. Missionaries, traveling with the explorers and traders or following closely after them, were faced for the first time with the problems of religious and cultural diversity on a world-wide scale. Most missionaries, understandably ignorant of the cultures they encountered, approached them with pessimism and mistrust. In fact, their theology made it very difficult for them not to disdain the non-Christian cultures and religions in these new lands.

Beginning with the papal privileges granted to Portugal in the mid-fifteenth century--to peacefully occupy all lands of the unbelievers that might be discovered along the west coast of Africa --successive kings of Portugal and Spain were endowed by the Pope with the right of patronage in regard to both colonial and missionary enterprises. They had the duty to evangelize, to send to these lands "wise, upright, god-fearing, and virtuous men... capable of instructing the indigenous peoples in good morals and in the Catholic faith." They further had the right to put down armed opposition to the Gospel, even to the extent of occupying the territory of "obstinate pagans."[4] The Portuguese and Spanish missionaries were supported, according to the royal patronage system, by the sovereigns at home and the local governors or viceroys in the colonies. But as explorations and conquests were accompanied and followed by a quest for wealth and power, subject peoples were exploited. Missionaries often found themselves "caught in the middle" as they attempted to defend their newly converted natives and at the same time please their powerful patrons. For the most part, missionary activity had the appearance of being a part of the work of colonization. The Church and colonial conquest went hand in hand.[5]

Protestant missionary activity began to expand only in the seventeenth century, when the East India Companies of the Protestant English and Dutch began to push to the ends of the earth. After the Reformation the primary concern of the Protestant churches had been survival. Moreover, the solu-

tion of the Treaty of Westphalia, <u>cuius regio,
eius religio</u>, made it difficult to envision a
broad missionary obligation. Negative theories
were even proposed. Johann Gerhard expressed the
view that the Great Command of Christ to preach
the Gospel to all the world ceased with the Apostles. In the Apostolic period, the offer of salvation had been made to all nations. To those who
had refused it, there was no need to renew the offer.[6]   Luther himself had said that after the
Apostles, "No one has any longer such a universal
apostolic command, but each bishop has his
appointed diocese or parish."[7]

Another factor that curtailed Protestant expansion in the area of missions was the absence of
religious Orders. Luther had done away with them
and, as Jaroslav Pelikan has pointed out, "It was
the Orders that made possible the conversion of
Europe, and the absence of anything similar to
them has persistently hindered Protestant mission."[8]   One might say that later the denominational and interdenominational missionary societies among Protestant groups functioned somewhat
parallel to Roman Catholic missionary Orders.

Protestant missionaries traveling with the
trade companies for the most part did not differ
from their Roman Catholic counterparts. Nor were
the trade companies of the Protestant English and
Dutch any less autocratic than the Catholic Portuguese and Spanish in their direction of the
Church. Dutch missionaries, for example, were civil servants. Their primary responsibility was to
minister to the Dutch traders and merchants, but
at the same time they were to evangelize the indigenous peoples. A cash bonus was even awarded
the minister for each person baptized. As with
the Portuguese and Spanish, special privileges
were held out to those who embraced Christianity,
making the political motive at least as strong as
the religious for conversion.[9]

According to this "accompanist" perspective, therefore, it was governments and commercial companies that for the most part controlled and directed this early missionary enterprise. Not until the Pietist's missionary activities of the latter part of the eighteenth century did a new and dynamic trend begin to develop in the missionary field. It reached its peak in the following century, the century that has been labeled "the great era of missions."[10] In the nineteenth century for the first time Christianity was propagated very largely without the direct patronage of governments or even colonizing agencies.[11]

Although the nineteenth century has been called the great era of missions, the outlook for the Church becoming universal was not very promising at the beginning of the century. The Church had spread beyond Europe and into the New World, but in regard to the great non-Christian religions and civilizations set-backs more than matched earlier successes. The Catholic Church, especially, had been sapped spiritually by Jansenism and politically by the French Revolution. Further, the papacy suffered humiliation at the hands of Napoleon. In the missions, the rivalry among religious Orders, the lack of indigenous clergy, and the misunderstanding arising from the efforts of Rome to centralize more extensively all missionary work contributed to the problem. It seemed the Church did not have the energy or the resources to meet the demands of missions. The final blow came when the Jesuit Order was dissolved by the Pope in 1773. At least three thousand missionaries were forced to leave their mission posts.[12]

It was the Industrial Revolution more than anything else that gave Europe its great penetrating force. As van Leeuwen describes it, the Industrial Revolution became "a kind of irresistible bulldozer forcing a way for Western civilization into the non-Western areas of the world."[13] The scientific advances which made it possible for man to harness power for manufacturing and travel, set Europe out to conquer with a new sense of confidence and a new sense of mission to the world.

Earlier traders, especially to the East, had no intentions of establishing dominion over the lands they visited. But with the competition for trade growing and the need for expanding markets for manufactured goods increasing, the idea of an empire or colonialism on a grand scale came to the fore. Originally, exploration was accompanied by exploitation; thereafter, trade was accompanied by the establishment of colonial rule.[14]

The outburst of European economic and imperial activity coincided with the awakenings that were widespread in the West. Because the great flourishing of missionary activity in the Church accompanied the age of industrialism, capitalism and colonialism, it is not surprising that Great Britain, and later the United States--countries that took the lead in the Industrial Revolution--should also take the lead in the Protestant missionary endeavor. Because of the great British colonial expansion in the nineteenth century, Alec Vidler speaks of a _pax_ _britannica_ which was extremely advantageous for English missionaries.[15]

On the Catholic side, those countries or areas that adopted mechanization and industrialization first and profited from them most--France, Belgium, Germany, and Northern Italy--also shouldered the nineteenth century missionary task. The Catholic Church in the United States was a late-comer to the missionary movement, being considered by Rome as missionary territory itself until 1908. The French Church, especially, recovering from the paralysis of the French Revolution, gave birth to many new Orders of men and women dedicated to missionary work. The Jesuit Order was reconstituted in 1814 and the Congregation for the Propagation of the Faith was reorganized and centralized in

Rome in 1817. In addition, there was an attempt
to interest the laity in the work of the missions,
as the Protestants had done in their missionary
societies, through organizations such as the
Society for the Propagation of the Faith, founded
in France in 1817.[16]

It is ironic that, at the same time as there
was an upsurge in zeal and devotion to carry the
Gospel to all nations, European churches, both
Catholic and Protestant, seemed to be losing their
hold on their own people at home. They seemed unwilling or unable to meet the new challenges to
Christian belief and to adapt their outlook and
their structures to the social, political and economic revolution that was taking place.[17] On the
other hand, the evangelical revival, John Wesley's
Methodist movement, as well as other spiritual
awakenings which cut across denominational lines,
led to that new phenomenon of the nineteenth century, the interdenominational or nondenominational
missionary society. The cooperative ventures of
these societies served, moreover, as the seeds of
the beginnings of the ecumenical movement.[18]

2. The Spirit of Christianity: The Matrix of Colonialism

A second approach to the question of the
interrelationship of colonialism and missionary
activity sees in Christianity the very seeds of
colonialism. From this perspective, the Christian
faith is inextricably bound to Western economic
and political systems. The great century of missionary expansion was not only the great century
of industrialization, capitalism and colonialism,
but the former gave birth and impetus to the latter. The historian, Latourette, says that the new
life which expressed itself in learning, industry,
commerce and territorial expansion also showed itself in the propagation of the Christian faith.

He suggests that "this was probably because that new life had, in part (although by no means fully), Christian origins."[19]   Van Leeuwen is more confident.   He credits the world-wide spread of the Gospel during the nineteenth century to "the revolutionizing forces perpetually at work within Western civilization" which "ultimately derive their impetus from that particular history which reaches out from Zion to the very ends of the earth."[20]   In other words, van Leeuwen is saying that there is a theological explanation for Western civilization and, indeed, an overall theology of history.

According to van Leeuwen's thesis, the expansion of the West is a unique phenomenon in world history and, although the outward success of Christianity which accompanied this expansion is relatively small, Christianity is actually spread by Westernization itself.   Although Western civilization and Christianity cannot be identified as one, still the very process of emancipation from religious constraints, which van Leeuween refers to as "secularization," is the unique product of Western civilization.   The religious constraints which van Leeuwen mentions refer to those taboos and superstitions which sacralize nature and the universe, identifying them with the gods.   In contrast, the Judeo-Christian tradition de-sacralizes creation, looking upon it as something humans are to subdue, use, and change for their own good.

If secularization is the product of Western civilization, Western civilization, in turn, was set in motion and nurtured in the course of Christian history.   Modern technology, science, democracy, capitalism, socialism, nationalism, even communism, are fruits (good or bad) of a civilization which was formed and driven forward by the spirit of Christianity.[21]

This spirit of Christianity has resulted from a merging of the characteristics of Israel with those of Graeco-Roman civilization, and later with the converted "barbarians" of Europe. Van Leeuwen sees in this merging a combination of the superiority complex of the Greeks with the global outlook of Israel derived from the Bible. The superiority complex of the Greeks carried with it a sense of responsibility for educating and civilizing the barbarians and later those being colonized. The global view of Israel included Israel's notion of exclusiveness and election. Wedding the superiority complex of the Greeks with Israel's global view had mixed blessings, according to van Leeuwen. It led at times to "outbursts of colonial fanaticism under the guise of various motives of a religious, nationalistic, racial, social or economic character, and [was] accompanied at times by repulsive manifestations of hypocrisy.[22]

At other times, the genuine concern for lifting the "natives" and "uncivilized peoples" up to the level of Western civilization was pursued with missionary fervor. Christianity was "sure of its task and its call to spread the Light amid the darkness of heathendom."

> The assault on social evils, the use of medicine to relieve physical distress, the lifting of men out of their backward state, out of their poverty and ignorance, their liberation from the bonds of social tyranny and pagan customs, the introduction of an enlightened, democratic idealism—all of these have found their deepest inspiration, consciously or unconsciously, directly or indirectly, in the biblical promise of salvation for all.[23]

For van Leeuwen the influence of Israel in the expansionist attitude of the West is dominant; the global outlook drew its deepest inspiration from the Bible. But this does not mean that the Greek and barbarian influences are unimportant. "Western peoples," he states, "whose boast it is that they have spread the light of civilization and salvation around the world, were in origin themselves barbarians--only caught up in the progress of the Gospel from Jew to Greek, from Greek to barbarian, and thus Christianized."[24]

Raymond Panikkar expresses a somewhat similar position when he describes Christianity as "ancient paganism or, to be more precise, the complex Hebrew-Helleno-Greco-Latino-Gothico-Modern religion converted to Christ more or less successfully."[25]   And what is at the heart of this conversion?   The central Christian belief in the Incarnation.   As Denis de Rougemont has expressed it:

> Word, and not silence; made flesh and not
> concept; Grace, instead of merit or spir-
> itual techniques. Faith, and not direct
> knowledge of the divine; History, instead
> of Myth.   Recognition of the flesh and
> hence of matter as realities of our pres-
> ent life. Paradox, tension, dialectic...
> And love of one's neighbor as oneself,
> corresponding with the love of God, re-
> placing the sacred and founding the
> person.[26]

From the "matrix" perspective, this was the spirit which became intertwined in Western culture, urging it on and being carried itself by that which it helped form. This was the spirit behind the great era of missionary activity.

Which of the two perspectives is the true one? It is not my intention here to decide. But perhaps a clue to the solution could be found in the approach which Max Weber used in his famous study, THE PROTESTANT ETHIC AND THE SPIRIT OF CAPITALISM.[27]   Weber did not claim that Reformed Christianity was the cause of modern capitalism. But he did see in Calvinistic Christianity a creative religious breakthrough in which God's call was experienced as a secular calling. It was in their dedication to hard work and personal enterprise that Christians could experience the meaning and power of the Gospel, and they regarded their successes as God's approval and blessing. This new "worldly asceticism" provided the milieu, the justification, and the impetus for the expansion of free enterprise in industry and commerce. Calvinism, then, was a cause in the rise of capitalism.

An analogy between Weber's approach and the interrelationship of missionary activity and colonialism can perhaps be drawn. The Christian Gospel was not the cause of colonial expansion, but certain expressions of Christianity did provide a milieu, a justification, and an impetus for the expansionist policies of "Christian" states.

Some would label all the Church's missionary activity of the past several centuries, and especially the nineteenth century, a prostitution to Western imperialism. Missionaries represented European domination in the same way that the traders and administrators did. But that is hardly a balanced judgment of the missionary movement. As Neill points out, for many people in the nineteenth century the alternatives were not independence or enslavement, but total destruction (by unscrupulous exploiters or through the slave trade) on the one hand, or survival in a state of colonial dependence on the other.[28]

Actually, the degree of independence that the missionaries maintained and the direct confrontations with colonial governments which resulted from this, cannot be passed over. This is especially remarkable when one considers that, with notable exceptions, missionaries were politically quietist or conservative.[29] The colonizing powers themselves were supposedly "Christian" powers, yet so often they pressured missionaries into compromising situations.

Christopher Dawson perhaps captures the built-in dilemma of this period of colonial/missionary expansion when he states that the discovery of the New World and the opening of the new route to India were at once the result of "the old mediaeval crusading ideal and of a very modern interest in cheaper grocery, and this combination of incongruous motives characterizes the whole history of European colonial development." He designates the Spanish conquests in the Americas as the work of "predatory adventurers and devoted missionaries, partially controlled by a remote government which was itself divided and frustrated by conflict between its sense of Christian responsibility and its lust for power and wealth."[30]

Unquestionably, the Church and its missionaries were at times less than faithful to the prophetic and liberating mission of Jesus Christ. Thus, when the political consciousness of the people in many areas under colonial domination began to be awakened--often through the education offered by the missionaries--the reaction against the West, against foreign and colonial exploitation, was bound to include reaction against the religion that came with Western domination.

We say that the era of colonialism is, for the most part, past. Van Leeuwen has called it a necessary phase that has left a deep impression, but one that has resulted not in harmonious cooperation but in a radical anticolonialism.[31] In order to clarify further the present missionary situation, we shall examine what effect colonialism has had on the colonized, how that era came to an end, and what vestiges of it remain. We shall begin with the movement toward decolonization because it has only been after achieving independence that rising nations have begun to analyze the effects of colonialism and neo-colonialism.

THE RISE OF NEW NATIONS:
DECOLONIZATION

The early twentieth century brought with it a series of events which were to dash forever the confident claims of European nations that they had a monopoly on Christianity and civilization. In the First World War, most colonized peoples fought dutifully under their European rulers. But there was an underlying resentment among many Indians and Africans, for instance, that they had been drawn into a conflict that was not of their making nor of their deep concern.

The great anti-Christian force that was set loose in the world with the Russian revolution also caused the Church to reassess the ties it had in its missionary outreach with western expansionism. Although the atheist "Russian menace" was to engage the energies of many in the Church during the succeeding decades, still, as Neill points out, a certain self-questioning did take root in the Christian Church: "Were the Marxists not in part right? Was not the colonial epoch in reality a period of shame rather than of glory for the western world?"[32]

The Second World War only broadened and deepened the resentment of colonized peoples, as virtually all of them were drawn into the circle of violence and suffering. With the extermination of millions of Jewish people in Nazi Germany and the wholesale destruction of the people of Hiroshima and Nagasaki by American atomic power, the moral pretensions of the West were shaken to the core. Was it any longer possible to speak of the "Christian West?"

A wave of nationalism among colonized peoples began to swell as a result of these and other developments but the road to emancipation and political independence was not simple. When fifty-one States signed the United Nations Charter in San Francisco in 1945, only thirteen were Asiatic or African; only four were newly independent. But by 1960, after the United States and Russia stopped vying with one another in creating obstacles to admission of new members, there were forty-five Afro-Asian states out of ninety-nine members. Today, if we include the Latin-American countries which were founding members but have become more and more closely linked to the Third World, then the statutory two-thirds majority automatically belongs to these new and developing states. However precarious the stability of some of these new nations may be, it is as nation-states that they must be dealt with in the international forum.[33]

Although this radical change in the complexion of the United Nations is not reflected in the powerful Security Council, still the developing nations have made effective use of their majority in the General Assembly. The initial endeavor of the Third World majority has been to pressure for the dismantling of colonialism. Although the resolutions of the Assembly are subject to the veto of the five great powers, the Third World countries have used their resolutions to bring pressure to bear on some important factors in the decolonization process.[34]

The Third World nations focused their attention on the sections of the United Nations Charter that dealt with the "trust system" and "non-self-governing territories." The Charter states that those territories under the trust system have the right to achieve independence or some freely chosen autonomous regime. This provision is linked, however, with the requirement of a minimum of cultural, economic, and political development. Without this, the Charter states, the first right cannot be exercised effectively. But to the developing nations this was just a continuation of colonialism and of the "sacred mission" with which the Western powers deluded themselves. They therefore worked for definite cut-off dates for trust agreements and procedures for lifting of trusts, aimed at transition to independence.[35]

The question of non-self-governing territories was a more difficult one. Although according to the Charter the interests of a territory's people were primary, there was no mention of independence. Even the definition of what was a "non-self-governing territory" was initially left to the colonial powers themselves to decide. This led Spain and Portugal to claim, as late as 1965, that their colonies should be regarded as "overseas provinces."[36]

The first attempt to form a united front in the fight for decolonization came at the Bandung Conference in 1955. There, the Afro-Asian countries declared that the arrangement whereby their countries were governed by political decisions made by colonial powers was the primary cause of underdevelopment. Against the argument that political independence should await economic viability, as stated in the United Nations Charter, they argued that economic growth depended largely on political decisions, and until they were responsible for their own destiny, the local effort and initiative would lack the spontaneity necessary for real development.[37]

The most resolute and bold intervention by developing nations concerning decolonization was the "Declaration on the Granting of Independence to Colonial Countries and Peoples," introduced and passed by the United Nations General Assembly in 1960. It called for a rapid and unconditional end to colonialism, which it declared, was a "denial of fundamental human rights..., contrary to the United Nations Charter," and compromising to "the cause of world peace and collaboration." It insisted, moreover, that all peoples have the right to determine their political status, and the lack

of preparation is never to be a pretext for delay-
ing independence.[38]

Some argued that this declaration was illegal,
that it contradicted directly certain parts of the
United Nations Charter. The Third World countries
based their rebuttal on that section of the Charter which requires respect for the "principle of
the priority of the inhabitants' interests."[39]

Although this declaration had no binding
force, it has had an effect on the decolonization
process. To ensure its implementation, the Assembly secured the creation of a Committee on Decolonization, which continues to be concerned with
affairs such as the Portuguese African colonies'
recent transition to independence.[40]

LINGERING COLONIALISM UNDER A NEW GUISE:
NEO-COLONIALISM

Once the process of decolonization was well
under way, attention shifted to an analysis of the
effects of colonialism and the dangers of the so-
called neo-colonialism. Neo-colonialism refers to
that type of economic and cultural domination
which, it is claimed, keeps the Third World countries in a state of dependence.

"Orthodox" Marxists, as we might call them,
and those who employ their critique, argue that
all colonialism and imperialism can be explained
from the economic point of view. The very nature
of capitalist development, according to this analysis, demands expanding markets--above all, markets for capital.[41] Others have argued that some
colonial enterprise arose from an embittered nationalism. In other words, European powers were
determined to make up overseas for losses of power
they experienced at home.[42] But even if economics
were not always behind the original colonial

thrust, economic colonization or exploitation has accompanied political colonization, and has lingered on long after countries have won their political independence. One only need consider the Latin-American situation where economic dependency has continued even though political independence was achieved at the beginning of the nineteenth century.

In attempting to assess the effect of political colonization or domination on the economic question, Calvez states that colonial governments were not the cause of underdevelopment, but they certainly have perpetuated it.[43] To the extent that effective, stable government is a condition for economic progress, colonial rule in the technical sense was often an improvement. Missionaries, too, welcomed the order and stability which colonial rulers brought to often-times warring and divided tribes and peoples. And yet, even apart from the moral question involved in imperialism, political domination did have an adverse effect on genuine socioeconomic and cultural development.

Colonizers (and missionaries) brought with them the conviction that they were superior in race, culture and religion to those whom they colonized. The sociocultural impact of being placed in an inferior position curtailed any energetic effort toward development. This superior/inferior relationship in the colonial situation was looked upon as being "natural" and therefore permanent. The type of education provided by colonial governments, usually through the missionaries, reflected and reinforced this mindset. As Gregory Baum has stated:

> When a Church that has become culturally dominant proclaims Jesus as the one mediator between God and man, invalidating all other ways of salvation, it creates a symbolic imperialism that no amount of personal love and generosity can prevent

in the long run from being translated into social and political realities. The symbols of exclusiveness belonging to a religion that has become culturally successful are objective factors that will affect the consciousness of a people and promote their cultural and/or political domination....[44]

Two separate societies emerged in these cases and, even when some degree of self-regulation was granted to the colonized communities, still they were ultimately protectorates. With full political life denied them, there was little incentive for creative initiative.

Economic domination did even more to stifle the initiative which development requires. The formation of plantations and the expansion of mining resulted in the displacement and relocation of many people. The movement of people to cities, especially port cities, destroyed the traditional economic unity of the village and caused areas of overpopulation. The skilled trades and small industries of the local people could not compete with the lower-priced, mass-produced Western products which the colonizers were anxious to sell. A traditional ecomony organized for subsistence and based on cooperation through the kinship system, was replaced by an exchange economy based on profit.

A distinction needs to be made between economic domination under the old colonial structures and the so-called neo-colonialism of more recent times. The old system was largely extractive. Raw materials were taken out of the colony and used by the industries in the home country. Neo-colonialism, on the other hand, often promotes industrialization in Third World countries. But the industries usually are of a kind that benefit only a small element in the society. Durable consumer goods such as automobiles, refrigerators, television sets and the like are produced; these can be purchased by only a small minority of the population. Furthermore, the technology as well as the technicians often must be imported for this type of production. The result of this "capital-intensive" rather than "labor-intensive" type of industry is the actual creation of unemployment. This type of industrialization is usually controlled by the huge multinational corporations whose actual power often outweighs that of the host country.[45]

As a result of this type of industrialization, modern cities have arisen around an enclave of foreigners and their native collaborators. They are surrounded by countless "marginals" whose conditions continue to deteriorate while the conventional economic indicators show continued growth. That more of the marginals do not share this prosperity is usually explained by their unregulated population growth.

The economy of these dependent countries develops, therefore, not along the lines of internal economic and social forces, but in the interest of the country or countries from which the foreign capital comes. This situation, which has been called "growth without development," or even "the development of underdevelopment," is perpetuated by an alliance between outsiders who make economic decisions which are not in the best interests of the developing countries and a local economic and political elite who, in turn, exploit their own people.[46]

This, in broad outline, is the situation which most Third World countries, most "missionary" countries, find themselves after successive periods of colonization, decolonization, and neocolonialism. In general, this is the "present situation" with which the missionary endeavor of the Church is confronted from the socioeconomic point of view. But the Church itself, so intimately identified with the West during its period of colonial expansion, has been going through a period of "decolonization" itself which has many parallels to the process of political and socio-cultural decolonization described above. We must examine this phenomenon.

DECOLONIZATION OF THE CHURCH:
THE DEMAND FROM CHRISTIANS IN NEW NATIONS

Protestant mission churches have been moving toward independence from their mother churches for some time. As early as the 1928 Jerusalem meeting of the International Missionary Council, the use of the term "younger churches" rather than "mission churches" was adopted. The World Council of Churches was predominantly Western in composition at its founding in 1948. As developing nations achieved their political independence, they demanded membership in the World Council, not through some parent church in another land, but as independent churches on an equal status with older churches. Not unlike the situation at the United Nations, Third World churches have forced the World Council of Churches to re-examine its predominately Western orientation and to take seriously the "rising expectations" and tense revolutionary climate in the Third World. This can readily be seen by the growing orientation toward the concerns of Third World churches in the pronouncements and studies of the World Council of Churches.

The concerns of the Third World churches began to be voiced in the early 1950s. Taking advantage of the results of Asian study conferences, the 1954 Evanston Assembly of the World Council of Churches was able to declare:

Society in Asia, Africa and some parts of Latin America today is characterized by the urge to national self-determination

in political and economic matters....
The people of these countries have awak-
ened to a new sense of fundamental human
rights and justice and they are in revolt
against enslaving political, economic,
religious and social conditions.[47]

Insisting on the need which emerging nations
have for economic and technical assistance, the
Assembly further asserts: "In the new context of
our age, relations between peoples hitherto 'subject' and 'ruling' should be one of partnership
and cooperation."[48]

At the New Delhi Assembly in 1961 the main focus was on developing nations, and the language in
pertinent documents reflects a growing urgency:

There are countries where economic progress has been slow or erratic because
they depend on the fluctuations of a market outside their control and--to remind
us that man does not live by bread alone
--there are wealthy societies plagued by
anxiety and frustration because the demands of people seem to be endless. Thus
a world strategy of development is over-
due....[49]

The Geneva Conference on Church and Society in
1966 dramatically showed that Third World representatives were beginning to have an equal voice
with spokespersons from the powerful nations. A
forceful address by Bola Ige from Nigeria reflects
the growing "decolonization" of the Church, that
is, the Third World churches speaking out on their
own behalf:

There can be no peace in the world where
seventy-five nations have their economic
(and therefore their political) future
dictated by the narrow self-interest of
Europe and America. There can be no peace

where the Soviet Union and the United
States arrogate to themselves the monopoly of directing the future of the world
and of other nations. And there can be
no peace as long as there is any colony
in the world, and as long as neo-colonialism remains more vicious than its
parent-colonialism.[50]

At the Geneva Conference the theology of revolution was in the forefront as delegates from some
Third World countries argued that the situation in
which they found themselves was so unjust that
there was no way to change without revolution.[51]

The Uppsala Assembly of the World Council of
Churches held in 1968 gave its answer to the findings and urgings of the Geneva Conference. It
withdrew from the radical concept of revolution in
favor of the term development.[52] But this does
not mean that the Third World representatives were
silenced. Perhaps the most radical and controversial sign of the Third World churches' presence
and power in the World Council came in 1970 when
the Executive Committee, following the mandate
given it by the Uppsala Assembly to act on the
question of racism, decided to give financial support to nineteen freedom movements in Third World
countries. Fourteen of these movements were in
Africa and four of them had used violence in their
resistance activities in Mozambique, Angola, and
Guinea. But the same four were also engaged in
education, social work, health services and economic aid. Reaction to the decision was severe,
especially in places like southern Africa and from
groups that are more evangelistic in orientation.
The Central Committee later clarified the decision
--the World Council did not identify itself with
any political movement, and the Central Committee
would make it possible for individual churches to
elect particular programs for direct support--but
it did not back away from its basic position.[53]
Earlier prophetic-sounding declarations were, for

the first time in this particular area, supported by actual deeds. The Third World churches had not only made themselves heard, but felt.

The fifth Assembly of the World Council of Churches which met in Nairobi, Kenya, in 1975 was, in a sense, the proof and the fruit of the phenomenon of decolonization of the Church. Meeting for the first time in Africa, the Assembly was influenced by African art, culture and concerns. African Christians were heard at Nairobi as never before in an ecumenical gathering. A cross-section of the Assembly reflected the increased participation of Asian, African, Carribean and Latin-American churches in the Council's activities.[54] There were more young people, more women, and more delegates from the Third World than ever before. They were there, not as external objects to be observed or discussed, but as internal subjective participants in the Council's operation.

Meeting under the theme, "Jesus Christ frees and unites," there was a deliberate attempt to be open to the new wave of evangelism discernible in the world, to reconciliation and dialogue rather than confrontation, to celebration and sharing. At the same time, the Assembly directed its General Secretary to see that the program on racism and development was not slowed down.[55] Nothing dramatic came out of Nairobi; many claimed that the Assembly lacked focus and thorough preparation. The presence of so many new faces (80 percent of the delegates had never attended such a gathering before) was bound to diminish the efficiency of operation, but at least the colonial missionary status of the member churches from the Third World seemed to have come to an end.

On the Catholic side, efforts to establish an indigenous episcopate and local leadership were pursued by Pius XI and even more vigorously by Pius XII. It was Pius XII also who enlarged the College of Cardinals and appointed a considerable

number of non-Europeans, among them several from
mission lands.[56] Pope John XXIII, in two encycli-
cals--MATER ET MAGISTRA (1961) and PACEM IN TERRIS
(1963)--focused the Church's attention on the need
of all peoples for social as well as economic development. In MATER ET MAGISTRA he reminded people that scientific and technical progress are not
supreme values, but are merely instruments to be
used for the betterment of the human family. In
PACEM IN TERRIS he declared that wealthier States,
in their varied forms of assistance to the poor,
should avoid any intention of political domination.[57]

Although the rising voice of indigenous church
leaders from "missionary" or Third World countries
was heard at the Second Vatican Council, the cause
of missions was still predominantly carried by
Western missionary religious Orders. Discussion
on development, for the most part, focused on humanization of technology in the industrialized
world and sharing of that technology and wealth
with poor nations. It was largely due to the
Third World leaders' criticism of the documents of
Vatican II as being too "Western" in orientation
that Pope Paul VI issued his encyclical ON THE
DEVELOPMENT OF PEOPLES (1967). But even in this
document, the emphasis is on what the powerful nations should do for the poor nations, rather than
what the developing nations, in justice, should
have the right to do for themselves. It is for
this reason that the Latin-American theologian,
Gustavo Gutierrez, calls the encyclical a "transi-
tional document."[58]

A shift can be seen in the MESSAGE FROM EIGHT-
EEN BISHOPS OF THE THIRD WORLD which came in direct response to the Pope's encyclical.[59] In this
and similar documents, the focus is no longer on
what the powerful are telling the powerful they
should do for the marginals, but rather what the
marginals are demanding in justice as rightfully
their own.

In the Roman Synods which have been called by the Pope since the Second Vatican Council, the Third World bishops have become increasingly vocal --even outspoken. This is true especially of the Synod held in 1974 to discuss the question of evangelization. Taking advantage of the teaching of Vatican II on collegiality, strengthened by the system of national and regional episcopal conferences which the Vatican Council had encouraged, and building on the previous Synod's declarations that work to transform the world toward a more just society was a "constitutive" element of the mission of the Church, the Third World bishops were determined that the Universal Church would hear their plight and their determination. As a result, after a month-long discussion, the Synod delegates were unable to come to an agreement on a declaration on evangelization. They declared that the richness they found in their exchanges "could not be easily unified without jeopardizing its integrity."[60] Instead, they offered a short statement of some fundamental convictions and a few of the more urgent guidelines, and asked Pope Paul to consolidate their discussions into a unified teaching.

Pope Paul's task was not an easy one, because the short statement the Synod issued amounted to placing in juxtaposition two quite divergent views on what evangelization means for the Church today. For example, it stated that the mandate to evangelize all people constitutes the essential mission of the Church. However, it also stressed that there is a mutual relationship between evangelization and the integral salvation or complete liberation of the person and peoples.[61]

Pope Paul issued his apostolic exhortation ON EVANGELIZATION IN THE MODERN WORLD in late 1975. In some ways it could be described in the words similar to those applied to Nairobi: there is no dramatic breakthrough; it seems to lack focus. The document is lengthy and repetitious. It describes evangelization in numerous ways, insisting that it is a complex process made up of varied elements such as the renewal of humanity, witness of explicit proclamation, inner adherence, entry into the community, acceptance of signs, and apostolic initiative. The Pope, disturbed by the remarks of some Third World representatives at the Synod, was determined to proscribe the limits and methods of liberation and development as secondary elements within the context of evangelization. Evangelization proclaims liberation and strives to put it into practice. "Nevertheless," the Pope insisted, "she [the Church] reaffirms the primacy of her spiritual vocation and refuses to replace the proclamation of the Kingdom by the proclamation of forms of human liberation."[62] Pope Paul had, in effect, brought the discussion full circle; the work of integration still lies ahead.

It was in the statements and speeches of Third World bishops at the 1974 Synod that the decolonization process in the Catholic Church became evident, however. Pursuing our parallel between the Third World spokespersons making their voices heard in the United Nations General Assembly and Third World religious leaders voicing their views in Councils and Synods, we could say that the bishops of the Third World made their voices heard in the "assembly," even though their views got "vetoed" in part by papal power.

Bishop James Sangu, speaking as a chairperson of the Tanzania Episcopal Conference, reflects the growing confidence of Third World church leaders. In words similar to those which would be heard from Africans at the Nairobi Assembly, he notes that the African church has reached a turning point, a "coming of age," and that it is "outdated" to regard these churches as "mission-lands."[63] "Christianity in Africa," Sangu declares, "is experiencing the greatest numerical growth on a sustained basis (seven and one-half million increase of Christians per year) of any

continent or of any period of history."[64] Bishop
Sangu says that the process of decolonization has
been one of the most important developments in
Africa in the last twenty years and that the "political wind of independence" has hastened the
localization and self-ministration of the Church.
He states:

> A parallel development has taken place in
> the Church. Formerly the missions were
> entrusted to missionary institutes which
> received from the Sacred Congregation for
> the Evangelization of Peoples, formerly
> the Propaganda, the 'jus commissionis.'
> During the last twenty years most of the
> missions have become dioceses and the
> hierarchy has been established....[65]

Sangu adds, however, that the church in Africa
is still largely under the Congregation for Evangelization and asks whether this Congregation
should not, perhaps, give up its former orientation and become a meeting place for local
churches, young and old. He calls for a new clarification of the boundaries and competence of the
local episcopal conferences and those of the
Vatican diplomatic corps, and he criticizes the
diplomatic corps for being "too Italian" and at
times forgetting its universal mission and suc-
cumbing to nationalism. Finally, he castigates
those nations still practicing colonialism,
apartheid, and/or racism--especially those claiming to be Christian nations--and urges the Vatican
to use its moral power to bring an end to such
injustices.[66]

All of this, it should be remembered, was said
at a Synod which had as its topic of discussion
evangelization. The bishop from Tanzania was well
aware of the fact:

> It is time for the church in Africa to
> speak out in defense of justice and

against oppression of any kind. The voice of the Church in such situations is a relief to the oppressed and the relevance of evangelization comes out clearer.[67]

Archbishop Picachy, speaking on behalf of the Indian Episcopal Conference, pointed out that in earlier times India had received the faith from other churches, but in the past twenty years it has been sending missionaries to other lands. He called on the bishops to begin a profound reflection on the theology of the local church and its relation to the Universal Church. He thanked the sister churches for their assistance in the form of personnel and money in the past, but declared that something more is expected of them today:

> They [the sister churches] have accepted and elaborated the principles of justice, liberation, and integral human development. Now we ask that they strive to bring it about that these principles effectively change the ways of thinking and acting of their governments so that in turn the plans of action, or programs and structures of international organization,...and of multinational corporations will be modified. Such work is indeed a form of cooperation of the utmost importance for the evangelization not only of India but of the whole of the Third World.[68]

It is clear from the statements and actions of church leaders in the Third World that, parallel to the decolonization which has been taking place in the political realm, there has been a decolonization process taking place within the Christian Church itself. This, too, is a sign of the times, one that those reflecting on the missionary endeavor of the Church must take seriously. Colonialism and Western expansion, emancipation and independence, neo-colonialism and dependency, plus the rising voice of Third World churches, all have contributed to the present state of missions. And yet, underlying the missionary endeavor of every age is a theological rationale. We must examine what the theology was behind the "great era of missions" and then examine the "theological shift" that has taken place in the Christian Church which, I suggest, makes necessary a reformulation of missionary theology under the aegis of development.

SUMMARY OF CHAPTER ONE

Chapter One provides a glimpse of the close ties between churches and governments, and points to the recognition of the political, economic, and sociocultural realities that must be confronted in the analysis of, and the theological reflections on, missions.

As a prologue to the study of the theology of missions in the modern world, we note the correspondence between the rise and fall of Western political colonization and Christian missionary expansion. Since both movements originate in the technologically developed Western countries (First World) and operate in the technologically under-developed "mission" lands (Third World), we can draw a parallel between them:

Political Colonization	Christian Expansion
Colonization	Great era of missions
Decolonization and the emergence of "new" nations conscious of their influence when functioning as a Third World bloc	Development of local church leadership and growing self-awareness and self-determination within Third World churches

NOTES ON CHAPTER ONE

[1]Stephen Neill, A HISTORY OF CHRISTIAN MISSIONS (Baltimore: Penguin Books, 1964), p. 140.

[2]For discussion on the role of the Church in guaranteeing the social system and thereby legitimizing the political sphere, see Francois Houtart and Andre Rousseau, THE CHURCH AND REVOLUTION, Violet Nevile, trans. (Maryknoll, New York: Orbis Books, 1971), chap. 9, esp. pp. 322-25. In basic agreement with this position but from a different approach, see Arend T. van Leeuwen, CHRISTIANITY IN WORLD HISTORY, H. H. Hoskins, trans. (New York: Charles Scribner's Sons, 1964), pp. 301-03.

[3]Foreword to THE THEOLOGY OF CHRISTIAN MISSION, Gerald Anderson, ed. and intro. (New York: McGraw-Hill, 1961), p. xi.

[4]Neill, HISTORY OF CHRISTIAN MISSIONS, p. 141. See also Joseph Masson, "Missions" in SACRAMENTUM MUNDI, 6 vols., Karl Rahner et al., eds. (New York: Herder and Herder, 1969), 4: 68-69. The Papal bulls of Martin V in 1430 and Nicolas V in 1542 gave Portugal the exclusive right not only to develop missions and carry on commerce, but also to pursue the slave trade in Africa. According to S. Cerqueira, "L'Eglise Catholique Portugaise," in LES EGLISE CHRETIENNES ET LA DECOLONISATION (Paris: Armand Colin-Bourrelier, 1967), p. 468, quoted in Houtart and Rousseau, THE CHURCH AND REVOLUTION, p. 246, for more than seventy years after 1560, Angola became the chosen land for the Jesuits and the slave traders. The Jesuits, declared champions of the "expansion of faith and the empire," legitimated by their evangelizing activities the conquest of the land and the sale of Africans to Brazil: "The best way to convert the blacks [being] to sell them so they can be introduced to Christianity through the dignity of their labor in the American plantations." Houtart and Rousseau also cite J. Duffy, PORTUGAL IN

AFRICA (London: Penguin Press, 1967), p. 54, to the effect that even in the nineteenth century the Bishop of Luanda gave collective baptism to the cargos of slaves in a ceremony known as "baptism of freedom" (p. 246).

[5]Rome, recognizing the doubtful advantages and certain disadvantages of the patronage system, was determined from the early seventeenth century to establish its own control over the missionary enterprise. With this objective in mind, the Congregation for the Propagation of the Faith was established in 1622. This led to a long controversy with Spain and Portugal over Vicars Apostolic and priests being sent by the Propaganda to check on missionaries in countries under the patronage system and reporting on what they considered unlawful adaptation of rites and questionable missionary techniques. The famous Chinese rites controversy arose as a result of this practice, along with a jealous struggle between the Dominicans and the Jesuits. See Neill, HISTORY OF CHRISTIAN MISSIONS, pp. 191-94. Also see "Missions," SACRAMENTUM MUNDI, Vol. 4, pp. 64-65; 69.

[6]Neill, HISTORY OF CHRISTIAN MISSIONS, p. 221. Neill notes that Robert Bellarmine, the famous Catholic apologist in the post-Reformation period, included among the eighteen marks of the true Church its missionary activity, and reproached the Protestants for having no missionary outreach comparable to that of the Roman Catholic Church (CONTROVERSIES, Book IV).

[7]Quoted in Gustav Warneck, OUTLINE OF A HISTORY OF PROTESTANT MISSIONS FROM THE REFORMATION TO THE PRESENT TIME, George Robson, trans. (Edinburgh and London: Oliphant, Anderson and Ferrier, 1901), pp. 14-15. For a brief discussion on the slowness with which the Protestant missionary activity began, see William R. Hogg, "The Rise of Protestant Missionary Concern, 1517-1914," in THEOLOGY OF CHRISTIAN MISSION, Anderson, ed.,

pp. 95-111. K. S. Latourette, A HISTORY OF THE EXPANSION OF CHRISTIANITY, 7 vols. (New York: Harper and Row, 1937-45), suggests six reasons for Protestantism's lack of missionary activity: (1) Its struggle to establish itself, (2) its involvement in the wars of religion, (3) the Reformer's eschatological stance, (4) the indifference of Protestant rulers to spreading the faith, (5) the absence of Protestant missionary machinery, and (6) the relative lack of contact with non-Christian peoples by predominantly Protestant countries until the latter part of the seventeenth century (3: 25-28).

[8]THE RIDDLE OF ROMAN CATHOLICISM (Nashville: Abingdon Press, 1959), p. 88.

[9]Neill, HISTORY OF CHRISTIAN MISSIONS, p. 224.

[10]Ernst Benz, "Pietist and Puritan Sources of Christian World Mission," CHURCH HISTORY 20 (1951); 28-55. Latourette is the one who has labeled the nineteenth century the "great" missionary era. See A HISTORY OF THE EXPANSION OF CHRISTIANITY IN A REVOLUTIONARY AGE, 5 vols. (New York: Harper and Row, 1958-62).

[11]Van Leeuwen, CHRISTIANITY IN WORLD HISTORY, p. 267. The author admits there was considerable indirect support of the missionary enterprise by governments: "The protection afforded by the military and naval authorities and the diplomatic representatives of Great Britain and the United States to missionaries...--especially in China--...gave rise to grave misunderstandings where the independence of missionary activity was in question." He notes further that governmental assistance to Christian schools and hospitals in the colonies was fully justified in the context of general educational and social policy, but indirectly at least it was facilitating the spread of the Christian religion.

[12]Neill, HISTORY OF CHRISTIAN MISSIONS, pp. 204-07.

[13]CHRISTIANITY IN WORLD HISTORY, p. 317.

[14]In the course of the nineteenth century Britain established dominion, direct or indirect, over the whole of India, Burma and Ceylon. France annexed Indo-China; Holland completed its takeover of Indonesia. Japan maintained its independence by an almost overnight transformation into a modern military power. China was not wholly colonized, mainly because the colonial powers could not agree on their stakes in the division. France occupied Algeria in 1830, then moved into Tunis. Morocco was divided between France and Spain, while Britain established almost complete control in Egypt. Italy took over Tripoli and Libya. Then the powers turned toward Africa. Britain, France and later Germany and Belgium virtually carved the whole of Africa into colonies under their rule. The islands of the Pacific were soon to fall into the hands of Western colonial powers. See Neill, HISTORY OF CHRISTIAN MISSIONS, pp. 245-248.

[15]THE CHURCH IN THE AGE OF REVOLUTION, Vol. 5 of THE PELICAN HISTORY OF THE CHURCH (Baltimore: Penguin Books, 1961), p. 247.

[16]See de Vaulx, HISTORY OF THE MISSIONS, pp. 126-28. Also see "Missions," SACRAMENTUM MUNDI, Vol. 4, pp. 69-70, and Neill, HISTORY OF CHRISTIAN MISSIONS, pp. 397-401. In the eighteenth century France had begun to replace Portugal and Spain as the main sources of missionary personnel; Holland and Ireland followed later.

[17]Vidler, THE CHURCH IN THE AGE OF REVOLUTION, p. 248.

[18]William Carey, a British Baptist, stands as the pioneer and symbolic figure of the beginning of modern Protestant missionary activity. He was

instrumental in forming the Particular Baptist Society for the Propagation of the Gospel amongst the Heathen. Its outlook was universal, not colonial. Carey was convinced that there should be only one missionary agency, and he proposed a world missionary conference to encourage coordination in the missionary endeavor. Carey's correspondence from India, where he himself served as a missionary, stimulated the founding of the interdenominational London Missionary Society. His AN ENQUIRY INTO THE OBLIGATION OF CHRISTIANS TO USE MEANS FOR THE CONVERSION OF THE HEATHEN has been called the charter of modern missions. See comments by Hogg, ECUMENICAL FOUNDATIONS (New York: Harper and Row, 1952), pp. 5-8, 17. Other societies soon began to spring up in Scotland, New England and elsewhere, all stemming basically from Pietism. See Neill, HISTORY OF CHRISTIAN MISSIONS, pp. 251-53, also Ruth Rouse and Stephen Neill, A HISTORY OF THE ECUMENICAL MOVEMENT: 1517-1948 (published on behalf of the Ecumenical Institute Chateau de Bossey by S.P.C.K. in London, 1954). On John Wesley, see Martin Schmidt, THE YOUNG WESLEY: MISSIONARY AND THEOLOGIAN ON MISSIONS (London: Epworth Press, 1958), pp. 5-11.

[19]A HISTORY OF THE EXPANSION OF CHRISTIANITY, Vol. 4, p. 19.

[20]CHRISTIANITY IN WORLD HISTORY, p. 268. Lesslie Newbigin, "The Gathering Up of History into the Church," in MISSIONARY CHURCH IN EAST AND WEST, C. C. West and D. M. Paton, eds. (London: SCM Press, 1959), p. 83, makes a similar point: "The ferment of change which arises from the impact upon ancient cultures of the Gospel, or at least that kind of life which had its origins within Christendom, is the force which is giving an irreversible direction to that which was static or merely cyclical."

[21]Van Leeuwen, CHRISTIANITY IN WORLD HISTORY, p. 16. The author notes further that what perhaps

was once forced upon people under colonial domination, they seem to be taking up on their own initiative now. "For him who has once eaten of the tree of Western civilization," writes van Leeuwen, "there can be no turning back...." (p. 14).

22IBID., p. 264.

24IBID., p. 265.

25"The Relation of Christians to their non-Christian Surroundings," in CHRISTIAN REVELATION AND WORLD RELIGIONS, Joseph Neuner, ed. and intro. (London: Burns and Oates, 1967), p. 169. Panikkar sees Christianity as the fulfillment through conversion of every religion.

26MAN'S WESTERN QUEST (New York: Harper and Row; London: Allen and Unwin, 1957), p. 28.

27T. Parsons, ed. (New York: Charles Scribner's Sons, 1958). Weber states, "We have no intention whatever of maintaining such a foolish and doctrinaire thesis as that the spirit of capitalism... could only have arisen as the result of certain effects of the Reformation, or even that capitalism as an economic system is a creation of the Reformation.... On the contrary, we only wish to ascertain whether and to what extent religious forces have taken part in the qualitative formation and quantitative expansion of that spirit over the world" (p. 91).

28HISTORY OF CHRISTIAN MISSIONS, p. 249. For an overly optimistic interpretation of the history of missions during this period, see Delavignette, CHRISTIANITY AND COLONIALISM, pp. 49-52; 63-78.

29Vidler, CHURCH IN THE AGE OF REVOLUTION, p. 251.

30Christopher Dawson, UNDERSTANDING EUROPE (New York: Sheed and Ward, 1952), p. 135.

[31]CHRISTIANITY IN WORLD HISTORY, p. 41. Indian
diplomat and historian, K. M. Panikkar, in his
book ASIA AND WESTERN DOMINANCE (London: Allen and
Unwin, 1953), pp. 479-80, has argued that Christian missionary work in Asia--"the last Crusade"
he calls it--is merely a temporary phenomenon accompanying Western political and economic expansion. With the current retreat of the West, the
missionary effort and consequently the influence
of Christianity in Asia will also recede. He
maintains that the work of missions has been, in
the end, a failure.

[32]HISTORY OF CHRISTIAN MISSIONS, p. 453.

[33]Jean-Yves Calvez, POLITICS AND SOCIETY IN THE
THIRD WORLD, M. L. O'Connell, trans, (Maryknoll,
New York: Orbis Books, 1973), p. 10. For a more
detailed discussion of the question of United Nations membership, see Stephen S. Goodspeed, THE
NATURE AND FUNCTION OF INTERNATIONAL ORGANIZATION,
2nd edition (New York: Oxford University Press,
1967), pp. 136-40.

[34]Calvez, POLITICS AND SOCIETY, p. 15. These
factors include the encouragement of native movements for independence, influencing public opinion
in the mother countries, and pressuring the super-
powers by multiplying public debates on the problems of decolonization, thus keeping the matter
before the public.

[35]IBID., p. 16. See also Goodspeed, INTERNA-
TIONAL ORGANIZATION, chap. 15, "The Trusteeship
System and Non-self-governing Territories," pp.
528-65.

[36]Calvez, POLITICS AND SOCIETY, p. 17. For a
brief account of the tragic history of Portugal's
African colonies and their struggle for freedom,
as well as the Catholic Church's unfortunate identification with Portuguese domination, see Houtart
and Rousseau, CHURCH AND REVOLUTION, pp. 245-63.

[37]Calvez, POLITICS AND SOCIETY, pp. 8-9.

[38]Calvez, POLITICS AND SOCIETY, p. 18. For more detailed discussion of the declaration and the process by which it was adopted and then implemented, see EVERYMAN'S UNITED NATIONS, 8th ed.

[39]Calvez, POLITICS AND SOCIETY, p. 19.

[40]IBID., p. 20. For a brief summary of this committee's accomplishments and current projects, see section on decolonization under "United Nations" in 1976 BRITANNICA BOOK OF THE YEAR (Chicago: Encyclopedia Britannica, Inc. 1976), p. 690.

[41]IBID., p. 218. Calvez quotes Jules Ferry, LE TONKIN ET LA MERE PATRIE (1890): "Colonial policy is the daughter of industrial policy..., the manifestation of the eternal laws of competition." For a critique of this basically Leninist theory, see Peter Berger, PYRAMIDS OF SACRIFICE (New York: Basic Books, 1974), pp. 50-56.

[42]Calvez, POLITICS AND SOCIETY, p. 218. The author refers to a study by Henri Brunschivig, FRENCH COLONIALISM, 1871-1914; MYTH AND REALITIES, W. G. Brown, trans. (New York: Praeger, 1964, 1966). Berger, PYRAMIDS, p. 53, makes a similar point: "France... acquired most of its colonial empire after its domestic development had reached an advanced stage of industrializing capitalism, and it is an open question whether that empire, taken as a whole, was more of an asset or a liability economically."

[43]Calvez, POLITICS AND SOCIETY, pp. 221-22. The question of a causal relationship between imperialism and underdevelopment is a matter of dispute. If one accepts without question the Marxist-Leninist theory of imperialism, then one must say that colonial powers caused underdevelopment because of the built-in exploitative nature of capitalism.

Gunnar Myrdal, THE CHALLENGE OF WORLD POVERTY (New York: Vintage Books, 1971), pp. 275-85, argues more cautiously that because the theory of international trade was worked out without considering the desire or need of colonized peoples to develop, it contains a theoretical bias opportune to people in the developed countries. Characterized by the predilections of harmony of interests, laissez-faire, and free trade, international trade and capital movements based on this theory tended to breed inequality rather than any equilibrium which could imply a trend toward an equalization of incomes. Mydral states, "By circular causation with cumulative effects, a country superior in productivity and income will tend to become more superior, while a country on an inferior level will tend to be held down at that level or even deteriorate further...." (p. 279). In the sense that colonial powers disrupted the "structures" of traditional society, as will be explained in the succeeding paragraphs of the text, it can be argued that they "caused" underdevelopment. On this point Calvez and Myrdal do not seem to be in basic disagreement. For more extensive discussion of the dispute, see Robert Rhodes, ed., IMPERIALISM AND UNDERDEVELOPMENT (New York: Monthly Review Press, 1970); also, Andre Gunder Frank, CAPITALISM AND UNDERDEVELOPMENT IN LATIN AMERICA (New York: Monthly Press Review, 1967).

[44]Introduction to Rosemary Ruether, FAITH AND FRATRICIDE (New York: Seabury Press, 1974), p. 14.

[45]Berger, PYRAMIDS, pp. 48-49. There is a growing supply of literature on the question of multinational corporations. See, for example, United Nations, Department of Economic and Social Affairs: MULTINATIONAL CORPORATIONS IN WORLD DEVELOPMENT (New York: United Nations, 1973). Also see Hugh Stephenson: THE COMING CLASH (New York: Saturday Review Press, 1972) and Richard Barnet and Ronald Muller, "A Reporter at Large: Multinational Corporations," THE NEW YORKER (2 and 9

December 1974): 53ff. For a brief "state of the question," see Richard D. N. Dickinson, TO SET AT LIBERTY THE OPPRESSED (Commission on the Church's Participation in Development, Geneva: World Council of Churches, 1975), pp. 25-30.

[46]Andre Gunder Frank, CAPITALISM AND UNDERDE-VELOPMENT IN LATIN AMERICA, coined the phrase "the development of underdevelopment." This is the basic argument against development ideology (developmentalism) as it has arisen especially in Latin America. Also see the fine analysis of the forces of exploitation--foreign forces always relying on the help of internal feudal structures--in Kwame Nkrumah, NEO-COLONIALISM, THE LAST STAGE OF IMPERIALISM (New York: International Publishers, 1969). For a sample of the vast literature in this area, see Berger, PYRAMIDS, pp. 64-65. n. 11.

[47]EVANSTON SPEAKS: REPORTS FROM THE SECOND AS-SEMBLY OF THE WORLD COUNCIL OF CHURCHES, 1954 (Geneva: World Council of Churches, 1955), p. 35. Quoted in Paul Bock, IN SEARCH OF A RESPONSIBLE SOCIETY: THE SOCIAL TEACHINGS OF THE WORLD COUNCIL OF CHURCHES (Philadelphia: Westminster Press, 1974), p. 200. (For convenience, reference to World Council of Churches documents appearing in Bock will be given.)

[48]IBID., pp. 42-43. Bock, RESPONSIBLE WORLD SOCIETY, p. 200.

[49]THE NEW DELHI REPORT: THE THIRD ASSEMBLY OF THE WORLD COUNCIL OF CHURCHES, W. A. Visser't Hooft, ed. (New York: Association Press, 1962), p. 95. Bock, RESPONSIBLE WORLD SOCIETY, p. 209.

[50]WORLD CONFERENCE ON CHURCH AND SOCIETY (official report), M. M. Thomas and Paul Abrecht, eds. (Geneva: World Council of Churches, 1967), p. 18. Bock, RESPONSIBLE WORLD SOCIETY, p. 209.

[51]Bock, RESPONSIBLE WORLD SOCIETY, p. 82. The author further discusses the role of the Third World delegates at this conference and a subsequent consultation held in Zagorsk on the question of violent revolution, pp. 81-85. Important study volumes prepared for the Geneva Conference include: CHRISTIAN SOCIAL ETHICS IN A CHANGING WORLD, J. C. Bennett, ed.; RESPONSIBLE GOVERNMENT IN A REVOLUTIONARY AGE, Z. K. Matthews, ed; ECONOMIC GROWTH IN WORLD PERSPECTIVE, D. Munby, ed; MAN IN COMMUNITY, E. de Vries, ed. (all published by Association Press, New York, and SCM Press, London, 1966).

[52]For a discussion of the significance of the Geneva Conference for Uppsala as well as pre-Geneva dialogue with Catholics on Vatican II's CHURCH IN THE MODERN WORLD, the intervening consultations at Zagorsk and the joint consultation of the World Council of Churches and the Vatican Commission on Justice and Peace in Beirut—SODEPAX, Society, Development and Peace—see Ronald Preston, "A Breakthrough in Ecumenical Social Ethics," in TECHNOLOGY AND SOCIAL JUSTICE, R. H. Preston, ed. (Valley Forge, Pennsylvania: Judson Press, and London: SCM Press, 1971), pp. 15-40. The Official Report of the Beirut Conference, WORLD DEVELOPMENT, CHALLENGE TO THE CHURCHES (Geneva: The Ecumenical Center, 1968), urged peaceful change, but warned that obstruction to change could force peoples to violent action. It was not unlike Pope Paul VI's comments in his encyclical ON THE DEVELOPMENT OF PEOPLES. The Beirut document states: "There can be non-violent revolutions. All our efforts must be directed to change without violence. But if injustice is so imbedded in the status quo and its supporters refuse to permit change, then as a last resort men's conscience may lead them in full and clearsighted responsibility without hate or rancour to engage in violent revolution. A heavy burden then rests on those who have resisted change" (p. 20).

[53]See World Council of Churches, "Plan for an Ecumenical Programme to Combat Racism," Minutes of the Central Committee, Canterbury, August 1969, Appendix XX, pp. 270-77. These minutes plus other facts concerning the program are analyzed in Elizabeth Adler, A SMALL BEGINNING (Geneva: World Council of Churches, 1974). Also see TIME TO WITHDRAW: INVESTMENTS IN SOUTHERN AFRICA (Geneva: World Council of Churches, 1974). For a brief report on the Program to Combat Racism at the 1975 Nairobi Assembly of the World Council of Churches, see James W. Kennedy, NAIROBI 1975 (Cincinnati, Ohio: Forward Movement Publications, 1976), pp. 69-73. Also see Arthur J. Moore "Nairobi: Consolidation and Catching Up," CHRISTIANITY AND CRISIS 36 (February 2, 1976): 5. Moore notes that the attempt to exclude grants to liberation movements was massively defeated.

[54]Kennedy, NAIROBI 1975, p. 116.

[55]IBID., p. 102.

[56]See Rene P. Millot, MISSIONS IN THE WORLD TODAY, J. Holland Smith, trans., Vol. 100 of the TWENTIETH CENTURY ENCYCLOPEDIA OF CATHOLICISM (New York: Hawthorn Books, 1961), pp. 12-39. Also see CATHOLIC MISSION: FOUR GREAT MISSIONARY ENCYCLICALS, J. M. Burke, ed. (New York: Fordham University Press, 1957).

[57]PACEM IN TERRIS (New York: American Press, 1963), par. 123. For an overview of Catholic social teaching since Pope John, including documents, see THE GOSPEL OF PEACE AND JUSTICE, presented by Joseph Gremillion (Maryknoll, New York: Orbis Books, 1976) and RENEWING THE EARTH, David O'Brien and Thomas Shannon, ed. (Garden City, New York: Image Books, 1977).

[58]A THEOLOGY OF LIBERATION, Sister Caridad Inda and John Eagleson, trans. and eds. (Maryknoll, New York: Orbis Books, 1973), p. 34.

[59]Reprinted in BEYOND HONESTY AND HOPE: DOCU-
MENTS FROM AND ABOUT THE CHURCH IN LATIN AMERICA,
ISSUED AT LIMA BY THE PERUVIAN BISHOP'S COMMISSION
FOR SOCIAL ACTION, John Drury, trans. (Maryknoll,
New York: Maryknoll Publications, 1970), pp. 3-12.
Latin-American bishops meeting in Medellin in 1968
attempted to interpret the Vatican documents from
the point of view of poor countries in a continent
of misery and injustice. They described the Church
in Latin America as living in a revolutionary climate. See THE CHURCH IN THE PRESENT-DAY TRANSFOR-
MATION OF LATIN AMERICA IN THE LIGHT OF THE COUN-
CIL: THE MEDELLIN DOCUMENTS (trans. and made
available through the U.S. Catholic Conference Division for Latin America, Washington, D.C., 1970).
2 vols.

[60]"A Declaration from the Synod," reprinted in
ORIGINS 4 (November 7, 1974), p. 305.

[61]IBID., p. 308.

[62]Article 34. ON EVANGELIZATION IN THE MODERN
WORLD (The Publications Office, U.S. Catholic Conference, Washington, D.C., 1976).

[63]Excerpts from Bishop Sangu's report "The
African Church Comes-of-Age," in ORIGINS 4
(October 24, 1974): 276.

[64]IBID., p. 275.

[65]IBID., p. 276.

[66]IBID., p. 278-79.

[67]IBID., p. 278.

[68]Text of Archbishop Picachy's address to the
Synod, "India: Vital Perspectives," in ORIGINS 4
(October 24, 1974): 281-83.

CHAPTER TWO

THE TRADITIONAL THEOLOGICAL RATIONALE BEHIND MISSIONARY ACTIVITY

PROTESTANT AND CATHOLIC APPROACHES: METHODOLOGICAL SIMILARITIES

Behind all missionary activity is some theory or, more accurately, some theology of missions. A specific theology of missions depends, in turn, on the Church's understanding of itself and its total mission, its understanding of the individual person and his or her relationship to the world and ultimately to God. At the basis of all theology is a particular understanding of revelation—of how God is available to men and women in the world, of how God offers each one friendship and grace. At the heart of every theology is a concept of eschatology, that is, an understanding of the relationship among the Church, the world, and the expected Kingdom of God.

Revelation, as it was spelled out in the theology of "the great era of missions," dealt primarily with what was considered "revealed truth," with propositions known to be true on the authority of God revealing. For Protestants that revelation was located in the Bible as the inspired word of God; for Catholics it was primarily in the teachings of the Church.

Although impetus for missionary activity was provided on the Protestant side through the Evangelistic and Pietistic awakenings, and on the Catholic side by new religious Orders, still the understanding of revelation behind these movements was basically conservative.

51

From the eschatological perspective, the new "awakenings" did lay emphasis on education, health, and allaying social ills. But the underlying motive for missions was that of rescuing as many of the "heathen" as possible from damnation. This more traditional understanding of revelation and eschatology, in contrast to the subsequent liberal forms of Christianity, provided the main inspiration for missions. Indeed, when a more liberal theology about God's dealings with non-Christian religions began to develop, there arose a sharp counteroffensive on the part of mission-minded Christians. On the Protestant side it was expressed as follows: It is only through the biblical Christ that a person can know who one is and what one must do. Once confronted, a person is called upon to respond in obediential faith. Thus, Christianity becomes the crisis of all religions. This schema has found its most complete and convincing expression in modern times in the dialectical or kerygmatic theology of Karl Barth.[1] Its significance for a specifically missionary theology was set forth most dramatically in Hendrik Kraemer's THE CHRISTIAN MESSAGE IN A NON-CHRISTIAN WORLD. Kraemer states:

> The only valid motive and purpose of missions is, and alone can be, to call men and peoples to confront themselves with God's acts of revelation and salvation for man and the world as presented in Biblical realism, and to build up a community of those who have surrendered themselves to faith in and loving service of Jesus Christ.[2]

Kraemer's work was a deliberate and determined effort to stem the influence of liberal theology in Protestant missionary thinking. It came in direct response to a report entitled RE-THINKING MISSIONS which was prepared for the Laymen's Foreign Mission Inquiry by an appraisal commission headed by the noted American philosopher, W. E. Hocking.[3] This report which appeared in 1932, was the fruit of the commission's fact-finding travels in Asia and Africa on behalf of the American missionary societies. It expressed a theology of missions that was radically different from the formulations of the two great World Missionary Conferences held in Edinburgh in 1910 and in Jerusalem in 1928.

The Edinburgh Conference had declared that missionaries should attempt to understand non-Christian religions and approach them as far as possible with sympathy. The "nobler elements" found in these religions could even be used as stepping stones to higher things, and yet the universal and emphatic witness to the absoluteness of the Christian faith had to be maintained.[4] The Jerusalem Conference reaffirmed this Christocentric affirmation, but also spoke more positively of non-Christian religions:

> We rejoice to think that just because in Jesus Christ the light that lighteth every man shone forth in its full splendor, we find rays of that same light where He is unknown or even rejected. We welcome every noble quality in non-Christian persons or systems as further proof that the Father, who sent His Son into the world, has nowhere left Himself without witness.[5]

Even these statements were seen by some missionary experts as indicating a dangerous tendency toward syncretism. But the report, RE-THINKING MISSIONS, along with a number of other works which appeared shortly thereafter, was seen by many mission-minded individuals as a complete "sell out" of the Christian position. Reflecting the influence on nineteenth century liberal theology and that approach known as the "history of religions school," RE-THINKING MISSIONS sees the task of the missionary as that of seeking out, with people of

other lands, a true knowledge and love of God.
What has been learned by Christians through Jesus
Christ must be stressed in "life and word," and
yet "the Christian will regard himself as a co-
worker with the forces which are making for righteousness within every religious system." Joined
with those of other religious backgrounds in a
common search for truth, the missionary should
look forward, not to the destruction of non-Christian religions but to their continued co-existence
with Christianity, each stimulating the other in
growth toward unity in as complete a religious
truth as possible.[6] Missionary activity, according to this view, seems to be reducible to a type
of cross-cultural fertilization, which maintains
what Troeltsch called the "relative absoluteness"
of Christianity.

It was in response to such a position that the
International Missionary Council asked Kraemer to
prepare a report for its Third World Conference
(Tambaram, Madras, 1938). Encouraged by Kraemer's
CHRISTIAN MESSAGE IN A NON-CHRISTIAN WORLD, this
third great missionary conference declared
unequivocally that, while there are to be found in
other religions "values of deep religious experience and great moral achievements," still, "we believe that Christ is the Way for all, that He
alone is adequate for the world's needs.... We are
bold enough to call men out from them [other reli-
gions] to the feet of Christ. We do so because we
believe that in Him alone is the full salvation
which man needs."[7]

Kraemer's work became what might be called a
"modern classic" in Protestant missionary theology, as well as a restatement of the basic Protestant rationale behind missionary activity.
Kraemer's work stressed the absolute authority of
the Word, Jesus Christ, as discovered in the Bible
and seen through the eyes of faith. Although
Kraemer admits that God shines through the works
of creation and through the conscience of human

beings, still he claims that the "general revelation" can be discovered effectually only in the
light of "special revelation" and therefore is
itself an object of faith.[8] The only way, according to Kraemer, to keep the missionary movement
sound is to insist that the Gospel of Jesus Christ
represents not a more perfect stage of religious
development or production, but an entirely new
world of divine acts.[9] The only point of contact
between Christianity and the non-Christian religions is found in the attitude and disposition of
the individual missionary.[10]

On the Catholic side there are certain parallels to both the attempt to introduce elements of
liberal theology into missionary thinking, and the
subsequent reaction against it. There was an attempt in the nineteenth century to bring Roman
Catholic theology into harmony with the ideas of
Enlightenment. Early in the century, in Germany,
the Catholic theologians of the Tubingen school,
influenced in part by the thought of the liberal
Protestant theologian, Friedrich Schleiermacher,
attempted to approach the unit of natural and
revealed religion from the vantage point of human
experience. They investigated the tradition of
the Church, especially the writings of the Church
Fathers, and at the same time began to employ in
their work the developing science of biblical
criticism. But by midcentury, this creative theological impulse of the Tubingen school gave way to
a defensiveness in the wider church and to a renewed interest in scholasticism.[11] Historical and
biblical criticism were looked upon as threats to
the reality of faith which was regarded as a
timeless, changeless, metaphysical system. This
position found its official expression in the 1864
SYLLABUS OF ERRORS of Pius IX. A growing influence
of official "Roman theology," and an increasing
centralization of authority culminated in the 1870
dogma of papal infallibility. The missionary
activity of the Roman Catholic Church had long before been centrally coordinated by the Pope

through the Roman Curia. This centralization began with the establishment of the Congregation for the Propagation of Faith in 1622. Therefore, the few attempts to liberalize Roman Catholic theology had little effect on its missionary theology.

In England, John Henry Newman's exploration into the psychology of faith had no positive influence on the official "Roman theology." His formulation of a schema on the development of doctrine resting ultimately upon a "sensus fidelium" was to have its influence only much later. In France, the complicated struggles between the Catholic liberal and conservative groups in the early part of the nineteenth century had as many political as theological overtones. Later, at the beginning of the present century, the more strictly theological inquiry came to an abrupt halt with the condemnation of the so-called Modernists by Pius X in 1907.

The first specific theology of missions by a Roman Catholic was Joseph Schmidlin's KATHOLISCHE MISSIONSLEHRE IM GRUNDRISS, published in 1919.[12] It was based in a large part on the work of the Protestant scholar Gustav Warneck, who in 1897 published his famous EVANGELISCHE MISSIONSLEHRE.[13] According to Schmidlin, the primary purpose of missionary activity is the christianization of the non-Christians. Individual conversion was stressed. Because the newly converted people require ecclesiastical order, a local self-sufficient church should be organized. Schmidlin's method in formulating his theology of missions was to examine the textbooks of theology and extract from them, one by one, all that could more or less be related to missions. It was on Schmidlin's work, with certain adjustments and shifts of emphasis, that the so-called "manuals of missiology" were based prior the Second Vatican Council.

Kraemer's description of the purpose of missionary activity could fit the Catholic as well as the Protestant rationale for missions up until recent times, if the phrase "Biblical realism" in Kraemer's formulation were replaced by the "teachings or doctrine of the Church." Both positions represent what can be called a "positivist" approach to theology. That is, both positions assume that theology is essentially a matter of reflecting upon, explaining, defending and disseminating what is contained in its given primary source, be that Scripture according to the Protestant position, or tradition formulated in doctrines according to the Catholic view.

VATICAN II:
TRADITIONAL APPROACHES AND NEW ISSUES

It is interesting that what Kraemer was saying in 1938, the Second Vatican Council was to echo in very similar words in its DECREE ON MISSIONS in 1965. This similarity is evident not only in what was referred to above as a "positivist" approach to theology, but also in the strongly biblical foundation of the Vatican document. This pronounced biblical orientation, which had not been characteristic of earlier Roman Catholic missionary formulations, can be explained in this way: Catholic theology began to emerge from its strict doctrinal scholastic synthesis in the late 1940s and 1950s. It did so through an awakening of liturgical and biblical studies and in ecumenical contact, especially in Germany with Protestant kerygmatic or biblical theology. Biblical theology became "popular" in Catholic thinking.[14] The influence of this biblical movement was felt at Vatican II, not only in the DECREE ON MISSIONS, but also in a very important way in the DOGMATIC CONSTITUTION ON DIVINE REVELATION. It is important to look briefly at this latter document because, as was pointed out earlier, every theology depends ultimately on one's understanding of revelation.

Doctrinal theology, as clearly articulated at the First Vatican Council in 1870, understands revelation as "the sum of the truths disclosed by God for our salvation and preserved in doctrinal form by the one true Church."[15] Faith, according to this schema, is conceived as the response of the believer in the form of intellectual assent to these doctrines which contain universal and time-less propositional truths. Vatican II, attempting to move beyond this rather narrow, intellectual-istic understanding of revelation and faith, com-bined the kerygmatic or biblical and doctrinal positions. The Council describes revelation as happening in and through events of history, and in particular in and through the Christ event. "The obedience of faith" which "must be given to God who reveals," is described as an obedience "by which man entrusts his whole self freely to God...." That the individual must "entrust his whole self freely" involves a personal and con-tinuing commitment by the person to God. Never-theless, obedience of faith also demands "the full submission of intellect and will to God who re-veals."[16] We have here a clear example of a pro-cedure that was not uncommon at Vatican II – that of combining different perspectives not in the form of a synthesis but by mere juxtaposition.

Turning now to the DECREE ON MISSIONS, this juxtaposition of biblical and doctrinal theology makes its similarity to Kraemer's work striking. The opening article states that the two essential elements of missionary work are proclaiming the Word of God and planting churches. This is iden-tical with Kraemer's definition of the task of missions. The reasons given in the DECREE ON MIS-SIONS for this two-fold missionary task are the Gospel mandate, "Go into the whole world...," which is the same as Kraemer's, and, from a doc-trinal point of view, the very nature of the Church's universality.[17]

Chapter I of the DECREE ON MISSIONS amounts to a self-contained treatise. It presents in brief outline, with numerous biblical and patristic references, the theological basis for missionary activity. One might think that here would be the answer to the need for a new theological rationale for missions. But as we shall see, for the most part its foundations are in another age. The presence of some of the newer perspectives on the mission of the Church within this older rationale makes this document one of the most ambiguous of the Council. The first chapter can be briefly summarized as follows:

> The theological rational for missions is grounded in the mystery of the Trinity, in God's eternal saving plan (Art. 2-4). The specifically missionary activity which transmits salvation is distinguished from the general mission of the Church; the concepts, purpose, and methods of the mission and its varying forms are described in detail and contrasted with the pastoral and ecumenical service of the Church (Art. 5-6). As motives of missionary endeavors, it names the necessity of faith, baptism and the Church for salvation, love of God and glorification of God, and also the concrete fulfillment of human nature itself (Art. 7-8). Finally, the duration of missionary activity is given as the period between the Lord's first coming and His return, in which the Church works to gather together and convert the non-Christian nations. (Art. 9).[18]

Concerning Article 7 in the above summary, which states that faith, baptism and the Catholic Church are necessary for salvation, a further explanation seems appropriate. After quoting 1 Timothy 2, 4-5 to the effect that God wishes all to be saved and come to knowledge of the truth, and that Jesus is the one mediator, it then combines this statement with Acts 4, 12. Acts insists that there is no salvation in anyone other than Jesus. This is followed by a quote from Article 14 of the CONSTITUTION ON THE CHURCH, one of the most vivid examples of the older doctrinal theology: All must be converted to Christ as He is made known by the Church's teaching, for He himself "in explicit terms...affirms the necessity of faith and baptism, (cf. Mk. 16, 16: Jn. 3, 5) and through baptism, as through a door, men enter the Church. Whosoever, therefore, knowing that the Catholic Church was made necessary by God through Jesus Christ, would refuse to enter her or to remain in her, could not be saved."[19]

An even clearer picture of the older theological thinking that held sway in the DECREE ON MISSIONS of Vatican II can be shown by examining the three stages or degrees of missionary activity that are proposed in Chapter II, Articles 11-18. The first is the pre-kerygmatic or pre-evangelization stage. Here the important thing is the example of Christian living and practical demonstration of charity of the missionary. Because at this stage of missionary activity it may not be possible to preach the Gospel explicitly, it is all the more urgent for the missionary to display the attractiveness of the Christian life and to take an active and intelligent interest in the complete development of the people among whom he or she works.[20]

The point here is an important one. The "active and intelligent interest in the complete development of the people" is not stressed because it is valuable and right in itself. It is not stressed because it is part of the very saving mission of the Church, but only for the purpose of preparing the people for the second stage, the preaching or kergymatic stage. In very plain words, the maxim could be stated as follows: You cannot preach to people with empty stomachs, not that empty stomachs are a countersign to the message of Jesus that the Church proclaims, but that the hungry are not good listeners. Once again, Kraemer has said it before:

> All activities of the Christian Church and of missions in social service, in education, in rural construction, in medical work and so many things more only get their right missionary foundation and perspective if they belong as intrinsically to the category of witness as preaching or evangelization.[21]

The second stage, the kerygmatic, is, according to the DECREE ON MISSIONS, the heart of all missionary activity. By verbal proclamation it is hoped that a group can be led to explicit faith in Christ and to baptism. The decree does insist that "the Church strictly forbids forcing anyone to embrace the faith, or alluring or enticing people by unworthy techniques."[22] And yet, the very rationale behind the so-called "pre-evangelization stage" makes it difficult to distinguish it from an enticement. Finally, in the third stage, a community with its own hierarchy and clergy is formed and a new local church is established.[23]

From this overview of the first two chapters of the DECREE ON MISSIONS--which has much in common with what Kraemer was saying in 1938--it would seem that those dedicated to a continuation of missionary activity as it had come down to us would have few complaints. But this is not all that the Second Vatican Council said about the Church's missionary activity. From other Council documents, and even from parts of the DECREE ON MISSIONS which quote from these other documents, another perspective comes to light. This other perspective has provided much of the material for the questions which have been raised about the theological underpinnings of the Church's missionary endeavor.

The Council said that the whole Church, by its very nature, is missionary; that every disciple of Christ has the obligation to do his or her part in spreading the Truth. Furthermore, the responsibility to proclaim the Gospel throughout the world falls primarily on the body of bishops.[24] This last statement, especially, was not appreciated by religious Orders, who, in the past, have carried the load of the Catholic missionary enterprise, and because of their "exemption," worked directly under the Pope relatively free of the local bishop's jurisdiction.[25]

This refocus of the responsibility for missions represents one of the most significant but highly contested issues at the Council.[26] What it really signified was a recognition that the mission of the Church could not be identified univocally with the Church's "missions." The underlying question was a theological one concerning the collegial structure of the Church and, even more broadly, the task or mission of the Church as a whole. But it was the sociological or the actual situation of the Church in the world today that brought the theological question to the fore.

The situation which the Council Fathers faced was basically this: The Gospel mandate, "Go into the whole world..." had, from the geographical point of view, been carried out.[27] The Gospel had reached "the ends of the earth." The obvious question now arises, "Where do we go from here?" What makes this question even more timely is the accompanying phenomenon in the West of what some have call "dechristianization" of society. The Church, in almost every country, is entering into a "diaspora" situation. In light of the growing secularization and pluralism, the Church in the West is finding itself increasingly in "dechristianized" surroundings. The division of the world into "Christian" and "mission" countries makes less and less sense. The Church in the West is coming to the realization that it is in the missionary field on its own ground. Geography no longer is the decisive element for dividing the world into mission and non-mission territory. Furthermore, rapid transportation and instant communication make even the designations "far-off," "foreign," or "overseas" almost meaningless.

Some dedicated Christians, who have been or still are involved in missionary activity, were not and are not willing to accept such an analysis of the situation. At the Second Vatican Council the missionary "bloc" was strong and vocal. Those who had become accustomed to being regarded as the highly respected "foreign legion of the Church militant" were determined to maintain the distinction between the pastoral functions of the Church at home and the missionary functions abroad. They found many supporters among the non-missionaries, some of these in powerful positions and willing to speak on behalf of the missionaries. In an important speech before the Council, Cardinal Frings of Cologne opposed the use of the word "mission" for the Church's effort in "dechristianized" countries. Such analogical use of the term was, for Frings, misleading. Mission should be reserved to evangelization of places where the message of Christ had never been preached.[28]

This argument which ran deep and was one of the principal causes of ambiguity of the DECREE ON MISSIONS, did not end with the Council. One recent writer on missionary activity warns that if the distinction between "pastoral" and "missionary" work is not maintained things are sure to degenerate, for "...the Church's pastoral functions, home missions, social action, university students, workers, poor peasants, blind intellectuals, old folks, orphans, etc., may all be regarded as the proper objects of 'missionary activity.'"[29]

As strange and seemingly illogical as such a statement might appear for those who have not "manned the Church's farthest outposts," the writer is very serious and speaks for many others who are still fired by Pius XI's statement that among the many works of the Church "the greatest and holiest is that of missions."[30] They feel that today's theology has turned traitor to the missionary cause.[31] And yet, as has been suggested earlier, most of the conflicting issues which missionaries are having to face come from the Vatican documents themselves. Such issues can be summarized as follows:

If the human person has a right to religious freedom and is not to be forced in any way,[32] if the spiritual and moral good found among non-Christians is to be acknowledged, preserved, and promoted,[33] if (and this was shattering for many Roman Catholic missionaries) other Christian denominations are to be recognized as real churches,[34] if the laity as well as clergy and religious are responsible for spreading the Gospel,[35] if professing the faith and yet shirking earthly responsibilities is one of the more serious errors of our day,[36] then why missions, and why missionaries? Before any answer can be attempted, the theological reasoning behind these new issues and questions must be examined.

SUMMARY OF CHAPTER TWO

Chapter Two examines the traditional theological bases for missionary activity that continue to influence discussion on the conduct of missions. Although the surge of missionary activity took place in the 18th and 19th centuries, a specific theology of missions did not evolve until the late 19th and 20th centuries. When finally articulated, there existed a close similarity between Protestant and Catholic approaches. That is, both were source-dependent or "positivistic" - the Bible as the prime source for Protestant mission theology, and Church doctrine for the mission theology of Catholics. The Protestant approach was strictly Christocentric; the Catholic tended to be ecclesiocentric. The eschatological stance of both was "other-worldly." Attempts to liberalize these concepts were futile prior to Vatican II and the believed discontinuity between Christian and non-Christian religions provided the impetus for the continued influx of Christian missionaries into non-Christian lands.

Vatican II opened the way for consideration of new issues in the conduct of missions. Although the Council's DECREE ON MISSIONS remains theologically positivistic and ecclesiocentric, for the most part, other documents of Vatican II along with subsequent developments have forced us to rethink our theology of missions. The end of colonization, the "dechristianization" of the old bulwarks of Christianity, and the Council's admission that responsibility for spreading the Gospel rests with all the baptized and not just "special" missionaries, as well as the increasing recognition of the merits of all religions--Christian and non-Christian--provoked the radical question, "Why missions?"

NOTES ON CHAPTER TWO

[1]For Barth, there is only one revelation and that is Christian. He contrasts revelation with religion. Religion, according to Barth, is the human person's attempt to move toward God. See CHURCH DOGMATICS I/2 (Edinburgh: T. and T. Clark, 1956), pp. 301-02.

[2]THE CHRISTIAN MESSAGE IN A NON-CHRISTIAN WORLD (Grand Rapids: Kregel Publications, 1938. 7th printing, 1969), p. 292.

[3]RE-THINKING MISSIONS: A LAYMAN'S INQUIRY AFTER ONE HUNDRED YEARS (New York: Harper and Brothers, 1932).

[4]"General Conclusions" in The Report of Commission IV: The MISSIONARY MESSAGE IN RELATION TO NON-CHRISTIAN RELIGIONS, Vol. IV of THE WORLD MISSIONARY CONFERENCE, 1910 (Edinburgh and London: Oliphant, Anderson and Ferrier; New York: Fleming H. Revell Company, 1910), pp. 267-68.

[5]"The Council's Statement" in THE CHRISTIAN LIFE AND MESSAGE IN RELATION TO NON-CHRISTIAN SYSTEMS OF THOUGHT AND LIFE, Vol I of THE JERUSALEM MEETING OF THE INTERNATIONAL MISSIONARY COUNCIL (New York and London: I.M.C., 1928), p. 410.

[6]RE-THINKING MISSIONS, pp. 326-27. Also see pp. 40-47.

[7]"Findings of Tambaram Meeting" in THE AUTHORITY OF FAITH, Vol. 1 of THE TAMBARAM MADRAS SERIES (Published for the International Missionary Council by Oxford University Press, London, 1939), pp. 200-01.

[8]Kraemer, THE CHRISTIAN MESSAGE, p. 125. Kraemer has published other books on this same subject, among them RELIGION AND THE CHRISTIAN (London: Lutterworth Press, 1956), and WORLD CULTURES AND WORLD RELIGIONS: THE COMING DIALOGUE (London: Lutterworth Press, 1960), but his basic position has remained unchanged. His view of "general revelation" is that of Barth.

[9]Kraemer, THE CHRISTIAN MESSAGE, p. 402.

[10]IBID., p. 140.

[11]See Mark Schoof, A SURVEY OF CATHOLIC THEOLOGY, 1800-1970, E. Schillebeeckx, intro. and N. D. Smith trans. (Glen Rock, New Jersey: Paulist - Newman Press, 1970), esp. pp. 22-30.

[12](Munster: Aschendorff, 1919; 2nd ed., 1923). English trans.: CATHOLIC MISSION THEORY (Techny, Illinois: Mission Press, S.V.D., 1931).

[13]2 Vols. (Gotha: F. A. Perthes, 1897).

[14]For further discussion on the "biblical period" in recent Roman Catholic theology, see Richard McBrien, CHURCH: THE CONTINUING QUEST (New York: Newman Press, 1970), pp. 24-25.

[15]See discussion by Richard P. McBrien, DO WE NEED THE CHURCH? (New York: Harper and Row, 1969), p. 190; also see Avery Dulles, THE SURVIVAL OF DOGMA (Garden City, New York: Doubleday, 1971), pp. 154-57.

[16]DOGMATIC CONSTITUTION ON DIVINE REVELATION, Art. 5, in DOCUMENTS OF VATICAN II, W. Abbott, ed. (New York: Guild Press, 1966), p. 113. References to Vatican II documents will hereafter be made by article number as found in this volume.

[17]DECREE ON THE MISSIONARY ACTIVITY OF THE CHURCH, Art. 1. This Vatican document will hereafter be referred to as the DECREE ON MISSIONS.

[18]See Suso Brecther, "Decree on the Church's Missionary Activity," in COMMENTARY ON THE DOCUMENTS OF VATICAN II, 5 vols., H. Vorgrimler, ed. (New York: Herder and Herder, 1969), 4: 113.

[19]DECREE ON MISSIONS, Art. 7.

[20]IBID., Art. 11. Kraemer, THE CHRISTIAN MESSAGE, p. 140, makes a similar point.

[21]Kraemer, THE CHRISTIAN MISSION, p. 433. Kraemer rightly states that the main utterances of the Christian Church are worship, witness and ministry, and that the three terms must be understood in such a way that each of them partakes of the essential nature of the other (p. 405). It is difficult at times, however, to see how Kraemer keeps these three concepts in balance.

[22]DECREE ON MISSIONS, Art. 13. Also see DEC-LARATION ON RELIGIOUS FREEDOM of Vatican II, Arts. 2, 4, 6. The Jerusalem meeting of the International Missionary Council in 1928 likewise disavowed unequivocally all spiritual imperialism.

[23]The Vatican DECREE ON MISSIONS speaks extensively about the question of "adaptation." Art. 16 on the training of native clergy states that students should attempt to make contact with the particular way of thinking and acting characteristic of their people. They should in their philosophical and theological studies "consider the points of contact between the traditions and religion of their homeland and the Christian religion." Concerning the training of missionaries, Art. 26 insists that the missionary should not only have a knowledge of the people's religion and culture but a great esteem for their patrimony. It is clear that the Council Fathers were attempting to correct what had so often been the case before--the identification of Christianity with Western culture. For a similar position from the Protestant side and from the Third World, see THEOLOGICAL EDUCATION IN INDIA: REPORT OF STUDY PROGRAMME AND CONSULTATION, 1967-68 (Board of Theological Education of the NCC of India and Senate of Serampore College, 1968.) This report is quoted and discussed briefly by M. M. Thomas, "Toward an Indigenous Christian Theology," in ASIAN VOICES IN CHRISTIAN THEOLOGY, G. H. Anderson, ed. and intro. (Maryknoll, New York: Orbis Books, 1976), pp. 11-13.

[24]See the DECREE ON MISSIONS, Arts. 2, 23, and 29, with parallels in the CONSTITUTION ON THE CHURCH, Arts. 1, 17, and 23. Once again there was a similar and earlier movement among Protestant churches to locate the responsibility for missions at the center of the churches' corporate activity. This movement culminated in the 1961 merger of the International Mission Society and the World Council of Churches. The result was that for the first

time in history the Orthodox, Old Catholic, Anglican, and "main-line" Protestant churches of the world declared themselves officially to be, as churches, responsible for the evangelization of the world.

[25]Neill, A HISTORY OF CHRISTIAN MISSIONS, p. 558, makes the observation: "In all periods from the beginning, 'missions' have tended to be an adventure of inspired individuals, of religious Orders, of private societies, of groups of 'friends of missions.' Only rarely have they engaged the attention and whole-hearted support of Christian denominations."

Concerning the matter of "exemption" which religious Orders enjoy, it has had a long and interesting history in the Roman Catholic Church. Many bishops at the Council were unhappy with religious Orders operating within their dioceses and yet not under their control. From the missionary point of view, such exemption made it possible for the Pope to use religious Orders for the good of the universal Church. It was a mixed blessing, however, since rivalries among the Orders operating in the same region did arise, and at times the development of an autonomous local church was hindered by vocations going to the Order rather than to a local diocesan church. Moreover, missionary bishops who had been members of a particular Order often remained loyal to that Order. A strong diocesan clergy did not develop, and the local church tended to remain missionary. The shift of the burden of missionary activity from the missionary Orders through the Pope, to the Pope with the bishops, was part of the overall collegial thrust of the Second Vatican Council. For the Council's position on "exemption," see DECREE ON THE BISHOPS' PASTORAL OFFICE IN THE CHURCH, Art. 35.

[26]The history of the DECREE ON MISSIONS itself gives an indication of both the power of the missionary representation at the Council and the more

radical questions some of the Council Fathers had
on the Church's missionary theology. See COMMEN-
TARY ON THE DOCUMENTS OF VATICAN II, Vol. 4, pp.
87ff. At times among those who were responsible
for drafting the missionary schema, there appeared
to be "irreconcilable differences of opinion on
matters of principle." (p. 93) and many "perci-
pient and well-informed Council fathers even considered dispensing with a separate missionary
document." Everything concerning missionary activity, according to their thinking, should on principle be incorporated into the CONSTITUTION ON THE
CHURCH (p. 92).

[27]Eugene Hillman proposes a rather strange
interpretation of this text in his book, THE WIDER
ECUMENISM (New York: Herder and Herder, 1968). See
esp. chap. 8. Hillman claims that the Church is
meant to evangelize all the nations of the world,
and yet only consecutively. In other words, the
Church should see that the Gospel reaches the ends
of the earth, but it need not return to those nations which had accepted the Gospel at some time
in the past but later had allowed it to die. On
the contrary, "re-evangelization" according to
Hillman is against the Gospel mandate. For a different perspective on this Gospel mandate, see
Karl Barth, "Exegetical Study of Matthew 28,
16-20," in THE THEOLOGY OF CHRISTIAN MISSION,
G. H. Anderson, ed., pp. 55-71.

[28]See COMMENTARY ON THE DOCUMENTS OF VATICAN
II, Vol. 4, p. 99, n. 27.

[29]Quoted in Hillman, THE CHURCH AS MISSION
(New York: Herder and Herder, 1965), p. 29. No
further reference is given.

[30]Pius XI, RERUM ECCLESIAE (1926), quoted by
John Power in MISSIONARY THEOLOGY TODAY (Maryknoll, New York: Orbis Books, 1971), p. 3.

[31]For an overview of the discontent among many missionaries, see Power, MISSIONARY THEOLOGY TODAY, chap. 1. Power paraphrases the papers presented at the 1969 SEDOS Conference in Rome (Servizio documentazione e studi) and then attempts to weave together the divergent views of the contributors into some unified position. The inconsistencies of this book are pinpointed by Avery Dulles in "Current Trends in Mission Theology," THEOLOGY DIGEST 20 (Spring 1971): 26-34. The actual papers given at this conference, along with discussion which took place, have been published as FOUNDATIONS OF MISSION THEOLOGY, SEDOS, ed., John Drury, trans. (Maryknoll, New York: Orbis Books, 1972).

[32]DECLARATION ON RELIGIOUS FREEDOM, Arts. 2, 4, 6; DECREE ON MISSIONS, Art. 1.

[33]DECLARATION ON THE RELATIONSHIP OF THE CHURCH TO NON-CHRISTIAN RELIGIONS, Art. 2.

[34]DECREE ON ECUMENISM, Art. 3.

[35]CONSTITUTION ON THE CHURCH, Art. 17.

[36]CONSTITUTION ON THE CHURCH IN THE MODERN WORLD, Art. 43.

CHAPTER THREE

A THEOLOGICAL SHIFT AND ITS EFFECT
UPON THE CHURCH'S MISSION

REVELATION AND ESCHATOLOGY:
KEY CONCEPTS IN THE THEOLOGICAL SHIFT

We have examined the theological rationale behind the missionary activity during the colonial period. We turn now to the theological rationale behind the new perspective on missions which has been emerging from the documents of the Second Vatican Council and the statements of the World Council of Churches. Some missionaries contend that theology has compromised with the world, that it has "watered down" the clear biblical and doctrinal mandate, that it has "sold out" on the missionary enterprise.[1] On the other hand, many theologians would argue that theological thinking has changed because the conditions of the "missionary world" have changed. Instead of theology or theologians "selling out" on the missionary enterprise, they see the shift taking place today as an expedient attempt to pull together the pieces after the world and world view which supported the traditional theological rationale on missions have collapsed.[2] More accurately, however, the shift has resulted from a change in the method of doing theology--a method that accepts as an essential element dialogue with the contemporary world.

As mentioned before, any theology will depend ultimately on one's understanding of two key concepts--revelation and eschatology. Ecclesiology, in turn, and therefore a theology of missions, will reflect the fundamental understanding one has of revelation and eschatology.

73

Theology can be defined as the attempt to understand and articulate our presumed experience of God. This definition admittedly presupposes a number of things. First of all, it assumes that God is real and is available to us--that God reveals. It recognizes, further, that any disclosure by God to men and women is mediated through some element of human experience. It cannot be otherwise. "No one has ever seen God," St. John reminds us (Jn. 1, 18). Because God's self-disclosure is mediated through some facet of human life and history, the element of ambiguity is always present. We can only "presume" that a particular experience is revelatory, is grace-filled. Theology, speaking out of faith, must share something of the risk of faith. Further, the definition presupposes it is _our_ presumed experience of God. That is to say, there is a communal aspect to all theology. Our attempt to understand and articulate this presumed experience of God must be tested within the community of faith. This articulation must be manifested in deeds; it must be _practical_.[3]

Theology must begin from human experience.[4] God is available there. But as the community that proclaims that God has been revealed in a unique way in and through Jesus, our "present revelation" must be tested in and by the community of faith, both past and present.[5] Otherwise, theology runs the risk of becoming a mere self-reflection of those engaged in the enterprise.

Because the New Testament writings came into existence during the formative period of the Church, and were indeed constitutive for the community, they will always have a privileged position in the Church. If God willed a community to continue the word and work of Jesus, as Christians believe, then God must have willed the foundational writings of this community. For members of this community these foundational writings, as well as those taken over from the Jewish community, will

always have an irreplaceable position. They are
normative in the sense that they may never be forgotten or ignored; we must always be in dialogue
with them. Although not revelation themselves,
they point in an emphatic way to that unique revelation of God which early Christians perceived in
Jesus. They therefore serve all succeeding Christian generations in clarifying, deepening and
purifying their present experience of God.

Theology must also take seriously the post-
primitive tradition--the teachings of Church Councils, of popes and bishops, the articulations of
great theologians, as well as the reflection of
holy men and women through the ages. The reflections of the community down through history on
what they perceived as the "present revelation"
can also clarify our present attempts to do theology. As Gabriel Fackre has aptly said:

> Neither the Christian future nor present
> ...can dismiss what has taken place be-
> fore their time, although they always
> must put a question mark over it. But
> the source of that very mark is a strand
> of the past, the event of Jesus Christ.[6]

Such a method of doing theology can be described as reading the signs of the time, letting
this reading influence the way we interpret and
live the Good News of Jesus Christ that comes to
us through the community, and in turn letting the
Gospel influence the way we read the signs of the
times. It takes the present seriously; it builds
on the premise that God continues to be available
to men and women through present experience; and
it attempts to discern and then articulate that
presence in its theology. But it also takes the
past seriously--the history of the community of
faith and the documents that reflected in their
own time the community's perception of their
"present revelation." Still, this method moves
away from the narrower biblical and doctrinal

approach which sees its task confined to the interpretation, explanation and defense of tenets which have their origins in the Bible or in Church doctrines. Final authority or truth, for us, is confined neither to historical sources nor to present human experience itself, but the continuing dynamic interaction within the faith community between Christians' present experience of God and the recorded experience of those who have preceded them. This method we have been describing can, in a broad sense, be called the method of correlation as proposed by Paul Tillich.[7]

Such a method of correlation depends not only on an understanding of revelation as outlined above, but also on one's understanding of eschatology. For, if one is to take the present seriously, one also must be concerned about the future in the sense that tomorrow's "present" is a prolongation of today. The good of the present must, in turn, be sustained for the future, while the evil must be corrected in the hope of a better tomorrow. Indeed, being serious about the present ultimately entails being concerned about its relationship to the absolute future, the Kingdom of God.

There are a number of ways in which eschatology is formulated in current theology, but a basic contrast can be seen between most of these formulations and the understanding of eschatology in biblical and doctrinal theology. The basic contrast is this: In biblical and doctrinal theology, there is no real interest in history nor in the processes and future of history. Carl Braaten's description of Barth's eschatology is generally applicable to both the biblical and doctrinal theological methods:

> Eschatology, which has to do with the future destiny of this world, is lifted into the transcendental realm.... Eschatology thus is not a doctrine of the future,

neither of the future of man and his world, nor the future of God and his approaching kingdom. It is wholly absorbed into the transcendence and eternity of God, coming down vertically from above. The horizontal categories of history and the kingdom of God in the Bible are spiritualized into the beyond of eternity.[8]

The seventh chapter of the CONSTITUTION ON THE CHURCH of Vatican II, entitled "The Eschatological Nature of the Pilgrim Church and her Union with the Heavenly Church," reflects basically this same other-worldly, spiritualized understanding of eschatology: We are "exiles on earth" awaiting the return of our Redeemer (Art. 49). The "promised" restoration which we are awaiting has already begun in Christ," and is anticipated in some real sense through the Church. "There we learn through faith the meaning...of our temporal life, as we perform, with hope of good things to come, the tasks committed to us in this world by the Father, and work out our salvation" (Art. 48).

This perspective stands in stark contrast to the eschatological view expressed in the CONSTITUTION ON THE CHURCH IN THE MODERN WORLD:

Earthly progress must be carefully distinguished from the growth of Christ's Kingdom. Nevertheless, to the extent that the former can contribute to the better ordering of human society, it is of vital concern to the Kingdom of God. (Art. 39).

This same article further reminds us that the "expectation of a new earth must not weaken but rather stimulate our concern for cultivating this one." This is especially true since "the values of human dignity, brotherhood and freedom, and indeed all the good fruits of our nature and enterprise, we will find...again, but freed of stain, burnished and transfigured."

This latter view of eschatology reflects the correlative method of theology, in that it is vitally interested in exploring and explaining the interrelationships among history, the Church and the Kingdom of God. It is important to note that the Kingdom of God in this perspective is not identified with the Church. In doctrinal theology, especially, the Church and the Kingdom were identified with each other. Here, in contrast the Church serves as the herald, the sign, and the servant of the Kingdom. The Kingdom of God provides a measure against which every major area of Christian faith can be focused.[9] It is, according to Braaten, "the most powerful symbol of hope in the religious and social history of mankind." Combining social, political and personal dimensions of fulfillment, the concept of the Kingdom unites spatial and temporal elements into an eschatological synthesis. It promises healing to bodily and spiritual illness, liberation from political and spiritual bondage, justice for the oppressed, righteousness for sinners, and homecoming for exiles.[10]

The articulation of our presumed experience of God, therefore, must take place within the context of history, the Church, and the Kingdom of God. The understanding of the two key concepts, revelation and eschatology, as given above represents the background for the theological shift which has taken place in the Christian Church. As noted earlier, this shift has had a profound effect on the understanding of the nature and mission of the Church.

Several key passages from Vatican II's CONSTITUITION ON THE CHURCH IN THE MODERN WORLD reflect the tenor of this theological shift. In the introductory statement (Arts. 4-10) there is a conscious effort to relate the Christian message to

the actual situation of the world: "The Church has
the duty of scrutinizing the signs of the times
and of interpreting them in light of the Gospel."
The Church understands its primary task to be that
of "fostering that brotherhood of all men...," "to
carry forward the work of Christ Himself under the
lead of the befriending Spirit," and "to rescue
and not to sit in judgment, to serve and not to be
served."

After outlining some of the major changes that
have altered the complexion of the world situation
--spiritual, intellectual, scientific, biological,
psychological, social and technological--the document states, "Thus the human race has passed from
a rather static concept of reality to a more dynamic, evolutionary one" (Art. 5). The significance of this statement should not be overlooked.
The Thomistic-Aristotelian grip on theological
method has been loosened; doctrinal theology with
its timeless propositions has been shaken. For
the first time a processive and relational view of
history is detected in the Catholic Church's official declarations. Later in the same Constitution
governments are reminded that it is their duty to
take a "dynamic" concept of the common good as
their norm and goal (Art. 74).

Research and progress in various fields of
human endeavor and a new consciousness in humankind as a result of socialization and planetiza-
tion have brought about new and deeper insights
into the problem of God, into the way God reveals
and men and women respond. All of this has had a
profound effect on the theological thinking about
the Church's missions. The theological shift we
have been describing has not taken place overnight, of course. One might say that on the Protestant side strains of the liberal theology of the
nineteenth century--from Schleiermacher to Ritschl
--have begun to surface again after the devasting
blow given it by Barth's neo-orthodoxy. On the
Catholic side many of the questions which the

Modernists were asking (and perhaps attempting to answer from an inadequate, one-sided point of view) have emerged once again, even though it was assumed by Rome early in the present century that they had been forever banished.

MAURICE BLONDEL:
A SOURCE IN THE THEOLOGICAL SHIFT

Gregory Baum, in MAN BECOMING: GOD IN SECULAR EXPERIENCE,[11] traces one strain of this theological shift back to Maurice Blondel who, he claims, has had a growing influence on the doctrinal evolution which has been taking place in the twentieth century. Indeed, Yves Congar and Bishop Butler have affirmed that Blondel, more than anyone else, stands behind the doctrinal evolution at Vatican II.[12]

It will be helpful at this point to examine what Baum calls the "Blondelian shift" in order to demonstrate how the theological shift we have been describing is reflected in a specific author. Baum's book itself is a serious and worthwhile attempt to reflect in a systematic way on the new manner in which men and women of our age experience the Gospel and how, in turn, this experience can help us interpret and transform our culture along what Baum calls the lines of its own deepest dimension. While Baum is not alone in this endeavor, nor even among the first,[13] still his approach will be useful here because his understanding of the Church and its mission provides a position against which we can project our own attempt to spell out a theology of missions under the aegis of development.

At the turn of the century and in the midst of the heated Modernist controversy, we find Blondel, the French philosopher-theologian, attempting to forge a new Christian philosophical synthesis which would be open to the conditions and thought of his day.[14] His dynamic understanding of existence makes his thought surprisingly contemporary, even today. He was convinced that God is present to human history and that this presence is the source of new life in the aspirations, conflicts, and thought forms constituting the human reality in every generation. Therefore, to understand the meaning of God as revealed in Christ, one must be open to dialogue with contemporary culture.

The "Blondelian shift" about which Baum speaks is basically this: Blondel understood the human person as a dynamic reality. In his famous thesis, L'ACTION, which caused so much controversy at the Sorbonne in 1893, Blondel dealt with man's and woman's need for the transcendent.[15] He attempted to show that a systematic reflection on human life and development leads to an acknowledgment of the divine. By this reflection, one is brought to the threshold of the Christian Gospel. Truth, for Blondel, is present in the action of men and women, and action refers not only to their doing, but to their willing and choosing, as well as to their creative thinking. Action is that very self-affirmation by which men and women become themselves and determine their own history. To act, for Blondel, is to strive to achieve an agreement among knowing, willing and being. From the first moment of life, men and women are summoned to action, and they become themselves, remain who they are, and enter into their destiny by involving themselves in life through action.

Revelation, for Blondel, is not new truth that is added to human life from without, nor is God to be understood as a divine being facing human beings from beyond. This Blondel labels "extrinsicism." For the person of today's world it is impossible to accept truth which has no intrinsic relationship to life or does not in some way correspond to his or her experience of reality. As

Blondel states it, "Nothing can enter man that does not somehow answer in him a need for expansion, whatever the origin or the nature of that appetite may happen to be."[16]

If the transcendent is present in the finite, which Blondel believed to be the case and which he labeled the "method of immanence," then it should manifest itself in the structures of human action.[17]   Briefly, it works in this way: Men and women are carried forward by the logic of their action to an important option in their lives which determines what they will be. Their capacity for willing, which cannot be exhausted in a finite universe, leads them to wider and wider action. They discover the world in which they live and they attempt to organize it; they come to love other persons and to assume responsibility for their own lives and the lives of others; they expand their love to include family, nation and the whole human race. Still, the deep willing at the core of their being is not exhausted. The dynamism of the inner dialectic of human action lures them on to a goal which lies beyond their power to achieve but which, if it were to be offered to them as a gift, would be genuine fulfillment. Finally, they are summoned to an inevitable option: either they open themselves to the infinite or enclose themselves in the finite order and thereby violate the thrust of their own action.

Men and women may open themselves to the infinite either by acknowledging an infinite, self-revealing God, or, if they have not heard of God, by refusing to invest the finite with infinite value. In other words, they avoid idolatry. Openness means they place nothing in the way of divine grace and they rely on it for further action. This grace is gift-like, that is, although people need an order beyond the finite if they are to be fully themselves, they are at the same time totally incapable of achieving this by their own resources. Therefore, the transcendent, present in the finite, is clearly distinguished from it.

Recognizable here is a theology of universal grace, or a version of the ancient Logos theory Christology. It is the divine Logos that is creating the cosmos and redeeming humankind. Because of the omni-presence of the Logos, divine grace and, therefore, salvation is available to people wherever they are. This theology of universal grace was revived by Protestant thinkers of the nineteenth century, and among Catholics has found a strong advocate not only in Blondel but in theologians such as Teilhard de Chardin, Henri de Lubac, and Karl Rahner.[18] This position influenced the teaching of Vatican II and created the doctrinal basis for the Catholic Church's openness to world religions and to secular culture. Although Rahner admits only an indirect influence of Blondel on his own thought, the two men who, he does admit, had a direct influence on him—Marechal and Rousselot—were in turn influenced by Blondel.[19]

DEFINING THE CHURCH:
A BROAD OR MORE RESTRICTED VIEW

1. A BROAD UNDERSTANDING OF CHURCH

If the option to open oneself to the infinite is offered to men and women everywhere, if divine grace is present to human history, then the question arises once again, "Why missionaries?" "Do we really need them?" Or, even more basically, as Richard McBrien has asked DO WE NEED THE CHURCH?[20]

There are two ways of approaching this question. One is to broaden the understanding of Church to include all those who respond to this divine option, even if they are not specifically conscious of it. The Church then exists wherever "there is light amidst darkness;" it includes anyone in whom the Spirit creates new life. The second way is to maintain a more restricted or more specific understanding of Church. The Church consists of those who explicitly confess the Lordship of Jesus of Nazareth, who ratify that faith in baptism and thereby commit themselves to membership and mission within the sacramental community of faith.

Both of these conceptions or models of the Church can stress the diaconal or servant aspect of the Church's mission. But from the point of view of the missionary endeavor and the Church's role in world development, it is evident that the broad or restricted understanding of Church will be a vital determining factor in the focus and scope of the Church's mission.

Gregory Baum tends toward the broad understanding of Church.[21] He suggests that it is possible to affirm the universality of grace and at the same time speak of Church in a meaningful way. However, his description of the Church carries an ambiguity as he states, "The Church is the community where God's universal redemptive presence is proclaimed, celebrated and possessed in Jesus Christ...." That is a restricted definition. Then he adds, "...the Church is the community where humanity has become fully conscious of its divine destiny and hence the community which has the mission to serve this destiny in the world." This statement would also appear restricted when read with the earlier definition. But Baum also acknowledges that, because the same "marvelous things" that happen in the Church are also available outside, it can be said that the fellowship produced by the Spirit of the Church extends beyond its visible boundaries. "Church", then, according to Baum's perspective, is "the divine message about man's life in community."[22]

It follows from this that ecclesiology is not simply the theological study of the Christian Church and its mission, but "the critical study, based on divine revelation, of what happens in human society;" it is "the study of the Spirit's presence to sick society;" or simply "the theological study of human society."[23] Baum therefore broadens the concept of Church to include not only those who specifically proclaim, celebrate and witness the universal redemptive mystery which has become incarnate in Jesus Christ, but also all those individuals and human communities in whom the Spirit creates new life.

Van Leeuwen basically comes to this same position, although by a different route. In discussing the role of the Church in the technological, secular world, he describes it at times in a specific or restrictive sense, and yet overall he clearly calls for a broad understanding of Church. He notes that Christian churches in non-Western countries have generally formed tiny minorities out of touch with the political emancipation and economic and social transformations which mark the "incognito Gospel" present in secularization and technology. This isolation must end, according to van Leeuwen.[24] In preaching the Gospel the Church must not be concerned with the survival of any particular religion, but simply with the future of man.[25] "The whole Church must bring the whole Gospel to the whole world," is his famous conclusion.[26] Understood in light of van Leeuwen's overall view, this statement could be interpreted to mean "the spirit of Western civilization [the Church] is to bring secularization [the incognito Gospel] to the whole [non-Western] world." The more specific and temporary task of the Church as van Leeuwen sees it will be discussed later.

Max Stackhouse, in ETHICS IN THE URBAN ETHOS,[27] employs an ecclesiology similar to that of Baum and van Leeuwen. Although he uses traditional theological terms in nontraditional ways, still his "sociotheological analysis and reconstruction of a polity for the liberated city of mankind" provides many valuable insights for the reformulation of missionary theology under the

aegis of development. In a chapter entitled "Ecclesiology and the Cosmopolitan Polity," Stackhouse outlines the polity for an ecumenical ecclesiology which can, perhaps provide the groundwork
for a united Christian effort in formulating a
theology of missions as development.[28]

According to Stackhouse, all major theories of
urban polity are rooted in "credos." Any fully
developed "credo" must have at least three ingre-
dients: eschatology--a peculiar concept of the
"good" future; doctrine--a formal model by which
what is "right" gives normative order to human
existence; and polity--a structured constituency
whereby visions and doctrines are made "fit" and
operational in the transformation of social life.
The "ecclesia," or that body of like-minded people
called out and organized around a common purpose
or vision, is the decisive category by which urban
power and organized constituencies are to be
understood.[29]

Stackhouse sees the changes and the new period
into which the Church is moving as a "highly significant and prophetic development...." On the
one hand, it represents "the Church's relative
success in both responding to the modern world and
transcending the parochial loyalties of nation,
race, special tradition and ideologized polity."
On the other hand, Stackhouse sees in this new
development the "redefining [of] 'ecclesia' in
such a way that it is no longer confined to
'churchiness.'"[30]

Like Baum, Stackhouse broadens the understanding of ecclesiology. He defines ecclesiology as:

>...the critical analysis and reconstruc-
>tion of the operative patterns of crea-
>tive order, identity formation, and
>enspirited community among those who are
>called out of ordinary existence to actu-
>alize a vision of life as transformed un-

der the conscious influence of the ultimate and most worthy power or powers of
existence. The organizational support
system for those on the way to fulfill
the human vision of a transformed future
under a doctrine of 'right' is the
focus.[31]

This broad view of ecclesiology, and therefore
of the Church, which Stackhouse admits "may turn
much of the study of the Church on its head" cuts
across religious traditions and includes non-
Christians as well as Christians:

Those groups who participate in the process of transforming life in nonapocalyp-
tic and nonutopian ways and who accent
creative order, transformed identity and
enspirited community are faithful to the
project and the doctrine whether or not
the members of such a group confess a
particular religious tradition or use the
terms 'God' or 'Christ.'[32]

Stackhouse insists, however, that the "ecclesia"--the "enspirited community" that is faithful
to the project and the doctrine--have good social
organization and organized group activity. Furthermore, because of his very broad understanding
of Church, Stackhouse can insist on the traditional formula extra ecclesiam nulla salus est
(outside the Church there is no salvation).[33] As
an organized movement, the "ecclesia" must have a
symbol or language system, a polity, an economy, a
pattern of mores, and constituent members. It will
be a "meta-system, a parallel organization to the
whole society." It will have a close relationship
with the host society and yet will attempt "to integrate the various levels of its internal structure (and sometimes those of the whole social
system) in a way that is consistent with its
vision of the future and its understanding of
ultimate patterns of worth and power."[34]

In these three examples of a broad understanding of Church, there appear definite similarities and certain common weaknesses. In Baum's Church as the "human communities in whom the Spirit creates new life;" in van Leeuwen's in which the concern is "simply with the future of man;" and in the formulation of Stackhouse in which the Church is described as the "enspirited community" of "like-minded people called out and organized around a common purpose or vision," we find the common desire to include within the Church all peoples, groups, movements and events in which the action of the Holy Spirit is discerned. They might be described as ecclesiologies of the institutionalized Spirit. And yet that one vital element which alone sets the Christian Church apart from other communities, organizations or movements, has lost its central position--that is, the profession of the Lordship of Jesus of Nazareth and, following from this, the celebration of His Lordship within the community of faith in word and sacrament.

The legitimate objectives of these broadened ecclesiologies and the uniqueness of the Christian Church could both be maintained if these writers were to make clear the distinction between the Church and its mission, on the one hand, and the Kingdom of God on the other. Actually, in spite of the awkwardness of the term, it is "kingdom-ology" rather than ecclesiology which these authors are formulating. This is more than a matter of mere quibbling over terminology. A definition of Church is especially important in this attempt to formulate a theology of missions which will take as its focus the Church's role in world development.

Stackhouse insists that the broadened definition of ecclesiology is "a very critical point at which to take the pulse of significant movements in society." This broadened definition, according to Stackhouse, enables Christians to argue that

secular movements and activities are not in fact
marginalizing and displacing the Church in relation to important cultural-political innovations
that are taking place.[35] But, however commendable
this effort is to "locate" and define the Church
in such a way that it is not "marginalized" and
"displaced" in modern society, still the Christian
Church ceases to be the Christian Church when its
distinguishing mark is no longer the profession of
the Lordship of Jesus of Nazareth. The restricted
or more specific definition of Church, which will
be employed here, will enable us to maintain the
uniqueness of the Church of Jesus Christ and at
the same time to bring the specific responsibility
of the Church, as far as mission and development
are concerned, more in line with its real capabil-
ity. We must examine this restricted or specific
understanding of Church in more detail now.

2. A RESTRICTED UNDERSTANDING OF CHURCH

The restricted or more specific understanding
of Church insists upon the primacy of the position
of Jesus Christ and yet subordination of the
Church to the more inclusive concept of the Kingdom or Reign of God. Richard P. McBrien has defined the Church according to this understanding
in the following way:

> The Church is the community of those who
> confess the Lordship of Jesus Christ, who
> ratify that faith in baptism, and who
> thereby commit themselves to membership
> and mission within that sacramental com-
> munity of faith.[36]

McBrien insists that the primary reality is
the Kingdom of God and that the existence and
function of the Church make no sense apart from
it. The mission of the Church, therefore, is
definable only in relationship to the Kingdom.

Stated by McBrien, the Church's mission is:

> To proclaim in word and sacrament the
> definitive arrival of the Kingdom in
> Jesus of Nazareth (kerygma), to offer it-
> self as a test case of its own proclama-
> tion, as a group of people transformed by
> the Spirit into a community of faith,
> hope, love, and truthfulness--a sign of
> the Kingdom on earth and an anticipation
> of the Kingdom of the future (koinonia),
> and finally to realize and extend the
> reign of God through service in the
> sociopolitical order (diakonia).[37]

The Church, therefore, is never an end in itself. Rather it is meant to continue the work of
Jesus Christ--that is, to announce, to be a sign
of, and to serve the Kingdom of God to which all
humankind has been summoned. The Christian community believes that the Kingdom of God has broken
into our history in a definitive way in Jesus of
Nazareth. Because of the life, death and resurrection of Jesus, the Christian community confi-
dently expects the final realization of the
Kingdom through him. Because of what God has
already accomplished in Jesus Christ, the faith
community is given hope for the future of Jesus,
that shalom promised throughout the Old Testament,
that "fulfillment of the promised righteousness of
God in all things, the fulfillment of the resurrection of the dead that is promised in his resurrection, the fulfillment of the lordship of the
crucified one over all things that is promised in
his exaltation."[38]

Signs of the Kingdom of God are present even
now in mystery in those situations where men and
women of good will strive together to establish
understanding and respect, justice and peace. The
Kingdom is already present in history, as Rahner
says:

...wherever obedience to God occurs in grace as the acceptance of God's self-communication. And this does not take place solely in the Church as the socially constituted, historically visible society of the redeemed. It does not take place solely in the secret inwardness of conscience, in meta-religious subjectivity, but in the concrete fulfillment of an earthly task, of active love of others, even of collective love of others.[39]

The Church, then, is the community that specifically proclaims and celebrates the "good news" that the hidden involvement of God in humanization and salvation of the whole human family has become definitively manifest in Jesus Christ. People are drawn to the Church by the haunting figure of Jesus of Nazareth, but both the gift-like invitation to membership in the Church and the possibility of commitment to mission are hidden in the mystery of election. Election to membership in the Church, in turn, brings with it not privilege but a responsibility to service. The call or election to membership does not necessarily mean that those who respond will achieve God's Kingdom, nor that those who have not been called or have not heard the call will be lost. For, as St. Augustine has said, "Many whom God has, the Church does not have; many whom the Church has, God does not have."[40] Neither can it be maintained that those who are not in the Church are in a position of disadvantage in the pursuit of a full and mature life here and now, nor of future existence in the Kingdom. As McBrien points out, "...biblically, the counterpart of election is simply non-election--not reprobation or reduction to a disadvantaged condition."[41]

ECCLESIOLOGY AND CHRISTOLOGY:
A FURTHER PROBLEM

This distinction between all people being called to the Kingdom and only a certain few to membership and mission in the Church is of vital importance for two reasons. First of all, it offers an alternative to the perplexing and questionable position which Rahner and others have adopted concerning "anonymous," "implicit," or "incognito" Christians.[42] Secondly, it avoids the danger of relativizing Jesus as the Christ, as the ultimate revelation of the Father--a danger which, it appears, some modern theologians such as Rosemary Ruether have not avoided.[43] Gregory Baum also seems to be sympathetic to this relativizing tendency in Christology.[44]

Basically, Rahner's position is that "graced" men and women are Christians whether they know it or not. That is, those people who, by their attitudes and lifestyle, are faithful to the will of God as expressed by Jesus, and yet do not profess his lordship nor become a member of his Church, are anonymous Christians. Implicit in this position, however, is what might be called a new ecclesiastical imperialism: All should be Christians; those who "measure up" to the Christian ideals are "on their way" to becoming Christians regardless of whether they know it, want it, or even outrightly deny it. What holds true for individual Christians likewise holds true for non-Christian religions. Inasmuch as they are authentic, they are implicit Christianities destined to be superseded by explicit Christianity. The further they move along the way of divine grace, the closer they come to being displaced by the Christian Church. Rahner likens other world religions to the religion of Israel in the Old Testament. Like Israel, they anticipate the grace of Christ and prepare for his total manifestation in the Christian Church. Salvation is available to people within the religion they find themselves in until such time as they are confronted in an existential way with the revelation of Jesus Christ.[45] Therefore, these religions have relative validity. While such a position may be unobjectionable as long as Christians are talking to one another, it is hardly conducive to broader dialogue with non-Christians.

Gabriel Fackre is another who attempts to deal with Christ's relationship to the Church and to the rest of the world.[46] He tries to reconcile the broad (or what he calls "radical ecclesiology") and the more specific understanding of the Church. Although he explicitly denounces any ecclesiastical imperialism, he does end up in a position not unlike that of Rahner.

Fackre sees in the Emmaus episode of the New Testament an analogy for understanding the relationship of Christ to the Church and to the world. Even as then there were those whose "eyes were kept from recognizing him" while they were on the road, and those whose "eyes were opened" in the breaking of the bread, so today some encounter the "incognito Christ in the Church invisible," while others "know Christ" in the visible community of faith. Fackre suggests that perhaps we can speak of the two "faces" of Christ.[47] He speaks hesitantly about the "incognito relationship as participation, in some sense, in the Church." Those who do not acknowledge his name and yet are his co-workers are designated as members of the "doing church," while those in the "knowing church" have a deep, personal communion with Christ in a type of bride-bridegroom relationship. Fackre suggests that the concept of the "invisible church," translated into fresh terms, can designate those who do not "know" Christ but nevertheless do his worldly will.[48]

On the other hand, Fackre insists upon the Church as the sacrament of God, as the Body of Christ. The celebrating and worshipping community is "a community of _memory_ of the Events that give it identity;" a community of hope and vision. Because its Herald and Embodier is the Head of the Church, the community already experiences in some way the goal toward which it is moving. As Fackre states it, "The celebrating community which looks forward to the coming of God with appetite whetted for the reconciliation of the world, is by dint of his presence, a downpayment, a 'firstfruit' of the Kingdom which comes."[49]

Fackre attempts to reconcile the broad and specific understanding of Church. But the Christological difficulties raised by terminology such as "the 'two' faces of Christ" and "the incognito Christ in the Church invisible" are almost greater than the questions they attempt to answer. But by making the distinction between the Church and the Kingdom of God--all are called to the Kingdom but not all are called to the Church--and by admitting that there are other ways to the Kingdom than through the Church, the designation "anonymous Christian" or "incognito Christ in the Church invisible" becomes unnecessary.

The second reason why the distinction between the Church and the Kingdom is important concerns the relativizing of the position of Jesus. Rosemary Ruether, in an attempt to establish a doctrinal basis for religious pluralism, stresses the incompleteness of God's revelation in Jesus.[50] With a strong futurist eschatological focus, Ruether sees the need to translate into eschatological terms both the absolute claims which the Church has made for Jesus and the Church's own historical existence. Placing in central position the doctrine of the second coming, and distinguishing between "fulfilled and "unfulfilled" messianism, Ruether claims that Jesus is the Christ only in the proleptic sense. Divine redemption is finished in Christ only by way of anticipation. His life and work are a token, a pledge, a first installment of the complete redemption promised in Scripture. From this point of view, which Ruether calls unfulfilled messianism, Jesus will be Lord, but Jesus is not yet Lord in the definitive sense.[51] It follows from this that the Church is not the unique vehicle of grace, and room remains in the world for

other ways of grace, for many religions, and especially for the other biblical faith, Judaism. Fulfilled messianism, according to Ruether's point of
view, forgets about the meaning of the second coming; it teaches that the promises contained in
Scripture are fulfilled in Jesus and, therefore,
ultimately lead to religious imperialism.

Ruether's approach may be attractive, especially for those attempting to clarify the relationship between Christianity and Judaism, but it
negates the very purpose for which the Christian
Church exists—to profess that God has acted decisively and definitively in human history through
the person of Jesus of Nazareth; that Jesus is the
exalted Lord now and that he will come again to
finalize the Kingdom and to deliver it to the
Father. By relativizing God's revelation in Jesus,
Ruether in effect pulls the foundation from beneath the Christian Church. Either Jesus is Lord
and the power released by his Resurrection is the
source of the Church's faith, its hope and its
love, or the Church is a mere humaninzing community—one among many—and the ideas of Christ, the
Kingdom, the Church, community and eucharist become mere expressions of men and women. This
latter position has in fact been adopted by
Ruether.[52] For Ruether, the eschatological future
is still so outstanding that it is impossible for
the community to claim any "church time" or to
"fashion structures for its own historical
perpetuation."[53]

Richard McBrien contends that by maintaining
such a position, Rosemary Ruether has placed herself outside the Christian tradition. Avery Dulles
concedes that she is somehow Christian because she
claims to be.[54] Gregory Baum, on the other hand,
calls Ruether a Christian theologian whose work is
brilliant.[55] From her relativistic Christological
position, it should be evident that Rosemary
Ruether would not accept the restricted or more
specific definition of Church worked out above.

THE MISSION OF THE CHURCH:
DIALOGUE

The understanding of Church as distinguished from the Kingdom maintains the unique and definitive position of Jesus of Nazareth and still allows for a religious pluralism. Christians elected to membership and mission in the Church enter and remain within the community because they see in Jesus "the goal of human history, the focal point of the longings of history and civilization, the center of the human race, the joy of every heart, and the answer to all its yearnings."[56] Because they believe this, they are bound to share this perception, the "Good News," with others. But with the awareness that God is indeed present and available outside the Church, with the conviction that all have been called to God's Kingdom and that men and women are summoned and graced by what is best in their own religious traditions, proclamation of the Gospel can perhaps best be accomplished in our day through dialogue.

To say that other world religions can reasonably be called "ways of salvation" and we should approach them through dialogue, does not make the question of truth superfluous. As Hans Kung has stated in ON BEING A CHRISTIAN:

> If Christian theology today asserts that all men--even in world religions--can be saved, this certainty does not mean that all religions are equally true. They will be saved, not because of, but in spite of polytheism, magic, human sacrifice, forces of nature. They will be saved, not because of, but in spite of all untruth and superstition.... However much truth they exhibit in certain respects, which Christians must affirm, they do not offer the truth for Christians.[57]

Kung says the Church in its mission must be fully alert to syncretist indifferentism but include tolerance; it must claim absolute validity but be ready to revise its own standpoint whenever this turns out to be in need of revision.[58] None of this is possible without dialogue.

The Church must listen to others before she can speak to them; she must discern God's presence in the religions, cultures, and value systems that she encounters. Archbishop Picachy of Calcutta, India, speaking at the 1974 Roman Synod, stressed the fact that interfaith dialogue should be the normal expression of evangelization:

> India has cradled and nourished many ancient creeds, which even now are a source of inspiration for the religious life of millions of their followers. We in India are daily witnesses to the religious experiences of these men, whose deep sincerity often puts us to shame. We can testify from experience to the presence of the Holy Spirit in the aspirations and undertakings of the adherents of these great religious traditions.[59]

The Archbishop sees in this dialogue something good in itself. Through it, God calls religious souls onward to a higher spirituality and a profounder commitment to their creator. He insists, however, that such dialogue does not prevent Christians from proclaiming the Word revealed in Christ Jesus. Still, there is need for humility, for often those with whom Christians open a dialogue and to whom they want to bring the Good News are more deeply steeped in God than the Christians themselves. "Hence it follows," the Archbishop explains, "that they respond more than we do to the Spirit and are able to manifest him in their lives better than we.... It can happen that we are called through them to turn to God more than they are through us."[60]

Dr. Philip A. Potter, General Secretary of the World Council of Churches, addressing the bishops at the same Synod, pointed out that dialogue is not an intellectual exercise nor a means of discovering how others think and speak so that we can adapt our ready-made, traditional, and oftentimes dogmatic answers. Rather, it is a form of existence, and only if the churches and Christians live this dialogue among themselves as a normal manner of existence can it be credible to those without faith.[61]

Dialogue seems to be the only way in which committed people in a multireligious world can actively promote that shalom, that peace and development for which the human family yearns. Some writers warn against using dialogue as a "tool for mission."[62] Such an expression, however, arises out of the former understanding of the Church and its mission. Christians should enter into dialogue confident of their own position and commitment, yet aware that the Church exists to foster "that brotherhood of all men which corresponds to this destiny that is theirs." That is how Vatican II's CHURCH IN THE MODERN WORLD viewed dialogue. It states further:

> By virtue of her mission to shed on the whole world the radiance of the gospel message, and to unify under one Spirit all men of whatever nation, race, or culture, the Church stands forth as a sign of that brotherliness which allows honest dialogue and invigorates it.[63]

Dialogue with nonreligious ideologies is necessary and valuable also, as long as those encountered are willing to admit with us that the future is open and that the human person is not yet totally defined. The Christian-Marxist dialogues are a good example of this attempt.[64] Through such dialogue, the Church should strive to set up a continual dialectic or critique in the human community at large, by which men and women are summoned to an awareness of the divine mystery operative in their lives. Again, the Second Vatican Council has stated:

> ...the Church sincerely professes that all men, believers and unbelievers alike, ought to work for the rightful betterment of this world.... Such an ideal cannot be realized, however, apart from sincere and prudent dialogue.... Above all the Church knows that her message is in harmony with the most secret desires of the human heart when she champions the dignity of the human vocation, restoring hope to those who have already despaired of anything higher than their present lot. Far from diminishing man, her message brings to his development light, life, and freedom.[65]

The Church can never consider itself an exclusive "in" group, refusing membership to anyone who may seek it. Indeed, as Richard McBrien has pointed out, the Church should not shrink back with embarrassment at the approach of a non-Christian seeking admission into the community. Membership in the community that proclaims the Lordship of Jesus is a sublime vocation and can and should be a joyous, transforming experience, as well as a call to responsibility and to mission.[66] As Gabriel Fackre has said:

> The member of the visible Body has chosen a dangerous place to be.... 'To whom much has been given, from him much will be required.' In the language of another era of theology, transposed to this ecclesiological setting, 'It is a fearful thing to fall in the hands of the living God.'[67]

The Church must spread the Gospel through dialogue, confident that many who are in fact called or elected by God to membership in the Church will respond to that call and see where their true vocation lies. It must work unceasingly in this regard. But for the overwhelming majority of humankind, God's offer of salvation will be realized outside the Christian Church. Indeed, from a realistic point of view, the Church is not the "ordinary," but rather, the "extraordinary" means of salvation.[68]

The Christian community--Catholic, Protestant and Orthodox--numbers less than one billion in a world population approaching four billion. If we proclaim that all humankind is called to the Kingdom of God--and we do--it is inconceivable to imagine that at the present time three billion men, women and children could be outside the saving mercy of God.

THE MISSION OF THE CHURCH:
DEMONSTRATION

The new openness to other world religions and to secular culture in general has been made possible by the theological shift described earlier. Formerly the overriding thrust of the missionary endeavor was to incorporate and keep within the confines of the Church as many "souls" as possible so that their salvation might be assured. Today it is recognized that, while we continue untiringly to make the Good News of Jesus Christ available to people through dialogue, we must also aid the many who will never enter the Church to be converted to God within the framework of the religions they profess.

For this reason the former concept of "missions," with all the connotations about which we have been speaking, must now be seen within the context of the overall mission of the Church. That mission, task or vocation includes not only making known the Good News through dialogue, but also by the type of life Christians live together in community, demonstrating or showing forth to those outside the community that following Jesus Christ is not only possible, but that it makes a difference. The Church must be a test case of its own claims. Because of what God has done in and through Jesus Christ, we declare that the human enterprise is not futile, but hopeful; that the reconciling Word of God is present in the world; that the Spirit of love, justice, truthfulness, compassion and healing is indeed abroad in the world and is abounding in such a way that the forces of evil will not prevail.

The Church is, as the Second Vatican Council declared, "a kind of sacrament or sign of intimate union with God and of the unity of all mankind,"[69] or, as the World Council of Churches Assembly at Uppsala states, "the sign of the coming unity of mankind."[70] That coming unity is the Kingdom of God. The Church could not be a sign or sacrament of the Kingdom if that Kingdom were not in some way present within the Church. As a sacrament involves both a sign and a reality, each distinct but inseparable, so the Church and the Kingdom are distinct but inseparable. The Church is the "budding forth" of the Kingdom of God. It is the place where the creative and redemptive grace of God which permeates all the universe is celebrated through outward forms of expression--in prayer, confession, and worship.

The Church becomes the sacrament of God's hope for the world when, as Jurgen Moltmann says, "it freely chooses to make its own the groaning of the whole enslaved creation."[71] And it finds its strength, its hope and its resolve to do this primarily from its celebration of that great sign of reconciliation, anticipation and thanksgiving--the Eucharist. Gathered around the table of hope, the community, in word, sacrament and song, actualizes in a symbolic way the presence of the exalted Lord in their midst; they solidify their union one with another, and they anticipate sacramentally that eschatological banquet to which all humankind has been invited. "The Church becomes an event of grace as the lives of its members are transformed in hope, in joy, in self-forgetful love, in peace, in patience, and in all other Christ-like virtues."[72]

The Church, then, as a Spirit-filled community of worship and reconciliation, must demonstrate in a credible and historically tangible way that professing Jesus as the Lord does make a difference. Those outside the community should be able to say, "See how they love one another," and gain from the example of the Church, hope for the world. The Church as "an eschatological community pioneering the future of all mankind" is true to its vocation "only if it anticipates and represents the destiny of all mankind, the goal of human history...."[73] The Church must be "an aperitif of the Kingdom." It must be "the community of hope, par excellence." This is one of the vital aspects of the mission to which the Church has been called, and must be called again and again. That is to say, the Church must continually examine itself critically and take seriously the honest criticism of those outside who see it less than faithful to its claims. It must continually reform itself, realizing that its purpose and end lie not in itself, but in the Kingdom of God.

THE MISSION OF THE CHURCH: DEVELOPMENT

Finally, the Church must turn outward; it must engage in the affairs of the whole family of peoples. It does this, not according to the former rationale as a pre-evangelizing activity, but as an essential and integral part of its mission--the building up of the human community. As the 1971 Synod of Bishops declared, "Action on behalf of justice and participation in the transformation of the world fully appear to us as a constitutive dimension of the preaching of the Gospel."[74]

The Church, therefore, existing not as an end in itself but as a servant for the coming Kingdom, must work for integral salvation or the complete liberation of man and of peoples.[75] The term development designates in a comprehensive way the urgent task to which the Church has been called today. Although development can most readily be understood as a part of the Church's service to the world, or its _diakonia_, still the concept is broad enough to embrace within its meaning the first two aspects of the Church's mission as outlined above, namely, dialogue and demonstration. The term development does place emphasis on the Church's servant role in the world without, however, limiting the Church's mission to such service. In other words, dialogue and demonstration can be seen as a part of the Church's overall vocation to development. This will become more evident as the term development itself is clarified and the reasons are given why the Church's mission today can best be reformulated under the aegis of development. Before proceeding, however, the relationship between the first two aspects of the Church's mission--dialogue and demonstration--and the concept of development should be given.

DEVELOPMENT AND THE
FREUDIAN-MARXIST CRITIQUE:
A CLARIFICATION

As a context within which to further clarify the interrelationship among the three aspects of the Church's mission, we shall return to Blondel or, more accurately, to an addition that Baum makes to Blondel's thought. Baum claims to stand on the ground which Blondel has cleared, but he does not stand there uncritically.[76] Indeed, Baum declares that few theologians today would follow strictly Blondel's phenomenology of the human spirit. For his own part, Baum applies what he calls a "psychologically oriented phenomenology" to Blondel's position to show that human life is not as "neat" as Blondel would have it. It is, rather, a field of conflict betweeen forces of self-destruction and powers of creativity and new life. He also broadens what appeared to Blondel to be the single dramatic moment when God calls upon men and women to make their fundamental option. Thus, Baum gives more emphasis to the precariousness of life in this not-yet-fully redeemed world and also insists that people are open to divine mercy and grace in the many choices between life and death which constitute their history. People are open to ever greater development, but there is no assurance that this development will be continuous or steady.

By using the critiques of life and institutions of Freud and Marx, Baum attempts to show that people can enter into their own self-realization only if they are willing to wrestle with the enemy within and without.[77] Baum contends, further, that the Freudian and Marxian critiques must be applied not only to the emotional and political aspects of human life, but also to the Christian and the Church. Basically, Baum sees the value of the Freudian critique in this instance in uncovering the fact that in all expression of thought, of values, of religion, there is an element of defense. If men and women try to stress the intellect as the sole organ of truth (as the doctrinal-scholastic theology was prone to do), ignoring the emotions and personal life experiences, they will be unable to discover the hidden emotional factors in their knowledge and, therefore, incapable of submitting their knowledge to a critique. Baum concludes that without love, truth is not available, and that dialogue is the only possible way to deal with issues in a creative way. It is in dialogue that the participants acknowledge from the outset that their truth is still in need of redemption and thus open to a greater conversion to reality, to greater development. By making the Good News of Jesus Christ available through dialogue to those who have never heard it or have misunderstood it, and at the same time admitting their position can purify and deepen one's own, dialogue becomes a means of development.[78]

From the Marxist critique, which argues that every society or institution tends to create for itself a view of life, a set of values or a doctrinal system that will protect the centers of power in that society or institution and make it easier for those in power to rule, the Church should recognize that in all cultures and religions, including its own, there are ideological trends. Specifically, in the Church much of that which passes as religious ideals are subtly disguised ways of protecting a privileged institution and those in privileged positions within it.

Ideological trends occur when a doctrinal system presents the Church as a perfect institution above all others and as an end in itself. They occur when obedience to authority is stressed to the extent that any criticism is looked upon as a breach of faith. The papacy, for example, has at times been exalted as a position exempt from all criticism. Such ideological trends must be recognized and purified. In this way, the Church will demonstrate that it takes its side of the dialogue seriously. The Church must practice what it preaches. By continual reform, it will develop along lines of ever greater faithfulness to its mission. The sign that the Church offers the rest of the world, its celebration, koinonia, or demonstration, can be seen as a part of the Church's development. Being the world's light, and leaven can be seen as part of the world's development.

Baum points out that Christians can turn to Freud and Marx, who, when read critically, can clarify how the great fears of people and their inclination toward self-aggrandizement affect their very being, their culture, their religion, their Church. "The openness of man to this painful judgment, unsettling him in his presumed security, is God's gift to him. It is faith."[79] And God, according to Baum, "is what happens to man on the way to becoming human."[80]

Baum notes that since the process of a person's coming-to-be is one in which God is creatively present, it is tempting to extrapolate this view of creation to the whole universe. This would mean that the world comes to be through a process that, in its orientation and therefore its origin, is divine. In this process, there are special moments or pivotal points when the new is being created. Applied to the entire cosmic order, this would amount to a theory of evolution--an evolution that is not, however, the unfolding of reality according to a built-in dynamism, but rather an evolution that continues to depend on God's creative presence. Baum, however, limits the doctrine of God-as-Creator to statements about human life and to a new self-understanding about the individual and the community.[81] Baum's insights are helpful in clarifying the dialogic and demonstrative aspects of the Church's mission but he gives little emphasis to the Church's responsibility in the world. I insist the knowledge of God-as-Creator must also include men's and women's responsibility to build the earth. As Vatican II states:

> For when, by the work of his hands or with the aid of technology, man develops the earth so that it can bear fruit and become a dwelling worthy of the whole human family, and when he consciously takes part in the life of social groups,

he carries out the design of God. Manifested at the beginning of time, the divine plan is that man should subdue the
earth, bringing creation to perfection,
and develop himself.[82]

Moltmann has stated basically the same idea.
It is a necessary corrective to Baum's position:
"The Christian Church has not to serve mankind in
order that this world may remain what it is, or
may be preserved in the state in which it is, but
in order that it may transform itself and become
what it is promised to be."[83]

We must now turn and examine in more detail
the question of the Church as servant of the
coming Kingdom: we must look at the question of
development.

SUMMARY OF CHAPTER THREE

Chapter Three clarifies the transition between
the traditional and contemporary approaches to
theology and the consequent effects of this transition on the understanding of the Church's mission. The clarification focuses on the essentials
of any theology, namely, the understanding of
revelation, the perception and eschatology, and
the definition of ecclesiology. The salient differences between old and new approaches to
theology are brought out below:

A. <u>Traditional</u>   B. <u>Contemporary</u>
   (positivistic)   (correlative)

Revelation

Considered completed in   Understood and expres-
Christ and closed with   ed also in the <u>present</u>
the death of the last   tense--the availability
Apostle; hence under-   of God in present human

A. Traditional	B. Contemporary

Revelation
(Continued)

stood and expressed in the _past_ tense.	experience, without negating the _past_--the unique _revelation_ in Jesus, nor the _future_--Jesus' return in glory and the coming of God's Kingdom.

Eschatology

Historically _extrinsic_; a complete discontinuity between men's and women's striving for the more human future in this world and the coming of God's eschatological Kingdom.	Historically _intrinsic_; insists on an _intimate_ but not causal relationship between human efforts to establish the better future (development) and the gift of God's ultimate future (the Kingdom).

Ecclesiology

Church _equals_ the Kingdom of God; Church membership is necessary for salvation. The Church's mission: to incorporate as many within its confines as possible, in order to save their souls.	Church is subordinate to the Kingdom; call to membership is by God's mysterious election, which is neither a passport nor requisite for salvation but implies a responsibility for service in the name of Christ.

Chapter Three also clarifies the difference between the broad and restricted definition of Church and, insisting upon the latter, reformulates the Church's mission in terms of Dialogue, Demonstration, and Development, choosing the last of these as the appropriate aegis for a new theology of missions.

NOTES ON CHAPTER THREE

[1]See Chapter Two, p. 73, n. 31. Also, for a discussion of the heated worldwide debate following the Uppsala Report on "Renewal in Mission," see M. M. Thomas, "Salvation and Humanization," INTERNATIONAL REVIEW OF MISSION 60 (January 1971): 25-38. Thomas notes that Peter Beyerhaus has been outspoken in his criticism of the Uppsala Report for its "radical shift of center from God to man." Dissatisfaction with the World Council of Churches' posture led to the Congress on World Evangelization which met in Lausanne in 1974. Some saw it as the first step in organizing a conservative counterpart to the World Council of Churches. The final resolutions of the Congress did not, however, call for a withdrawal from the World Council of Churches. See discussion on this movement by Stephen Neill, "Ecumenism's Past and Future: Shifting Perspectives." Interview conducted by John E. Groh, CHRISTIAN CENTURY 92 (June 4, 1975): 568-72.

[2]According to this view, what is needed to overcome the crisis of missions is an adjustment, an accommodation with changed historical circumstances and current social challenges. It is the position developed by Hans Hoekendijk. See discussion of this position in Thomas, "Salvation and Humanization."

[3]As Karl Rahner states: "Theology is practical above all because it is oriented to the acts of

hope and love, which contain an element of knowledge which is unattainable outside them.... Orthodoxy and orthopraxis combine to influence one another in a basic inexpressible unity which can only come to light in practice, because knowledge is only sound when it has surpassed itself and become love...." See "Theology" in SACRAMENTUM MUNDI, Vol. 6, Karl Rahner, ed. (New York: Herder and Herder, 1969), p. 235. Also see Rahner, "The New Claims which Pastoral Theology Makes upon Theology as a Whole," THEOLOGICAL INVESTIGATIONS, Vol. 11 (London: Darton, Longman, and Todd, and New York: Seabury Press, 1974), pp. 115-36.

[4]McBrien, DO WE NEED THE CHURCH?, pp. 190-98. For a concise comment on the "current state of the question," see Roger Hazelton, "Homo Capax Dei: Thoughts on Man and Transcendence," THEOLOGICAL STUDIES 33 (December 1972): 735-47. Hazelton discusses the work of John E. Smith, EXPERIENCE AND GOD (New York: Oxford University Press, 1968) and gives reference to Gordon Kaufman and Herbert Richardson. He points out also the pertinence of Abraham Maslow's study of "peak experiences" for theology.

[5]I adopt the term "present revelation" from Gabriel Moran, THE PRESENT REVELATION (New York: Herder and Herder, 1972), but unlike Moran, I give more emphasis to the documents handed on to us from the earlier Christian communities, which, in turn, were the products of their reflections on their own "present revelation."

[6]HUMILIATION AND CELEBRATION: POST-RADICAL THEMES IN DOCTRINE, AND MISSION (New York: Sheed and Ward, 1969), p. 282.

[7]Tillich describes the method of correlation for systematic theology as follows: "...It makes an analysis of the human situation out of which the existential questions arise, and it demonstrates that the symbols used in the Christian

message are the answers to these questions."
SYSTEMATIC THEOLOGY, 3 vols., 1951-63. (Chicago:
University of Chicago Press, 3 vols. in one, 1967)
I: 62.   David Tracy, BLESSED RAGE FOR ORDER (New
York: Seabury, 1975), pp. 45-46, provides a useful assessment of Tillich's method. He states that
the contemporary theologian can accept Tillich's
articulation of the need for a method of correlation, but he or she cannot accept Tillich's own
model for theology as one which actually cor-
relates.   Tracy insists that, although Tillich's
formulation calls for investigation and correlation of both the "situation" and the "message," it
is only from the former that the "questions" arise
and only from the latter that the "answers" are
provided.   Tillich's own model is not capable of
correlating questions and answers from both sources and therefore does not provide a sufficiently
critical model.   Concerning what we have called a
"positivistic" approach to theology, Bonhoeffer
criticized Barth for his "revelational positivism."   See his letter of June 8, 1944 in LETTERS
AND PAPERS FROM PRISON, E. Bethge, ed., revised
ed. (New York: Macmillan Co., 1967, original
English ed., 1953), p. 171.   McBrien designates
both the kergymatic or biblical and the doctrinal
methods "positivistic" because of the preoccupation with "sources" and disregard for the "signs
of the times."   See CHURCH: THE CONTINUING QUEST,
p. 9.

[8]"The Gospel of the Kingdom of God and the
Church," in THE GOSPEL AND THE AMBIGUITY OF THE
CHURCH, Vilmos Vajta, ed. (Philadelphia: Fortress
Press, 1974), p. 7.   Braaten admits that in a number of essays Barth tried to break out of this
abstract dialectic of eternity and time, but in
the end he never did write the planned volume on
eschatology for the CHURCH DOGMATICS.

[9]McBrien, CONTINUING QUEST, p.14.   Reinhold
Niebuhr called "the great heresy of Roman Catholicism" that of "identifying the Church with the

Kingdom of God and making unqualified claims of divinity for this human, historical and relative institution." See BEYOND TRAGEDY (New York: Charles Scribner's Sons, 1946), p. 121. For a discussion of the development of "Church-centered theology" see chap. 4 of McBrien's DO WE NEED THE CHURCH? Also see Dulles, MODELS OF THE CHURCH (Garden City, New York: Doubleday, 1974), chap. 2.

[10]"The Gospel of the Kingdom," p. 4. Braaten credits Tillich with having made the greatest contribution to the interpretation of the doctrine of the Kingdom of God among the theologians of the last generations. He defined the problem of eschatology as the question of the meaning and goal of history, and therefore as the quest for the Kingdom of God.

[11](New York: Herder and Herder, 1970).

[12]See Gregory Baum, "Somerville's Blondel," CONTINUUM 6 (Spring 1968): 120.

[13]For discussion of others who have attempted to do theology from this perspective, see McBrien, DO WE NEED THE CHURCH? Part I: "The Secular Mood of Contemporary Theology." McBrien credits Bonhoeffer's LETTERS AND PAPERS FROM PRISON as the source of and inspiration for the secular mood of Christian theology. See also John Macquarrie, GOD AND SECULARITY, Vol 3. of NEW DIRECTIONS IN THEOLOGY TODAY (Philadelphia: Westminster Press, 1967); Langdon Gilkey, NAMING THE WHIRLWIND (Indianapolis: Bobbs-Merrill Co., 1969); and more recently, Gabriel Moran, PRESENT REVELATION.

[14]Blondel undoubtedly suffered from the fact that he was always associated with the Modernists, but his philosophy itself presented people with many difficulties. Alec Vidler, A VARIETY OF CATHOLIC MODERNISTS (Cambridge: University Press, 1970), p. 79, says, "...I find his thought obscure, his style insufferable, and his temperament

uncongenial." Paul Janet, one of the examiners when Blondel defended his thesis, L'ACTION, at the Sorbonne in 1893, said to Blondel, "Your thought is obscure; your way of writing obscures it still more. It takes me an hour to read one of your pages and then I fail to understand it." Quoted in THE LETTER ON APOLOGETICS AND THE HISTORY OF DOGMA, A. Dru and I. Trethowan, trans. (New York: Holt, Rinehart and Winston, 1964), p. 40. The following discussion is based on the first chapter of Baum's MAN BECOMING.

[15]L'ACTION (Paris, Alcan, 1893). For a good treatment of the thought of Blondel, see James M. Somerville, ed., TOTAL COMMITMENT: BLONDEL'S L'ACTION (Washington, D.C.: Corpus Books, 1968).

[16]This was Blondel's way of translating St. Thomas' principle: "Nothing can be ordained to a certain end unless there be in the thing a certain proportion to that end." Where Thomas speaks of proportion, relation and similarity, Blondel speaks of need. Although Blondel was an unceasing critic of scholasticism, in later years he made an attempt to reconcile his thought to some extent with that of Thomas. Basically, however, Blondel followed in the ways of inner experience, opened by St. Augustine. Blondel's immediate predecessor and professor was Leon Olle-Laprune; it was from him that Blondel received the incentive to work out his philosophy of action. For Olle-Laprune, as for Blondel, certitude is never that of the intellect alone, but of the human person. Complete certitude is personal. That which one knows, one should be and one should do. For further discussion of Blondel and his relationship to Olle-Laprune, see E. Gilson, T. Langan, and A. Maurer, RECENT PHILOSOPHY (New York: Random House, 1962), pp. 358-62.

[17]The "method of immanence" in Blondel is not to be confused with "a principle of immanence." The latter, according to Blondel, seeks to reduce

the supernatural to the rule of a supreme expansion of our being—to a total autonomy. The "method of immance," on the contrary, is to "place us face to face with ourselves and with God; it is to make us measure the infinite disproportion between the necessary and salutary heteronomy...." B. deSailly [Blondel], "La Notion et le Role du Miracle," ANNALES DE PHILOSOPHIE CHRETIENNE (July 1907), p. 346. Quoted in Avery Dulles, REVELATION THEOLOGY (New York: Herder and Herder, 1969) p. 88.

[18]See, for example, Teilhard de Chardin, HOW I BELIEVE, R. Hague, trans. (New York: Harper and Row - Perennial Library, 1969). This essay was written in Peking in 1934. For the thought of Henri de Lubac, see THE MYSTERY OF THE SUPERNATURAL, R. Sheed, trans, (New York: Herder and Herder, 1967 - original French, 1965). For Karl Rahner, see "Concerning the Relationship between Nature and Grace," THEOLOGICAL INVESTIGATIONS Vol. 1 (Baltimore: Helicon, 1961), pp. 297-317, and "Nature and Grace," THEOLOGICAL INVESTIGATIONS, Vol. 4 (Baltimore: Helicon, 1966), pp. 165-88. Numerous essays by Rahner could be added here. See esp. "Theology and Anthropology," THEOLOGICAL INVESTIGATIONS, Vol. 9 (New York: Herder and Herder, 1972), pp. 28-45, in which Rahner attempts to show "that dogmatic theology today must be theological anthropology, and that such an 'anthropocentric' view is necessary and fruitful." Rahner masterfully brings these ideas together in the opening chapters of FOUNDATIONS OF CHRISTIAN FAITH, W. V. Dych, trans. (New York: Seabury Press, 1978).

[19]Dom Patrick Granfield, "An Interview with Karl Rahner," AMERICAN ECCLESIASTICAL REVIEW 153 (October 1965): 221.

[20]McBrien's book has caused a considerable amount of anxiety, not so much among those who have read the work, but among those who are

threatened that such a question should even be raised. For McBrien's carefully formulated answer to the question posed in the title of this work, see pp. 228-30. See McBrien's further discussion of the matter in CATHOLICISM (Oak Grove, Minnesota: Winston Press, 1980), Vol. II, pp. 721-22.

[21]The following discussion is based on MAN BECOMING, chap. 3, "The Church in the New Perspective." Also see Baum, THE CREDIBILITY OF THE CHURCH TODAY (New York: Herder and Herder, 1968), p. 47, where Baum defines the Church as that which happens "whenever and wherever people become friends through God's presence to them."

[22]MAN BECOMING, pp. 67-68.

[23]IBID., pp. 68-69. Also see Baum, "Where is Theology Going?" THE ECUMENIST 7 (March-April 1969): 33-36.

[24]CHRISTIANITY IN WORLD HISTORY, p. 415. Van Leeuwen points out that the Church may waste her energies in adapting herself to aspects of an indigenous culture "already consigned to the past and doomed to become out of date." The critical question that the world-wide Church faces, according to van Leeuwen, is whether she is able and ready to serve her Lord amidst the needs of such a rapidly changing world as ours. The Church's task is to make ready, spiritually and materially, for the arrival of modern civilization (p. 424).

[25]IBID., p. 421. Speaking of India and what Christianity could offer should Hinduism disintegrate, van Leeuwen says, "The one and only thing that Christianity could offer India...would be a fully fledged, but secular, democratic state; and that is precisely what India has created already of her own initiative."

[26]IBID., p. 430.

[27](Boston: Beacon Press, 1972).

[28]IBID., pp. 142-173.

[29]IBID., pp. 142-43. Stackhouse develops the rationale behind his broadened conception of Church by a reinterpretation of the trinitarian theological tradition which he sees as the normative content of revelation (Chap. 6). He says that in face of cosmopolitan developments, the clash of cultures, and a quest for a new metaphysical hypothesis upon which to base civilization, the doctrine of the Trinity developed. It was superior to any other fundamental doctrine and represented in telescoped form the critical ideas that shaped the direction of civilization for hundreds of years. But in its ancient form, especially in its concept of the Spirit, it is inadequate. Stackhouse does not want to see all "Spirit" as continuously proceeding through the Son, but stresses a "two aspects" interpretation of the Spirit. "If the Athanasians saw Jesus Christ as of two natures, so also the Spirit has two aspects," even though, Stackhouse admits, this thought was not developed. Very soon the Spirit became identified with, or placed within, the Church. The priesthood became the true representative of Christ and the Spirit was seen as flowing through these channels to the collective Church (pp. 129-30). The author claims that the "two aspects" interpretation of the Spirit can provide a pluralistic civilizational force which is needed to allow diversity in unity for an urban ethos (p. 134). It is the Spirit-centered rather than Christ's body-centered Church that Stackhouse emphasizes.

[30]IBID., p. 146.

[31]IBID., p. 147. This definition embodies the trinitarian understanding of Church referred to in Note 29 above. In Stackhouse's reformulation, the "operative patterns of creative order," "identity formation," and "enspirited community" represent the traditional work of the Father, Son and

Holy Spirit, respectively. The "ultimate and most worthy power or powers of existence" describes the Godhead.

[32]IBID., p. 148.

[33]IBID., p. 149. See Hans Kung, "The World Religions in God's Plan of Salvation," in CHRISTIAN REVELATION AND WORLD RELIGIONS, Joseph Neuner, ed. (London: Burns and Oates - Compass Books, 1967), pp. 25-66. Also see McBrien, "The Necessary Ecumenism," COMMONWEAL PAPERS: 4, THE CHURCH IN THE YEAR 2000, XCI:5 (October 31, 1969): 145-148.

[34]Stackhouse, ETHICS AND THE URBAN ETHOS, p. 149.

[35]IBID., pp. 153-54. This is a concern shared by van Leeuwen. He warns that churches in Asia and Africa might continue to lead an existence "on the sidelines" instead of in the area where "the really strategic points for the Church in discharge of her apostolic obligation lie," that is, in the processes of "rapid social change" in the non-Western world (CHRISTIANITY IN WORLD HISTORY, p. 415).

[36]CHURCH: THE CONTINUING QUEST, p. 73.

[37]IBID., p. 73.

[38]Jurgen Moltmann, THEOLOGY OF HOPE (New York: Harper and Row, 1967), p. 229.

[39]"Church and World," in SACRAMENTUM MUNDI Vol. 1, p. 347.

[40]Quoted by Rahner in THE CHRISTIAN COMMITMENT (New York: Sheed and Ward, 1963), p. 35.

[41]DO WE NEED THE CHURCH? p. 170. For McBrien's disagreement with Rahner on this matter, see n. 3, p. 245 of the same work.

[42]See Rahner, "Anonymous Christians," THEOLOG-ICAL INVESTIGATIONS Vol. 6 (Baltimore: Helicon Press; London: Darton, Longman, and Todd, 1968), pp. 390-98. Also see "Atheism and Implicit Christianity," THEOLOGICAL INVESTIGATIONS Vol. 9, pp. 145-64. For discussion and comparison of current Roman Catholic and Protestant positions on the salvation of non-Christians, see George A. Lindbeck, "Fides ex auditu and the Salvation of Non-Christians: Contemporary Catholic and Protestant Positions," in THE GOSPEL AND THE AMBIGUITY OF THE CHURCH, pp. 92-123.

[43]See FAITH AND FRATRICIDE, pp. 246-51.

[44]See Baum's Introduction to Ruether's FAITH AND FRATRICIDE. Also see "The Jews, Faith and Ideology," THE ECUMENIST 10 (July-August 1972): 71-76. Ruether in her LIBERATION THEOLOGY (New York: Paulist Press, 1972), p. 10, insists that God's presence does not appear just in one time and place once for all, but wherever reconciliation is established and man glimpses his unity and the unity of the world with its transcendent foundations and meaning. According to Ruether, "a religious culture may pick out a particular place where this appearing is seen normatively--in Jesus or the Torah or Buddha--but this doctrine of incarnation is not just about this one place or person, but this one place or person operates as a norm for discerning the nature of the presence wherever it happens."

[45]See "Christianity and the Non-Christian Religions," THEOLOGICAL INVESTIGATIONS Vol. 5 (Baltimore: Helicon Press; London: Darton, Longman and Todd, 1966), pp. 115-34. The essays in CHRISTIAN REVELATION AND WORLD RELIGIONS by Hans Kung, Piet Fransen, Joseph Masson, and Raymond Panikkar adopt this same basic position. Kung clarifies (or alters) his position in ON BEING A CHRISTIAN, E. Quinn, trans. (Garden City, New York: Doubleday, 1976). He states, "The will of those who are

outside is not to be 'interpreted' in the light of our own interests, but quite simply respected. And it would be impossible to find anywhere in the world a sincere Jew, Muslim or atheist who would not regard the assertion that he is an 'anonymous Christian' as presumptuous. To bring the partner to the discussion into our own circle in this way closes the dialogue before it has ever begun'" (p. 98).

46See HUMILIATION AND CELEBRATION, p. 68ff.

47IBID., p. 268.

48IBID., pp. 272-73. Dorothee Solle, THE TRUTH IS CONCRETE, Dinah Livingstone, trans. (New York: Herder and Herder, 1969) takes a similar position in speaking of "the Church outside the Church:" "Isn't the 'Church outside the Church' simply a consequence of secularization, a hidden Church, in which Christ is present unrecognized as on the road to Emmaus?" (p. 103). In this hidden Church, according to Solle, "it does not make the least difference whether Christ is mentioned by name" (p. 105).

49HUMILIATION AND CELEBRATION, pp. 260-61.

50Ruether develops her position in an as yet unpublished work, MESSIAH OF ISRAEL AND COSMIC CHRIST. Baum discussed Ruether's position in his Introduction to FAITH AND FRATRICIDE. The following is based on the discussion. Also see "An Invitation to Jewish-Christian Dialogue: In What Sense Can We Say That Jesus Was 'The Christ'?" THE ECUMENIST 10 (January-February 1972): 17-24. This article will be the conclusion of Ruether's book, MESSIAH OF ISRAEL AND COSMIC CHRIST.

51In FAITH AND FRATRICIDE, Ruether states, "The attribution of an absolute finality to the heightened expectations surrounding the life and death of Jesus must be regarded as a flawed way of appropriating the real meaning of eschatological encounter." Jesus may be remembered as a paradigm of that final hope which has not yet been accomplished. "This memory may then be reexperienced as a paradigm again and again...providing the pattern for experiencing the eschatological in history" (p. 248). The exact meaning of this last statement is difficult to determine. It appears to contradict Ruether's strong statement that Christianity has illegitimately historicized the eschatological by making absolute claims about the life, death and resurrection of Jesus. See Part 4 of Chap. 5 in FAITH AND FRATRICIDE, "The Key Issue: Christology," pp. 246-51. Dulles, MODELS OF THE CHURCH, p. 101, places Ruether close to Moltmann in her futurist eschatological stance (which I find questionable) and designates both their positions as "verging on the denial of Christianity." Even Baum, in his Introduction to FAITH AND FRATRICIDE, p. 18, states "The Christian reader may feel that the author of FAITH AND FRATRICIDE had paid too little attention to the resurrection of Jesus...and hence has left herself in a situation where she could be accused of having abandoned the center of the gospel, i.e., of no longer being a Christian theologian." Baum attempts to defend her position and purpose, but not very successfully.

[52]"A New Church?" COMMONWEAL, 90 (April 4, 1969): 66.

[53]THE CHURCH AGAINST ITSELF (New York: Herder and Herder, 1967), p. 56.

[54]For McBrien's critique of THE CHURCH AGAINST ITSELF and Ruether's basic position, see CHURCH: THE CONTINUING QUEST, pp. 52-54. For Dulles, MODELS, p. 101.

[55]Introduction to FAITH AND FRATRICIDE, p. 20.

[56]THE CHURCH IN THE MODERN WORLD (Art. 45).

[57]ON BEING A CHRISTIAN, p. 104.

[58]IBID., p. 114.

[59]"India: Vital Perspectives," reprinted in ORIGINS 4 (October 24, 1974): 281.

[60]IBID., p. 283.

[61]"A Way for the Church to Be," excerpts from Potter's address, reprinted in ORIGINS 4 (October 24, 1974): 284.

[62]See J. Samartha, "The Progress and Promise of Inter-Religious Dialogues," JOURNAL OF ECUMENICAL STUDIES 9 (Summer 1972): 472-73.

[63]THE CHURCH IN THE MODERN WORLD (Art. 92)

[64]For a discussion of the Christian-Marxist dialogue, see Paul Oestreicher, ed., THE CHRISTIAN -MARXIST DIALOGUE (London and New York: Macmillan, 1969). John Macquarrie, THREE ISSUES IN ETHICS (New York: Harper and Row, 1970), notes that the Christian-Marxist dialogue is confined to a very few persons on either side and that some of the Christian contributions have been extraordinarily naive. Macquarrie says that some enthusiasts for dialogue ignore profound differences between Marxism and Christianity. Also see the discussion on dialogue by Rahner, "Reflections on Dialogue within a Pluralistic Society," THEOLOGICAL INVESTIGATIONS Vol. 6, pp. 31-42; Rahner, "Dialogue in the Church," THEOLOGICAL INVESTIGATIONS Vol. 10 (New York: Herder and Herder, 1973), pp. 103-21, and by Baum, MAN BECOMING, pp. 41-47.

[65]THE CHURCH IN THE MODERN WORLD (Art. 21).

[66]See DO WE NEED THE CHURCH? p. 172.

[67]HUMILIATION AND CELEBRATION, p. 271.

[68]Heinz R. Schlette develops this line of thought in TOWARDS A THEOLOGY OF RELIGIONS (New York: Herder and Herder, 1966). For a critique of Schlette and Rahner, whom Schlette follows, see Wolfhart Pannenberg, "Toward a Theology of the History of Religions" in BASIC QUESTIONS IN THEOLOGY: COLLECTED ESSAYS, Vol. 2. George H. Kehm, trans. (Philadelphia: Fortress Press, 1971), pp. 65-118.

[69]CONSTITUTION ON THE CHURCH (Art 1).

[70]THE UPPSALA REPORT (Geneva: World Council of Churches, 1968), p. 17.

[71]RELIGION, REVOLUTION AND THE FUTURE, M. D. Meeks, trans. (New York: Charles Scribner's Sons, 1969), p. 216.

[72]Dulles, MODELS, p. 65.

[73]Pannenberg, THEOLOGY AND THE KINGDOM OF GOD, p. 75.

[74]JUSTICE IN THE WORLD: Third International Synod of Bishops, Rome, 1971 (Washington, D.C.: United States Catholic Conference, 1971), Introduction, para. 6.

[75]"A Declaration from the Synod," printed in ORIGINS 4 (November 7, 1974): 308.

[76]The following discussion is based on MAN BECOMING, pp. 106-14.

[77]Once again Baum is not the only, nor the first, to propose such a critique. The protagonists of "political theology"--Metz, Moltmann, and liberation theologians--Gutierrez, Segundo and most others, make use of the Marxist critique. The German theologians have been turning more to the critical theories of Marcuse and the Frankfurt School. For good introductory articles, see

Edward Schillebeeckx, "Critical Theories and Christian Political Commitment," CONCILIUM 84 (April 1973): 48-61; Charles Davis, "Theology and Praxis," CROSS CURRENTS 23 (Summer 1973): 154-168; Willi Oelmuller, "The Limitations of Social Theories," in RELIGION AND POLITICAL SOCIETY, The Institute of Christian Thought, ed. and trans. (New York: Harper and Row, 1974), pp. 121-69. For a more extensive treatment of the psychological and political liberation of human persons see the last two chapters of Moltmann's THE CRUCIFIED GOD (New York: Harper and Row, 1973).

[78]Pope Paul VI has suggested that "the spirit of dialogue is friendship, and even more, it is service." See ECCLESIAM SUAM, para. 87.

[79]Baum, MAN BECOMING, p. 113.

[80]IBID., p. 40.

[81]IBID., pp. 220-21.

[82]THE CHURCH IN THE MODERN WORLD (Art. 57).

[83]THEOLOGY OF HOPE, p. 327.

CHAPTER FOUR

DEVELOPMENT, LIBERATION, REVOLUTION AND POLITICS:

AN EXAMINATION OF TERMS

THEORIES OF DEVELOPMENT:
A HISTORICAL PERSPECTIVE

Before attempting to elaborate on the servant aspect of the Church's mission, that is, on the Church's role in integral human development, it is necessary to provide the rationale behind the choice of the term development in this study. If missionary theology itself has become a quaestio disputata, it is no less true to say that the concept of development has become the center of much disagreement and debate. Selecting it as the linguistic vehicle for discussing the Church's missionary thrust is definitely "going against the stream" of popular theological jargon. The attempt to fashion a theology of development is simply passe among many Christian thinkers who are interested in the current theological ferment about the role of the Church in society, the disparity between the rich and poor nations, and the dehumanizing and denaturing effects of uncontrolled technology. Political theology, for the most part, is localized in Europe, especially Germany; the theology of revolution seems to have had its day; but liberation theology, which is most critical of any theology of development, occupies the center of attention for many at the present time. One might say that "liberation" has replaced "hope" as the theological password to popularity. Nonetheless, the position adopted in this study is that when "the smoke has cleared," when liberation theology itself has been liberated from a self-imposed provincialization, it will be recognized that development is still the most comprehensive and practical term for theological reflection in working out the Church's diaconal role in the comtemporary world.[1]

1. SOCIAL EVOLUTION:
A DETERMINIST'S VIEW

Although the term development has taken on a new significance in the sociopolitical and economic realms in recent times, it has a rich and varied history, the roots of which are found in philosophy. If development in its most general meaning can be defined as any process of progressive change, most modern philosophers would consider that development of some kind or other characterizes all things, both in the physical and biological fields. This conception stems from the earliest days of philosophy--Heraclitus' contention that all natural things are constantly changing. There was a contrasting view, of course, embodied in the speculations of Democritus. He was convinced that the world is made up of changing combinations of atoms which themselves are not subject to change or development. This latter view dominated the early scientific age in Europe, but the last hundred years have brought discoveries in the biological and physical sciences which have caused opinion to swing back to the Heraclitean emphasis on the importance of process and development.

Albert Einstein's theory of relativity contended that time and space are united in a continuum which implies that all things are involved in time, and therefore in development. Similarly, the philosopher Alfred North Whitehead was important in charting this transition from the nondevelopmental view in which time was an accidental and inessential element to an essentially dynamic perception of reality.

When we turn to the question of human history or of change in societies, we find also that there have been various theories of development. Perhaps the most persistent has been the theory of social evolution. According to Robert Nisbet,[2] the premises the various theories of development of major social evolutionists are all drawn from the metaphor of growth, from the analogy of change in society to change in the growth processes of the individual organism. Nisbet points out six of these premises which he claims are most constitutive and far-reaching in their relation to the various theories of social evolution: Change is natural, it is directional, immanent, continuous, necessary, and it proceeds from uniform causes. I shall comment briefly on these premises, especially as they are evidenced in the thought of Karl Marx.

For all the social evolutionists, the overriding problem in the study of society was that of finding the proper reconciliation between order and change. For Auguste Comte, whom Nisbet calls "in most respects the subtlest and most theoretically sophisticated of all the social evolutionists in the nineteenth century," order is order-in-change, and change is simply the incessant realization of a higher level of order. Nisbet declares:

> What was true of Comte was equally true of the others in the century--Hegel, Marx, Tocqueville, Spencer, Morgan, Newman, and Taylor, to name the principal exponents of the theory of development--who similarly proceeded from the assumption that change is as natural to a social entity as any of its elements of structure.[3]

Nisbet notes that the entity for Comte was human knowledge fundamentally, although he widened this in later work to civilization in its entirety; for Hegel it was freedom; for Marx, the means of economic production through the ages; for Tocqueville it was democracy in the West; for Spencer, each of the whole range of society's principal institutions; for Newman, it was Christianity; for Morgan, the entity was the idea of kinship, of property and of civil government; for Taylor it was culture generally, and religion specifically.

In his discussion of the premise "change is directional," Nisbet defines change as "a succession of differences in time within a persisting identity." He notes that we observe the succession of changes but that it requires analysis and deduction, or metaphor, or analogy, to bind the plurality of observed changes into a single, ongoing process. It requires further analysis and deduction to reach the conclusion that this single, ongoing process has a beginning, middle and end--that is, direction in time. The social evolutionists had to specify this direction for whatever entity of development was claimed. It is in this specification, according to Nisbet, that we are given the sequence of stages, which for most of us today remains the single most distinctive aspect of the theory of social evolution.

We have, therefore, Comte's Law of Three Stages, under which knowledge could be seen as having passed from the religious to the metaphysical to the positive or scientific. We have Hegel's dialectic view of the spirit of freedom moving from its beginnings in the Orient with ever-widening scope to what he believed to be its ultimate and widest manifestation in the Prussian state of his day. We have Marx's depiction of the direction of economic evolution from ancient slavery--with some form of primitive communism preceding it--through feudalism to capitalism and, eventually, to socialism and mature communism. Past, present and future were thus connected in a single, directional series.[4]

Change is immanent. This premise is at the core of the whole theory of social evolution. This does not mean that social evolutionists were unaware of changes that were induced by outside accidents or interference. But what they were anxious to discover was that kind of change which, assuming no interferences or mutational accidents, could be seen as inherent, as a function of the particular entity itself. Nisbet notes that Comte's so-called laws of social dynamic, Spencer's "development hypothesis," and Marx's "economic law of motion of modern society," all had in common a conviction on the part of their authors that the processes of cumulative directional change with which they were concerned were immanent to the social systems that were being studied. Marx, for example, according to Nisbet, assumed that in capitalism there is a natural course of development, one that can be decelerated temporarily by alien forces or accelerated by a revolutionary vanguard of the proletariat, but that cannot, in the long run, be abrogated by human decision.

When Nisbet discusses the premise, "change is continuous," he cautions that he is not using the term in the common sense of the constant or omnipresent, but in the stricter and older sense of logical gradation of steps within a single series. The concept of continuity is one of the fundamental ideas of Western thought. Its importance in the theory of development is obvious; change can hardly be declared directional or predictable, save on the grounds of continuity. According to Nisbet, the law of continuity, expressed by Leibniz as "nature makes no leaps," made its way "from Liebniz's monadology to areas as far flung and distinct as Marx's theory of revolution and Darwin's theory of natural selection. Nisbet's comments on Marx are interesting. He claims that, despite a theory of revolution that many would regard as an assertion of the very opposite of continuity, Marx is an "apostle of genetic continuity." He quotes what he calls Marx's rendering of the Leibnizian law of continuity:

> And even when a society has got on the right track for the discovery of the natural laws of its movement--and it is

the ultimate aim of this work to lay bare the economic law of motion of modern society--it can neither clear by bold leaps nor remove by legal enactments the obstacles offered by the successive phases of its normal development. But it can shorten and lessen the birth pangs.[5]

Contrary to what might be assumed, Nisbet insists that Marx's view of revolution does not reflect a renunciation of the slow, gradual, and cumulative idea of evolution and the assumption of continuity on which it is based. Nisbet states:

...Marx and Engels--at least in their systematic theory--saw revolution as but a final, triumphant, and more or less dramatic stage of growth just as continuous in its sequence or stages as anything to be found in Comte, Darwin, or Spencer. Revolution, in the Marxian sense, is feasible and theoretically rational only when the shape of the new social order is already substantially formed within the womb of the preceding order.[6]

Nisbet then quotes Marx's words: "No social order ever disappears before all the productive forces for which there is room in it have been developed, and new, higher relations of production never appear before the material conditions of their existence have matured in the womb of the old society." Nisbet concludes, "Acceleration of a process, even by armed uprising, does not bespeak discontinuity."

Commenting on the premise of the social evolutionists that change is necessary, Nisbet states, "Necessity is one of those golden words of the nineteenth century, nowhere more golden than in the theory of development". He cautions, however, that when the social evolutionists are speaking about a given sequence of development as necessary, they are talking not about history in the aggregate but about the system or systems they are studying. Marx is an exception. He seems willing to extend the idea of necessity of development from the constructed system that is his rendering of capitalism to the specific areas of historically formed nations. After speaking about laws and tendencies "working with iron necessity towards inevitable results," Marx adds that the nation "that is more developed industrially only shows, to the less developed, the image of its own future."[7]

Finally, Nisbet suggests that the social evolutionists operated on the premise that change proceeds from uniform causes. This principle, like the others, finds its roots most directly in the theory of natural history--nature must be consistent and uniform in her working. Darwin accepted this theory in conjunction with his doctrine of natural selection: biological change in time has been the work of a uniform process--the "survival of the fittest." In economics Adam Smith proposed that the uniform cause of development was competition; for Rousseau, examining human institutions in general, development could be explained by the ceaseless operation of human beings' vices, avarice, ambition, etc. Nisbet states, however, that it probably was Immanuel Kant who was most responsible for putting the idea of endemic, uniform conflict in the form most usable to the study of developmental change. Set forth in the form of a "fourth thesis" in his IDEA FOR A UNIVERSAL HISTORY (1784), Kant declared: "The means employed by Nature to bring about the development of all the capacities of men is their antagonism in society, so as this is, in the end, the cause of a lawful order among men."[8]

Like Kant, Hegel found internal conflict to be the effective cause of the development he studied in terms of the idea of freedom. According to Hegel, through the dialectic, by which thesis and antithesis are resolved into synthesis, the spirit is "at war with itself." Marx saw this notion of endemic conflict or tension of internal elements as the developmental process in economic society. Class struggle is, and will remain, a constant and vital element of all societies until, through a long-range development of the social order, private property and social class will be abolished once and for all. Thereafter, motivation for change will lie in the consciousness of men and women.

For the social evolutionists, according to Nisbet, this uniform mechanism of change, built into the developing entity, rendered superfluous any dependence upon either a Providence above or external and unique events below, to explain the course of human development.

2. HISTORICAL CONSCIOUSNESS: A DYNAMIC VIEW

There were, and are, theories of development which do not depend on social evolution with its analogy of change in society to change in the growth processes of the individual organism. These theories depend primarily on the emergence of the phenomenon that has come to be known as the "historical sense" or "historical consciousness." This phenomenon stems from the period of Enlightenment and is first reflected in the writings of historians like Giambattista Vico and Johann Gottfried von Herder. Vico was caught up in a cyclical theory of human history in which societies, or nations, as he called them, pass through determined stages, but he combined with this a theory of knowledge which underlined humans as historical beings whose powers and capacities do not conform to a fixed or static pattern, but are necessarily subject to change and development. He distinguishes between knowledge acquired by observation of the nonhuman, natural world, and knowledge gained from that which men and women achieve on their own, that is, their history. This latter knowledge is more valid, according to Vico, because in order for humans to know something fully, they must in some sense have participated in the making of it.[10]

Herder was likewise caught up in the Enlightenment preconceptions of humans as progressive beings, but he did introduce into his thought the idea that human actions and achievements must be viewed from a standpoint which took proper account of "time, place and national character"--in other words, cultural milieu and the inevitable limits imposed by historical situation and circumstances. He insisted that past thought and action could not be treated as if they were manifestations of an unchanging human consciousness.[11]

A more open, dynamic understanding of history and social change is reflected in the works of sociologist Max Weber and philosopher Ernst Bloch. Weber did not accept the theory of social evolution. He did not think that scholars had enough evidence to speak scientifically of a necessary direction implicit in the historical process. Rather, Weber saw many diverse and irreconcilable values present in the human world, all deserving loyalty. They could never be brought together in a single synthesis. As Gregory Baum describes Weber's perspective:

> Every development in one direction, faithful to a certain ideal, would inevitably neglect other values, irreconcilable with it, and hence ultimately produce a reaction, a new movement, possibly mediated by religious breakthrough that

would seek to recover some of these neglected values.[12]

For Weber, history is undefined and open.
Through charismatic persons and the countervailing
movements created by them, freedom is inserted into the historical process. Each social order
creates its own opposing movements. According to
Baum, Weber--like Marx and Hegel--saw a type of
dialectic relationship between society and consciousness, or between infrastructure and supra-
structure. But for Weber, these dialectics did
not carry history forward in a clearly defined
direction. Although he does speak of the eventual
"iron cage" into which functional rationality will
lead society, he also speaks of the application of
reason in another way. Rationality eventually
moves beyond the functional questions of means to
that of meaning. People urged on by charismatic
leaders, are able to react against the alienation
that increasingly rigid bureaucracy inflicts.[13]
The possibility of charismatic leadership renders
social change or development, as used here, for
Weber, dynamic and open.

Ernst Bloch, a revisionist Marxist, distinguishes between what he calls the "cold" current
of Marxism which stresses the scientific, deter-
minist aspect in the development of history, and
the "warm" current which recognizes the elements
of phantasy, imagination, and human longing in the
process of world development. According to Bloch,
the future is never created according to fixed
laws; it is produced by a process that involves
people's freedom and their imagination.[14]

It is out of this second perspective on
history and social change that I shall fashion the
meaning of development as the aegis under which to
construct a theology of the Church's mission. It
must be said that the proponents of the use of
other terms which we shall critique--revolution,
liberation, politics--also write from this general

historical perspective. That is, they look upon history not as determined but open; they view the development of societies from a dynamic perspective, and look upon the future as something for which the human family somehow has responsibility. Even from the theological point of view, they would agree that somehow God is acting in history and that history itself has some discernible meaning and hoped for goal. But it is the way in which they formulate their views and, even more, the theological presuppositions behind their formulations that is the object of my critique. Furthermore, some of these presuppositions are evident in the very terminology they choose to employ. Words are important and carry with them implications and nuances that are more than a matter of mere semantics. I have chosen the concept of development as the aegis under which to interpret theologically this common dynamic understanding of history and under which to outline the contribution that the Christian Church can and should make in directing change toward goals that are beneficial for the whole human family.

Development, as I shall employ it here, encompasses the whole spectrum of changes that must take place in individuals and in societies as they move toward a condition regarded as more fully human. In theological terms, that movement is toward the Kingdom of God. The concept of development does not necessarily specify in particular instances how this movement is to take place. It can, therefore, take the best from the theories of revolution, liberation, and politics without being absorbed by them. The term development has frequently been associated with economic and social matters which, in turn, presuppose the political realm. But it applies as well to growth in freedom and to the fulfillment of the individual within the community.[15]

Unlike the term liberation, development has no direct identification with biblical motifs. On the surface this may appear to be a weakness, but in fact it protects those formulating a theology of development from the temptation of seeking to support their position by superficial and uncritical biblical references or parallels. This is something that the theologians of liberation and revolution have not always been able to avoid.[16] Furthermore, avoiding direct biblical language facilitates dialogue with those outside the theological circle of the Church or even the Judeo-Christian tradition. Development does have a relationship to the theological concepts of creation, revelation, eschatology and ecclesiology; it does lend itself to theological elaboration, as will be shown later, and yet it also provides a bridge for dialogue between the Church and the rest of the world.

DEVELOPMENT AND DEVELOPMENTALISM

The understanding of the term development, as I intend to use it, is of fairly recent origin. After the Second World War, with the founding of the United Nations and the remarkable recovery which Europe made with the help of the Marshall Plan, the operational concept of development became widely used among Western nations. As a result of World War II, virtually every area of the world was touched by Western technology. The contrast between industrial and traditional societies, between developed and underdeveloped nations, became apparent. New possibilities seemed at hand. By economic aid and technology, "backward" countries could be transformed and modernized. They could "catch up." This outlook has aptly been labeled the "myth of development." Economic aid was thought to be the essential element in getting poor countries moving. Once started, they would progress through the various stages of development that the rich countries had experienced.[17]

In this perspective, development was synonymous with economic growth. It could be measured by comparing the gross national product or the per capita income of developing nations with those countries regarded as highly developed. The short-comings of such a measure in traditional societies are obvious. The root causes of underdevelopment and stagnation were not analyzed. The expectations of the poor were raised and then frustated as unrealistic plans for economic development faltered.

Gradually the term development took on a broader meaning. It began to be applied to the total social process--the interdependence of economic, social, political and cultural factors. Development or stagnation in one area would necessarily affect the others. This conception of development was behind the first "Decade of Development" proclaimed by the United Nations at the beginning of the 1960s. Barbara Ward has aptly summarized the philosophy behind the project.[18]

According to Ward, the plan was first of all seen as a genuine attempt to bring underdeveloped and developed nations together to do something constructive. The focus of the joint effort was to establish the rate of economic growth that developing nations had to maintain to keep ahead of their growth in population and still achieve a small surplus for investment in education, farming, and industrial development. Without such investment, a society or community cannot establish a modern economy in which self-sustaining growth is possible.

The problem of development must be attacked from many different sides simultaneously. One of the first steps, according to Ward, is to examine the pre-investment problem. This pre-investment problem can be explained as follows: In nearly every country, however poor, a very large part of its local resources, physical and human, is not used. The human element is even more important than the physical one. It is estimated that as much as sixty percent of development comes, not from capital, but from trained intelligence, the trained intelligence of a particular type, of course. Ward states that it is the trained intelligence

> ...of the managerial type, the honesty and steadfast dedication of the civil servant, the professional capacity of doctors, lawyers, and engineers, and then the skills at intermediate levels--young technicians who can help the fully trained engineers, the nurses and medical orderlies who help the doctors--and at every level, the teachers, on whose work all else depends.[19]

Both developed and underdeveloped nations have come to realize, moreover, that the whole question of aid must be tied to a re-evaluation and read-justment of the international trade policy. Finally, because full development planning is beyond the scope of many developing countries, a transfer of skills from developed to developing countries is essential if their ambitions are not to end in disillusionment. With the knowledge and experience acquired during the post-war period concerning the task of development, the United Nations planners saw in the Decade of Development a context for a joint strategy for global development.

The philosophy behind the Decade of Development reflects a "deep-rooted conviction that under the surface of the global processes of change exists a uniform trend which is called 'development,' a trend which will reach its ultimate goal of universal welfare and affluence, which is rational and can be understood, which can be steered and mastered."[20] The only problem was, and is, that the first Decade of Development fell pitifully short of its goals. Instead of closing the gap between rich and poor nations, the gulf between them widened. By 1970, two-thirds of the human family still struggled beneath the oppression of poverty. Frustration and bitterness grew. As Pope Paul warned in his encyclical ON THE DEVELOPMENT OF PEOPLES, the continued greed of rich countries would call down on them not only "the judgment of God," but "the wrath of the poor."[21]

In Latin-America, especially, the term development took on a pejorative meaning. DESARROLLISMO (developmentalism--some have suggested it be translated "growthmanship") became identified with ineffective and counterproductive measures which, instead of attacking the roots of underdevelopment, ensured the abiding dependence of the poor countries on the rich.[22] Underdevelopment, according to this viewpoint, is only a by-product of further development for the rich nations. The only possible way for poor countries to achieve development is to break the domination of the rich countries over them. Attempts to bring about changes within the existing order through reformism or modernization are futile. The economic, social, political and cultural dependence of the Third World countries must be overcome before any meaningful development can be achieved. This can be achieved only by struggle; it will involve conflict.

Evident in this critique of development is the Marxist or Marxist-leaning theory of capitalistic imperialism. However, much of the same critique is now widely accepted among a broad group of people, many of whom cannot be called Marxists or even "leftists" in any conventional sense.[23] But there is a parting of company when the means of ending domination are discussed. Most Latin-American liberationists pursue the Marxist analysis, insisting that the present private property system must be abolished and the control of the means of production placed in the hands of the "exploited" classes.

In the context of the failure of development programs to meet the raised expectations of the poor in developing countries and the failure of development philosophy to get at the root causes of underdevelopment, the concepts of revolution and liberation began to receive more emphasis from Third World activists.

Because those advocating the use of the term liberation are also the most vocal in criticizing the concept of development--much of the above critique of development or developmentalism comes from the liberationists--the term liberation will be examined first.

DEVELOPMENT AND LIBERATION

Gustavo Gutierrez, one of the chief proponents of a theology of liberation, speaks of liberation as being the term "more appropriate" and "richer in human content" than development. It expresses, according to Gutierrez, "the inescapable moment of radical change which is foreign to the ordinary use of the term development." Development "appears somewhat aseptic, giving a false picture of a tragic and conflictual reality." It is only within "the more universal, profound, and radical perspective of liberation, that development finds its proper place."[24]

Gutierrez does not discount the concept of development completely, but rather, places it within what he calls the more universal context of liberation. But in doing this, he identifies the term development with developmentalism and equates it with gradualism, reformism, and modernization. We suggest, on the contrary, that development is the broader and underlying concept. Liberation is a particular way of grasping, conceptualizing and formulating development at a certain time and place under certain historical circumstances.

Furthermore, Gutierrez' claim that liberation leads readily to biblical themes which can clarify theological problems obscured by the term development carries with it that danger mentioned earlier of applying biblical models uncritically to contemporary problems.

It is neither necessary nor accurate to identify development only with gradual growth and modernization. When this is done the liberationists have a valid criticism. Peter Berger has pointed out that concepts are not "made in heaven" and that all definitions are somewhat arbitrary. I shall distinguish, as he does, between development, on the one hand, and growth and modernization on the other. When this is done, the criticisms of the liberationists become invalid and the true value of the term development becomes clearer.[25]

Growth has to do with economics; it can be measured accurately by examining the society's gross national product and the rise in the per capita output. Economic growth is usually the result of the introduction or improvement in technological means of production and distribution. These technological and economic processes, in turn, affect the instituitions and the entire culture of the society in which they are introduced. This wider transformation that results is designated modernization. As Peter Berger states it, "Modernization refers to the institutional and cultural concomitants of economic growth under the conditions of sophisticated technology."[26] Growth and modernization, in the sense described here, can be designated as "value-free" concepts from the point of view of integral human development. That is, they can be meaningfully employed regardless of whether one evaluates these processes as good, bad, or indifferent from the ethical or moral point of view.

Development, on the other hand, rather than being identified with value-free concepts of either growth or modernization, as we have described them, carries with it "a much stronger undertone of positive evaluation."[27] Development implies a general improvement in the well-being of the population undergoing the process. Berger gives the following negative example to clarify this point:

> One may readily imagine a society based on slave labor of most of the population, which society nevertheless experiences rapid economic growth and modernizes its principal institutions. Very few social scientists would be prepared to speak of development in this situation (though, in a regrettable number of cases, they have in fact done so if the slavery was a bit camouflaged). Thus the notion of development is at least implicitly one of moral approval and political purpose. Put simply, development means good growth and desirable modernization.

Berger adds,

> People who speak of growth and modernization may do so in the role of neutral observers. People who speak of development should frankly admit that they are engaged in the business of ethics and, at least potentially, of politics.[28]

Berger's position expressed here, as well as his conception of development as a "religious category," will be discussed under the theology of development.

Our concern at present is with a clarification of terms. Berger's insight into the concept of development is invaluable for this purpose and seems to meet most of the liberationists' criticism of the term. Even Gutierrez admits that development policy is valid and necessary. The problem is that he places development within the context of liberation, while the position presented here considers liberation as a form of, and an element in, development. Further justification for this change in perspective will come as we consider the relationship between the terms development and revolution.

DEVELOPMENT AND REVOLUTION

In somewhat similar fashion to the way liberation has become the popular word in theological jargon today, revolution had its day in attempting to displace development as the perspective from which to consider the complex problems of the relationship between the Church and rest of the world. The term itself has been applied to so many and so greatly contrasting situations...from the idea of "conversion," to armed political struggle, to change in sexual mores--that it does not lend itself easily to clear theological elaboration.

This fascination with, and struggle for, a theology of revolution flourished during the 1960s in both Protestant and Catholic circles. Harvey Cox, in his celebrated SECULAR CITY, proclaimed, "We are trying to live in a period of revolution without a theology of revolution."[29] Camilo Torres, the Colombian priest-turned-guerrilla, declared, "Every Catholic who is not a revolutionary, and is not on the side of the revolutionaries lives in mortal sin."[30] THE MESSAGE OF SEVENTEEN BISHOPS OF THE THIRD WORLD stated that the Church cannot but accept those revolutions which serve justice. They further defined revolution as "a break with some system that no longer ensures the common good and the establishment of a new order more likely to bring it about."[31]

Vatican II's teaching on revolution is ambiguous. It says that oppressed people should obey existing laws and yet it is lawful for them to defend their rights, "provided they observe the limits imposed by natural law and the gospel."[32] But Pope Paul VI's encyclical ON THE DEVELOPMENT OF PEOPLES contains a statement which was seen as an opening by those anxious for a theology of revolution. The Pope ruled out revolutionary uprisings "save where there is a manifest, long-standing tyranny...."[33] Later the Pope went to great pains to clarify and, to a large extent, withdraw the statement: "It seems to some that when we denounced in the name of God the very grave needs in which so many of humanity suffer, we had opened the way to the so-called theology of revolution and violence. Such an error is far from our thought and language."[34] Pope Paul returned to this same theme in his apostolic exhortation, ON EVANGELIZATION IN THE MODERN WORLD, by repeating what he had said at the Eucharistic Congress in Bogata in 1968: "We exhort you not to place your trust in violence and revolution: that is contrary to the Christian spirit, and it can also delay instead of advancing that social uplifting to which you lawfully aspire."[35]

At the World Council of Churches' Conference on Church and Society, held in Geneva in 1966, various dimensions of development were discussed, but the question of revolution dominated the most dramatic theological and ethical statements. Although Christians were urged not to resort to force, the question was raised "whether the violence that sheds blood in planned revolution may not be a lesser evil than the violence that, though bloodless, condemns whole populations to perennial despair."[36]

The specifically theological aspects of revolution are not our concern here. They will be examined later. But it is evident that at the Geneva Conference on Church and Society the term revolu-

tion symbolized that desire of many to break with
the past and hope for a new future. The most ar-
dent plea for a theology of revolution came from
Richard Shaull. According to Shaull, the crucial
questions of humanization or dehumanization in the
contemporary world are decided "on the frontiers
of revolution." In outlining a new strategy of
revolution, Shaull suggests a type of "guerrilla
warfare." This consists in "developing those bases
from which a system, unwilling to initiate major
changes when they are most urgently needed, can be
constantly bombarded by strong pressure for small
changes at many different points." At times the
Christian may have to take part in revolutionary
action which involves use of force. Above all
Christians must be involved "in those places in
the world where God is most dynamically at
work."[37]

That was Geneva in 1966. Yet even there, according to Trutz Rentdorff, "it was impossible...
to ignore the fact that the question of revolution
was only the extreme and politically explosive
form of the more complex problem of development."[38] The truth of this statement will become
clearer when we discuss van Leeuwen's contention
that development and revolution are dialectically
related.

The shift of emphasis back to the concept of
development came at the Uppsala Conference in
1968, when, as discussed in an earlier chapter,
the churches gave their answer to the proposals of
the Geneva Conference. Because of the interdependence of economic, social and cultural developments
and structural political changes, the Uppsala
Conference decided that development, not revolution, provided the basis for a far-reaching, ecumenical and theological concept of the future.
The term development is more rational and inclusive than the idea of revolution. It includes the
elements of design, planning, and consciously
thought out and deliberately effected change.

Scientific analysis and practical stimulus to action are part of the rational nucleus of the concept of development. It is not less dynamic or less political than the term revolution, but it does include reference to the interdependence and to the participation of all productive powers.

A further clarification of the role of revolution within the broader concept of development can be achieved by examining van Leeuwen's discussion of the relationship between revolution and development. Although my position is slightly different from van Leeuwen's, the two are not contradictory. Instead of seeing revolution as an aspect of development, van Leeuwen views the two concepts as mutually inclusive. They are like two sides of a single coin. Van Leeuwen argues that within the development processes there are contradictions and antithetical implications which could better be called revolutionary."[39]

Using Thomas Kuhn's theory of the structure of scientific revolutions as a tool, van Leeuwen analyzes the nature of radical social change and draws a parallel, as did Kuhn, between scientific and political revolutions.[40] A growing sense of malfunction in both political and scientific development could lead to a crisis. This crisis, which manifests itself in the form of frustration or inadequacy, is restricted to a small segment of the political community. This leads to a discarding of what Kuhn has termed a "paradigm" and it initiates the search for another. A paradigm is defined as a universally recognized scientific achievement that for a time provides model problems and solutions to a community of practitioners. Its parallels in the sociopolitical realm are the institutions that function to conserve and perpetuate normal social and political structures.

A new paradigm calls for a change in political institutions. But this change cannot take place without partially relinquishing one set of insti-

tutions in favor of another. Some will accept the
new institutional matrix within which political
change is to be achieved; others will not. Conflict is bound to result as both sides—old and
new—attempt to persuade society, often by force,
that their own functional view of things is the
most effective in meeting the present, and especially the future, problems of the community.
Each group defends its views from within its own
paradigm. It is the particular community that must
finally choose between one or the other paradigm,
since there is no higher standard than the community's assent. To a certain extent that assent
has to be based more on faith than on fact.

Van Leeuwen argues that Kuhn's insights help
explain why sociopolitical development cannot
always follow an unbroken line of gradual change,
and why revolutions sometimes explode the dominant
order in such a violent manner. The victory of one
paradigm of the sociopolitical order over another
will be viewed as progress or development by the
revolutionaries, but as chaos by the traditional-
ists. The post-revolutionary order will, in turn,
be threatened by new anomalies and crises. Because
of the essentially historical character of the
sociopolitical order, no permanent order can be
established. Van Leeuwen argues that the analogy
between scientific and sociopolitical revolutions
clearly indicates the interdependence of development and revolution, of gradual and evolutionary
changes as contrasted with sudden and violent
change.[41] Revolution, according to van Leeuwen,
is the dialectical counterpart of development. As
he states it:

> The process of development, in the socio-
> political realm as well as in the realm
> of science, may follow a continuous and
> uninterrupted course, as long as a given
> channel exists. But at the very moment
> when the adequacy of the traditional
> channel is being basically questioned and

the given system is no longer capable of responding to unprecedented challenges, what seemed to be the safeguard of continuity turns into the enemy of future development, carving out a new channel as it goes along. The established routes are not an unchangeable part of nature; they are historical realities, fixed by man in the course of history. The revolutionary character of development is determined by the historical character of human and worldly realities.[42]

The discussion by van Leeuwen concerning the interrelationship between development and revolution is indeed valuable and goes far in clarifying the dynamic concept of development that I am attempting to formulate here.

Most liberation theologians deliberately disassociate themselves from theories of revolution. Gutierrez claims that initially the theology of revolution was elaborated by theologians who had a first-hand knowledge of countries experiencing the revolutionary process, but then certain German theology became a sounding board for the theology of revolution. It was thereby taken out of its own context and then subsequently translated in Latin America. Gutierrez warns that such a theology of revolution runs the risk of becoming a revolutionary Christian ideology, of "baptizing" the revolution--something that many claim his own theology does not completely avoid. But most of all, according to Gutierrez's perspective, the theology of revolution--and he includes the theology of development as well--has the wrong starting point. Both attempt to further development or revolutionary action by applying a certain process of theological thought to certain aspects of the political world. Neither are grounded in "critical thought from and about the historical praxis of liberation, from and about faith as a liberating praxis."[43]

Gutierrez's theology will be examined more thoroughly in Chapter Six; our principal concern here are the terms themselves. However, in spite of the protests to the contrary by the liberationists, there is a definite, and indeed dangerous, relationship between the concept of liberation and the concept of revolution. Hugo Assmann, one of the more passionate liberation theologians, admits that the theology of liberation can be considered a part of the theology of revolution in the sense that "the theology of liberation seeks to be critical reflection on revolutionary action in both its overall aspects and its detailed circumstances, but it is not interested in discussing revolution as an abstract entity."[44]

DEVELOPMENT AND POLITICS

In a sense, the whole enterprise of world development and its specific forms of liberation and revolution can be considered under the aegis of politics. The term politics, however, or the understanding of the realm of the political, is fraught with difficulties. These difficulties stem in part from three fundamentally different perspectives on the meaning of the term political. The first perspective views the realm of politics or the political sector of society as a specific set of social institutions among other social institutions in a social system. A second perspective insists that the realm of the political is the basic meaning and structure of good order in a social system as a whole. Finally, there are those who look upon politics as the locus of the societal conflicts of interest groups. We shall examine each of these perspectives.

1. THE POLITICAL REALM:
A SOCIAL INSTITUTION WITHIN SOCIETY

The first perspective, that in which the political is understood as a set of social institutions among others in society, is reflected in a recent book by Jean-Yves Calvez, POLITICS AND SOCIETY IN THE THIRD WORLD. Calvez claims that societies and economies of developing countries are in the process of change precisely at the political level. On the international scene, within the world community, developing countries are making their presence felt as political states.[45] At every level it is as a social body that these young states are attempting to move forward with development. This social body is directed by a group of persons who are in the vanguard of the society as a whole. That is to say, it has not been the peasants, nor the entrepreneurs or industrialists, nor the labor unions, nor (in the case of Latin America) the Church that has taken upon itself the task of development; it has been the state--the state directed by a relatively small group of people.[46]

According to Calvez, "The state's role in development is one of the most characteristic aspects of the socioeconomic situation in today's developing countries." However, he points out that the state in this case means "a stratum of men, a kind of social class or rather a kind of caste which today almost exclusively plays the role of mover of society." This group is not always brilliant, according to Calvez, but it is generally the only dynamic one. It is this social group that has made development its objective.[47]

Calvez argues further that the understanding of the state as the prime mover in development among Third World countries cannot be explained by any alien socialist doctrines or ideologies. Whether the country officially espouses socialism or capitalism, the role of the state is still fundamental. Even in socialist societies, the Marxist theory of abolition of all private ownership of the means of production generally takes a less important place than development through state activity. This state activity takes the form of planning and intervention, the latter often by means of creating and managing many of the most important enterprises within the public sector.[48]

After examining a representative number of actual political regimes, Calvez states that they tend to be oligarchic, and if they are not impotent and corrupt they must be led by a personalist, charismatic leader.[49] Single parties are characteristic; the principal role of the party is to provide a means of communication from the leaders to the membership. Because the society in many of these countries is being built from the top down, according to future-oriented development plans conceived and directed by so-called experts, there are usually serious problems of national unification, integration and motivation.[50] Projects for land reform, population control, education and community development, to say nothing of overall economic progress, are often largely paper measures. Where implementation does take place, the results are often uneven, for neither ambitious plans nor proclamation of decrees can in themselves change customs, mentalities and institutions of traditional societies. Nevertheless, according to Calvez it is in the realm of the political--political understood as one of the social institutions among others in society, namely, the state or the government--that the direction for development is being determined. Any theology based on this understanding of politics could easily be accused of being a theological justification for state policy, that is, an ideology.

2. THE POLITICAL REALM: THE PUBLIC PLACE OF FREEDOM

To speak of the direction of development is to speak of objectives, means and goals. In keeping with the definition of development that we established earlier in the chapter, that is, when development is understood not merely as growth or modernization but as the overall betterment of peoples, then the objectives, means and goals involve particular human values. We are confronted with ethical and moral decisions, with what one might call political theology. In a sense political theology could be understood as the ethical or moral dimension of development. But political theology, as the term is generally employed today, represents something much broader and more theoretical. Its proponents, because they understand the term political in what we have designated the second perspective--politics is the basic meaning and structure of good order in a social system-- could not accept political theology as the ethical or moral dimension of development. Once again, our purpose at present is not to analyze or criticize the content of the theology, but rather to clarify the terms.

Jurgen Moltmann and Johannes B. Metz are two of the most prominent proponents of political theology today. Moltmann sees the field of politics as "the extensive field of constructive and destructive possibilities of the appropriation and utilization of nature's powers as well as of human relationships by human society." Noting that nature and human history come together in the process of civilization, Moltmann claims that for both human beings and nature, politics is becoming a common destiny.[51]

Moltmann traces the beginnings of this convergence of humans and nature toward the realm of politics to the late Middle Ages when men and women and their society, their science, their culture, and their economy began moving out of the theopolitical structures of medieval Christendom. This convergence continued with the emergence of national states and their struggle for autonomy. Philosophy threw off the tutelage of theology; natural science rejected the authority of the Christian understanding of the world. Finally, these various strands were consolidated in the age of Enlightenment. Metz states it succintly:

> The age of Enlightenment, on the one hand, and the political, social, scientific, and technological revolutions that began in it, on the other, show that the world now to a special degree and in a hitherto unknown way becomes the business of man, that he, man, now orders his affairs himself and takes them under the protection of his freedom and his political responsibility.[52]

The social structures of this world are looked upon no longer as God-given, but rather as the creation and the responsibility of men and women. Politics, or the political realm, becomes the focus for a theology of the world.

One might question at this point why the concept of politics, understood in this broad sense, was not chosen to be the aegis under which a new theology of missions could be formulated. There are several reasons why the term politics, thus understood, was not chosen. First, although it was suggested earlier that political theology might be considered the ethical dimension of development, both Moltmann and Metz insist that political theology is more than political ethics or the moral theology of politics. According to them, it reaches much deeper; it asks about the political consciousness of theology itself. It emphatically does not aim at giving religious support to political systems and movements. "Rather, political theology designates the field, the milieu, the environment, and the medium in which Christian theology should be articulated today."[53] It becomes, in a sense, a prologomenon to theology, taking the place of the old natural theology.[54] The starting point for the use of the term political, then, is not where the small stratum or social group of "movers" in a society

are attempting to direct development, nor where
social conflicts of interest groups or those advocating a particular paradigm arise, but in the
more theoretical public sphere in general. The
specific relationship between political theology
and political ethics will be examined more in
detail later, but for now it can be said that the
term political as it is employed by those advocating political theology is broader, more theoretical, and more ambiguous than the concept of
development as I have tried to define it in relationship to the Church's mission in the world.

Metz himself admits that the notion of political theology is ambiguous and therefore open to
misunderstanding. "It has," he notes, "been burdened with specific historical connotations."[55]
For this reason, he has had to defend and clarify
his terminology again and again. In Germany the
use of the term political theology brings to the
minds of many the book by Carl Schmidt POLITICAL
THEOLOGY (1922, 1934) which was used as the ideological justification of Hitler's National Socialist party.[56] In early Christian history the term
theologia politike or theologia civilis--distin-
guished in Stoicism from "mythical" or "natural"
theology--was the immediate successor of the religious state ideology of ancient Rome. The first
great outline of a Christian "political theology"
was attempted by Eusebius, the court bishop of
Constantine. His schema, "One God, one Logos, one
emperor, one empire," was severely criticized by
St. Augustine in his CITY OF GOD. Eusebius' theological sanctioning of the primacy of politics and
its authorization of the absolute claim of the
state was reflected later in Byzantine Caesaropap-
ism, in Machiavelli's and Hobbes' theories of
state and society during the Renaissance period,
and the French traditionalism of the last century.

Metz and other advocates of the current political theology argue that they are opposed to all
forms of theology which politicize directly. In

clarifying and defending his position, Metz makes a careful distinction between the state and society.[57] This distinction, according to Metz, makes it possible to differentiate the public sphere of the state as power from the public sphere in which the interests of all men and women as a social group are expressed. Metz insists that his approach has an essentially anti-totalitarian thrust and therefore is a safeguard against any authoritative, repressive political theologies. He says that by defining the political sphere in this way, the danger is removed from mixing politics and religion the way old political theology did.[58] The "modern history of freedom" (FREIHEITSGESCHICHTE) has taken on a central role in the political theology of Metz. Since the Enlightenment, Metz contends the category of politics has become identified with that of freedom; it is the democratic "public" place of the mediation of liberty.[59]

Even after the distinction has been made between the state and society and the political order has been conceived as the order of freedom, the concept of political theology still retains its own historical gravitation. As Hans Kung points out, "It can scarcely be given a new function by decree as a critical-revolutionary concept without misunderstandings." I agree with Kung when he says:

> Despite all the demarcations and dissociations put forward by recent advocates of a new 'political theology,' it is liable to be understood, not as a critical theological awareness of the social and political implications and tasks of Christianity, but--as the name itself implies --constantly in theory and practice as 'politicizing theology'. The term is an invitation to load on to 'political theology' from behind--so to speak--a political ideology (now of course 'left wing').[60]

The term political theology is, as we have seen, ambiguous and open to misunderstanding because it is "historically burdened." Another reason why the concept of politics as it is understood and used in contemporary political theology was not employed here is that it is too parochial for formulating an overall theology of the mission of the Church. That is, it originated and has remained too closely connected with a particular theological/historical situation in Germany.

This new political theology arose, first of all, according to Metz, as a critical correction of present-day theology. "Present-day theology" in this case refers primarily to the fruits of German exegetical studies known as <u>Formgeschichte</u> which have been interpreted in the categories of theological existentialism and personalism. The result is that the <u>kerygma</u> is understood as addressed to the individual person rather than to peoples and society. The message is privatized and the practice of faith, claiming to be completely ahistorical and apolitical, is reduced to the timeless decision of the individual person. Instead of answering the problem of the relationship between faith and social praxis, or religion and society, this prominent strain of modern theology simply bypassed the question. According to Metz "the de-privatizing of theology is the primary critical task of political theology."[61] This presumes, of course, that theological existentialism and personalism with their accompanying "privatization" of faith, have in fact permeated the universal theological scene. But many theologians, especially those from the Third World, would deny this is the case. Therefore, this premise upon which current political theology is built does not lend itself readily to universalization.

3. THE POLITICAL REALM:
THE LOCUS OF SOCIETAL CONFLICTS

Political theology takes as its task the attempt to formulate the eschatological message under the conditions of our present society. But here again, one might say that political theology is somewhat parochial. The "present society" that it analyzes is primarily the local German one, or at least the secularized, pluralistic, post-industrial and cybernetic society of the West. This leaves it open to certain legitimate criticism from those speaking from and for the Third World. Liberationists are not convinced that secularization and all that it entails has so completely permeated their societies. They do not see pluralism being readily accepted in their societies, nor do they view their economic situation as "post-industrial."

Gutierrez, for one, rejects Metz's claim that the world has become completely secularized. He denies that the unity of religion and society has been universally shattered. On the contrary, Gutierrez points to the Church in Latin America and insists that it still has a complex public dimension, exercising a significant role in support of the established order.[62] On the one hand, the Church is often the only institution with enough power to speak forcefully on behalf of the alienated and oppressed, but, on the other hand, it often finds itself tied to the established power structure. Even its silence indirectly enhances and legitimizes the status quo. It could be argued further that the complete privatization of faith, which political theology attempts to counteract, is not an accurate description of the situation in many African nations where traditional religions still dominate societies with what Kraemer calls the "primitive apprehension of the totality of existence."[63]

Gutierrez and others further accuse the proponents of political theology of reducing the problems of the world to a theoretical level of language, thus avoiding a real and effective commitment to the historical present.[64]

Metz and Moltmann see political theology as the theology of practice and realization of the

Christian mission in the world. Still, as eschatological theology--a theology drawn forward by
the hope of the future and interested in the
eschatological understanding of the history of humankind and the world--political theology determines its orientation to direct practice or action
in an indirect manner through political ethics.[65]
This qualification, which the liberation theologians do not wish to make, protects political theology from so uniting theory and practice that it
can no longer be self-critical. But to the liberationists this "eschatological proviso" seems to
be an invitation to abstention.[66]

Even when Moltmann, in the chapter in THE
CRUCIFIED GOD dealing with the political libera-
tions of people, states that he is writing in dialogue with the theology of liberation as developed
in Latin America, liberationist Jose Bonino accuses him of drawing back from "specific material-
izations" of God's presence into the refuge of a
"critical function" which is able to "remain above
right and left, ideologically neutral, independent
of structural analysis of reality."[67]

The root of this objection on the part of
liberationists is once again the basic understanding of the concept of politics. Among the proponents of political theology, as was pointed out
before, politics, or the political, is defined by
contrasting it with that which is private and individual. Politics in this sense is a human concern involving principles that relate to the
nature of the individual and the goals of society.
In liberation theology, on the other hand, political signifies--with certain nuances--the locus of
societal conflicts of interest groups, or the
third perspective on politics as we designated it
earlier.

Gutierrez, for example does recognize the universality of the political sphere, and yet he
claims that the revolutionary situation that

exists today, especially in the Third World, which is expressed in the radicalization of social praxis, has led liberationists to see the political arena as necessarily conflictual. Gutierrez states:

> More precisely, the building of a just society means confrontation--in which different kinds of violence are present-- between groups with different interests and opinions.... Concretely, in Latin America, this conflict revolves around the <u>oppression-liberation</u> axis.[68]

Gutierrez further suggests that those who wish to achieve or maintain a "low cost reconciliation" through a reformist's attitude toward the existing system are only advocating a justifying ideology for a profound disorder in society. Becoming aware of the conflictual nature of the political sphere should invite--even oblige--all people, and especially Christians, to join in the liberating struggle. Political theology, according to this understanding, is reflection on liberating praxis.[69]

At the deepest level, what is reflected here is a conflictual understanding of the whole historical process--basically a Marxist perspective. This is the "particular nuance" of the third perspective on politics mentioned earlier. Many North Americans would also accept, at least on the popular level, politics defined as the locus of societal conflicts of interest groups, but they would not reduce all of these conflicts to that of class. Rather, for them, politics denotes a pragmatic formulation of policies, a bargaining for support from various constituencies, and a compromising for the possible. Following from this third perspective on the term politics, political theology can easily be misconstrued as a justifying ideology for revolution on the part of liberationists or some devious attempt by the Church to interfere in matters of State on the part of North Americans.

It was stated at the beginning of this section that perhaps politics could have been the aegis for the reformulation of the Church's mission to the world. However, the foregoing critique has shown that the term politics is historically burdened and parochially associated with Western Europe, especially Germany. Furthermore, regardless of whether it must be or should be, political theology is commonly equated with a theology of practical politics. Thus, in the final analysis, I have elected the term development rather than politics as the aegis under which to reformulate missionary theology.

Our attention must once more turn to the more strictly theological question of the way in which liberation and revolution have been employed in in doing theology. Because my criticism of political theology is primarily on the level of terminology rather than theological method, I will focus my critique on the theology of revolution and liberation theology. Since liberation theology occupies the center of attention today and is, in turn, most critical of any theology of development, special emphasis will be placed on it. We will find that the majority of the theologians of liberation, although appearing to be liberal, even radical, in so many ways, make uncritical assertions or presumptions on the level of fundamental theology. The result is that there appears to be a certain ambiguity in the specifically theological character of their work. This is especially true of their understanding and elaboration of the two most basic elements in any theology--revelation and eschatology.

SUMMARY OF CHAPTER FOUR

Chapter Four contrasts the term development with liberation, revolution and politics from the contextual perspective, and presents the arguments for the choice of development as the thesis for rethinking a theology of missions. First a sketch of the history of the concept of development is presented, and then a clarification of its meaning and use in contemporary parlance is suggested. By freeing the term development from simple identification with technological and economic progress (developmentalism), and distinguishing it from the concepts of growth and modernization (which can be value-free from the perspective of true human betterment), development is described as the planned and desirable change in individuals and societies that must occur in moving the world toward the "more fully human"--ultimately, the Kingdom of God.

Unlike liberation, as defined by the Latin American theologian Gutierrez, which demands an absolute change in the present order, and revolution, as expounded by Richard Shaull, which emphasizes the radical process for achieving change, development recognizes no single process for attaining a condition considered more fully human. It does insist, however, that both specified goals and the means of obtaining them be open to broad critique, that the human cost always be given priority, and that results be weighed not by quantifiable measures but by identifiable values. In other words, according to the definition established here, development is intimately connected with human values; it is, as Berger says, "a religious category."

Concerning the choice of development rather than politics, a critique of three divergent understandings of the latter term, typified respectively by the positions of Calvez, Metz and

Moltmann, and, with certain nuances, Gutierrez and the average North American, the term was found to be ambiguous, historically burdened, parochially conditioned, and open to serious misunderstanding.

In choosing development rather than these other terms, my purpose is not to deny their legitimacy nor, indeed, to underestimate the valuable insights of those who employ them. Rather, I wish to show that the recent popularity of the term liberation is based on a narrow understanding of the concept of development, i.e., developmentalism, that revolution and liberation are prone to a "single solution" approach to very complex issues, and that the term politics, especially when combined with theological reflection, is too open to misunderstanding to be used as the conceptual model within which to reformulate the Church's mission.

NOTES ON CHAPTER FOUR

[1]This "provincialization" is not the result of emphasis on the uniqueness of the Latin-American cultural background and history, as much as the posture of "incommunication" which many Latin-American liberation theologians have assumed. Moltmann, "An Open Letter to Jose Miguez Bonino," CHRISTIANITY AND CRISIS 36 (March 29, 1976): 57-58, states: "Persons who know their own historical and socioeconomic borders are eager to experience that which is different and strange as it encounters them beyond their borders. African theology confronted us with something really new, for the African modes of thought have been entirely unfamiliar to us ever since Aristotle. Japanese theology, done in the Buddhist context, forces Western activists again and again to fundamental reorientations of their interests and thought forms. In North American Black theology we have

encounterd new forms of communication through the language and music of an oppressed community.

"But up to now scarcely anything comparable has come out of Latin America." Moltmann continues, suggesting that what Latin-American liberation theologians specialize in is criticism of Western theology and theology in general, and superficial instructions on Marx and Engels, as if these two Europeans were Latin-American discoveries.

Concerning political theology and its localization in Germany, it should be noted that there is a sense in which the political dimension must enter any attempt to theologize. On the level of fundamental theology the societal (political) context within which theologians work both affects and is affected by theological formulations. This basic fact is presupposed in the method of correlation that has been outlind in Chapter Two. Political theology as proposed by Moltmann and Metz implies something more than this.

[2]SOCIAL CHANGE AND HISTORY: ASPECTS OF THE WESTERN THEORY OF DEVELOPMENT (New York: Oxford University Press, 1969). The following discussion is based on Chapter 5, "The Theory of Social Evolution, pp. 159-88. Only page references to extended quotes will be given.

[3]IBID., p. 167.

[4]Nisbet notes that Durkheim, in his first major work, THE DIVISION OF LABOR, took the subject of social solidarity for evolutionary treatment, and found the normal direction to be from "mechanical solidarity" to "organic solidarity." He later abandoned this "panoramic" approach to social evolution, according to Nisbet, but not the cardinal elements of developmentalism. In subsequent works, he merely narrowed the focus.

[5]IBID., p. 177. The quote is from the Preface to the first edition of CAPITAL, Vol. 1, Frederick

Engels, ed. (New York: International Publishers, 1967). For a sympathetic critique of Marx and the implications of socialism for contemporary societies, see Michael Harrington, SOCIALISM (New York: Saturday Review Press, 1970, 1972). Harrington insists on a much less deterministic interpretation of Marx than Nisbet.

[6]Nisbet, SOCIAL CHANGE AND HISTORY, pp. 177-78.

[7]The quote is from the Preface to the first edition of CAPITAL, Vol. 1. Harrington, SOCIALISM, p. 86, claims that for Marx those laws which rule over the economy are themselves transitory, the creation of men and women who, once the preconditions of mastering them have been fulfilled, can change them.

[8]Quoted from Nisbet, p. 185.

[9]For a summary of the influence of Vico and Herder on the emerging sense of "historical consciousness," see article under "History, Philosophy of," ENCYCLOPEDIA BRITANNICA Vol. 8, 15th ed. (1977), pp. 962-63.

[10]See THE NEW SCIENCE OF GIAMBATTISTA VICO, abridged trans. of 3rd ed. (1744, T. B. Bergin and M. H. Fisch, trans. and intro. (Ithaca and London: Cornell University Press - Cornell Paperbacks, 1970), pp. 52-53.

[11]See Herder, OUTLINES OF A PHILOSOPHY OF THE HISTORY OF MAN, 4 vols., 1784-91, T. O. Churchill, trans. (New York: Bergman Publishers, 1966).

[12]Baum, RELIGION AND ALIENATION (New York: Paulist Press, 1975), p. 167. In chap. 8 of this work, "Creative Religion: Max Weber's Perspective," Baum presents Weber in a very favorable light. See also Weber, THE SOCIOLOGY OF RELIGION, E. Fisholl, trans., T. Parsons, intro. (Boston:

Beacon Press, 1963). Baum notes that it is possible, though probably misleading, to read Weber's sociology of religion as evolutionary theory. He accuses Talcott Parsons of doing this in his famous introduction to the English translation of Weber's book (pp. 166-67). S. N. Einstadt, in his introduction to Weber's ON CHARISM AND INSTITUTION BUILDING: SELECTED PAPERS (Chicago and London: University of Chicago Press, 1968), states that Weber did not use his vast knowledge to erect great evolutionary schemes of world history or of the progress of the human mind, but to "analyze systematically the great variety of human creativity in its social context, to analyze the most salient of the common characteristics and problems of different spheres of human endeavor, and to explore the conditions of emergence, continuity, change and stagnation of different types of social organization and cultural creativity." (p. xiv).

[13]Baum, RELIGION AND ALIENATION, pp. 173-75. Also see Weber, ON CHARISM AND INSTITUTION BUILDING, esp. Part II, "Charisma and Institutionalization in the Political Sphere," pp. 44-77.

[14]Ernst Bloch, DAS PRINZIP DER HOFFNUNG, 2 vols. (Frankfurt am Main: Suhrkamp Verlag, 1969). See sections of this work in English in Bloch, MAN ON HIS OWN, E. B. Ashton, trans. (New York: Herder and Herder, 1970); ON KARL MARX, J. Maxwell, trans. (New York: Herder and Herder, 1971); ATHEISM IN CHRISTIANITY, J. T. Swann, trans. (New York: Herder and Herder, 1972). Concerning the "cold" and "warm" trends in Marxism, see esp. "Hunger, Something in a Dream,' 'God of Hope,' Thing-For-Us," in ATHEISM IN CHRISTIANITY, pp. 264-73.

[15]See Denis Goulet, "Development--or Liberation?" INTERNATIONAL DEVELOPMENT REVIEW 3 (1971): 9. Goulet states, "The language of liberation remains, for many people in the 'developed world,' tactically unmanageable." He notes, "There can be no objection on principle...to granting tentative validity to 'development' as a hinge word." For a

discussion of the use and abuse of the term development, see Rene Laurentin, LIBERATION, DEVELOPMENT AND SALVATION. Charles Underhill Quinn, trans. (Maryknoll, New York: Orbis Books, 1972), esp. the Preface and Chap. 3, "The Word 'Development.'" Also see Denis Goulet, "That Third World," in WORLD DEVELOPMENT: AN INTRODUCTORY READER, Helene Castel, ed. (New York: Macmillan Co.; London: Collier-Macmillan, 1971), pp. 1-25: Philip Land, "What is Development?" in SEARCH OF A THEOLOGY OF DEVELOPMENT: PAPERS FROM A CONSULTATION ON THEOLOGY AND DEVELOPMENT, sponsored by SODEPAX and held in Cartigny, Switzerland, November, 1969 (Geneva: Committee on Society, Development and Peace, n.d.), pp. 180-203. Kenneth Kaunda, President of Zambia and one of the chief spokespersons of the Third World, defined development as follows: "The process of development implies shedding of traditional values, beliefs, and, indeed, behavior relative to membership of traditional organizations or socioeconomic and political groups." At the same time, he adds, "It involves the birth of new values and beliefs in relation to life and new institutions which give expression to new ideas and principles." (Quoted in Land's article listed above.) Richard D. N. Dickinson, TO SET AT LIBERTY THE OPPRESSED, is concerned about the gradual enlargement of the notion of development toward a broad and abstract understanding with a tendency to ignore or minimize economic aspects of social change. He claims that churches have retreated too quickly from economic analysis into the relative safety of more generalized statements about liberation and advocacy of "changed social structures." "What is needed," Dickinson says, "is to participate creatively in forging both new and economic perspectives, policies and instruments, on the one hand, and adequate instruments for technical guidance and evaluation, on the other." Also see Charles Elliot, THE DEVELOPMENT DEBATE (London: S. M. C. Press, 1971).

16One of the principal criticisms of liberation theology is the narrowness with which its proponents select and employ biblical images and themes. This will be brought out in my own critique in the following chapter. Also see John H. Yoder, "Exodus and Exile: The Two Faces of Liberation," CROSS CURRENTS 23 (1973): 297-309.

17This was the basic position adopted in the influential book by Walt W. Rostow, THE STAGES OF ECONOMIC GROWTH: A NON-COMMUNIST MANIFESTO (Cambridge, England: University Press, 1960). According to Gutierrez, A THEOLOGY OF LIBERATION, due to special circumstances and carefully planned methods of distribution, this work became widely known in the underdeveloped countries (p. 38, n. 8). According to Rostow's theory, poor countries would have to imitate the basic steps that rich Western societies had taken in their ascent to wealth. All societies, in their economic dimensions, are to be identified as lying within one of five distinct stages: the traditional society, the developing conditions necessary for growth, the take-off, the drive to maturity, and the age of high mass-consumption. For a useful discussion and criticism of Rostow's theory as a specimen of the highly developed countries' ideology, see Arend T. van Leeuwen, DEVELOPMENT THROUGH REVOLUTION (New York: Charles Scribner's Sons, 1970), esp. pp. 83-88.

18"The United Nations and the Decade of Development," WORLD JUSTICE 7 (March 1966): 317-26. The article is an address given by the author at Columbia University, April 2, 1964, and later published in a symposium, THE QUEST FOR PEACE - The Dag Hammarskjold Lecture Series, A. W. Cordier and W. Foote, eds. (New York: Columbia University Press, 1964)

19"Decade of Development," p. 321. A theme running through all the chapters of Gunnar Mydral's massive ASIAN DRAMA: AN INQUIRY INTO THE POVERTY OF NATIONS 3 vols. (New York: Twentieth

Century Fund and Pantheon Books, 1968), and one that he takes up again in THE CHALLENGE OF WORLD POVERTY, is that the noneconomic factors--attitudes, institutions, and the productivity consequences of very low levels of living--are of such importance in underdeveloped countries that they cannot be abstracted from in economic theory and in planning. He accuses most economists of doing just that (p. 11, with cross-reference to fuller discussion in ASIAN DRAMA).

[20]Van Leeuwen, DEVELOPMENT THROUGH REVOLUTION, p. 16.

[21]With commentary by B. Ward (Paulist Press, 1967), p. 57.

[22]See Gutierrez, THEOLOGY OF LIBERATION, chap. 2, "Liberation and Development," pp. 21-42. Berger, PYRAMIDS OF SACRIFICE, p. 46, refers to the suggested translation of desarrollismo as "growthmanship." For an assessment of the Decade of Development from an optimistic point of view, see Lester B. Pearson, PARTNERS IN DEVELOPMENT (New York: Praeger, 1969), popularly referred to as the PEARSON REPORT.

[23]Berger, PYRAMIDS, p. 46. For an overview of this position, Berger suggests Robert Rhodes, ed., IMPERIALISM AND UNDERDEVELOPMENT (New York: Monthly Review Press, 1970); for a contemporary critique of the Marxist theory, see Benjamin Cohen, THE QUESTION OF IMPERIALISM (New York: Basic Books, 1973).

[24]Gutierrez, THEOLOGY OF LIBERATION, pp. 36-37. The author speaks of the concept of liberation on three levels: It "expresses the aspirations of oppressed peoples and social classes, emphasizing the conflictual aspect of the economic, social and political process which puts them at odds with wealthy nations and oppressive classes." At a second level, liberation refers to

an understanding of history. Drawing on Teilhard de Chardin, Gutierrez sees the human person assuming responsibility for his own destiny. He speaks of the "unfolding of all men's dimensions," and the "gradual conquest of true freedom"--evolutionary concepts--but at the same time he speaks of "permanent cultural revolution" which leads to a "new way of being man" in a "qualitatively different society." Such a blending of radical and evolutionary vocabulary creates an underlying ambiguity. The third level of liberation connects it with biblical sources and Christ's liberation of humans from sin, alienation, injustice and oppression. Gutierrez insists that the three levels constitute a "single, complex process, which finds its deepest sense and its fullest realization in the saving work of Christ." Such a mixing of levels of meaning has prompted Richard Neuhaus, "Liberation Theology and the Captivities of Jesus," WORLDVIEW 16 (June 1973): 44, to declare that for Gutierrez the process of liberation in its most expansive sense comprehends the totality of God's purpose in history, but, more immediately, it might mean the student confrontation with the regime's police in the <u>plaza de armas</u> last Thursday afternoon. He concludes that, despite all Gutierrez's statements to the contrary, he ultimately equates the mission of the Church with the revolutionary struggle. Neuhaus states, "Thus, A THEOLOGY OF LIBERATION comes close to providing carte blanche legitimation for joining almost any allegedly revolutionary struggle to replace almost any allegedly repressive regime" (p.46). Andrew Greeley has also been critical of liberation theology. See "Theological Table-Talk: Politics and Polticial Theologians," THEOLOGY TODAY 30 (January 1974): 391-97.

[25]See Berger, PYRAMIDS, pp. 34-35. This definition of terms was developed in Peter Berger, Brigitte Berger, and Hansfried Kellner, THE HOMELESS MIND--MODERNIZATION AND CONSCIOUSNESS (New York: Random House, 1973). Contrary to my position

on the terms development and liberation, David Tracy, BLESSED RAGE FOR ORDER, states that Gutierrez "applies critical reflection on praxis ...with convincing power to the concept of 'development' in favor of the concept 'liberation'..." (p. 255, n. 35). Characterizing and localizing the concept of development as he does, perhaps Gutierrez is justified in his position, but I insist that development need not and should not be so defined.

[26]PYRAMIDS, p. 34.

[27]IBID., p. 34

[28]IBID., p. 35.

[29]SECULAR CITY (Rev. ed.; New York: Macmillan Co., 1966), p. 93.

[30]Quoted in George Celestin, "A Christian Looks at Revolution," NEW THEOLOGY NO. 6: ON REVOLUTION AND NON-REVOLUTION, VIOLENCE AND NON-VIOLENCE, PEACE AND POWER, Martin E. Marty and Dean G. Peerman, eds. (New York: Macmillan Co.; London: Collier Macmillan, 1969), p. 94-95. Camilo Torres became convinced that only violent revolution could change the corrupt and unjust situation in his country of Colombia. See John Gerassi, ed., CAMILO TORRES, REVOLUTIONARY PRIEST: THE COMPLETE WRITINGS AND MESSAGE OF CAMILO TORRES (New York: Random House - Vintage, 1971), p. 423.

[31]This Message is included in NEW THEOLOGY NO. 6 (see preceding note), pp. 243-54. It is also in BETWEEN HONESTY AND HOPE, pp. 3-12.

[32]THE CHURCH IN THE MODERN WORLD, Art. 74.

[33]ON THE DEVELOPMENT OF PEOPLES, Art. 31.

[34]Quoted in Richard McCormick, "Theology of Revolution," THEOLOGICAL STUDIES 29 (December

1968): 695. On his visit to Latin America in 1969, Pope Paul repeated this idea. See report by Francois Houtart and Andre Rousseau, THE CHURCH AND REVOLUTION, pp. 215-17. In the same article by McCormick, Bishop McGrath of Panama is quoted as saying, "We already have a theology of revolution, thanks to POPULORUM PROGRESSIO [ON THE DEVELOPMENT OF PEOPLES] but what we need is a theology of violence which makes precise that which is legitimate and that which is not" (p. 693).

[35]This apostolic exhortation, issued in December 1975, is available through the Publications Office of the United States Catholic Conference, Washington, D. C., 1976.

[36]WORLD CONFERENCE ON CHURCH AND SOCIETY, Report on Second Section, "The Nature and Function of the State in a Revolutionary Age," par. 84.

[37]Shaull has been called the most outstanding proponent of a theology of revolution. Shaull outlined his position in the first preparatory volume for the Geneva Conference, CHRISTIAN SOCIAL ETHICS IN A CHANGING WORLD, John C. Bennett, ed. (New York: Association Press, 1966). His essay in that volume is entitled "Revolutionary Change in "Theological Perspective." See discussion in J. M. Lochman, "Ecumenical Theology of Revolution," in NEW THEOLOGY NO. 6, pp. 103-22. The above references are taken from this essay, pp. 106-07. Also see the Shaull essay in this same volume, "Christian Faith as Scandal in a Technocratic World," pp. 123-34. See favorable comments on Shaull's theology in Charles West, ETHICS, VIOLENCE AND REVOLUTION (New York: The Council on Religion and International Affairs, 1969), pp. 52-53. Shaull's theological position will be examined in Chapter 5.

[38]"A Theology of Development?" in IN SEARCH OF A THEOLOGY OF DEVELOPMENT, SODEPAX, p. 207.

[39]DEVELOPMENT THROUGH REVOLUTION. Van Leeuwen sees development as the great revolutionary agent of modern history. He quotes Heilbroner, THE GREAT ASCENT, with approval: "Thus at the heart of the development process lurks a revolutionary potential--revolutionary not in the sense of a gradual redistribution of power and wealth such as accompanied the Industrial Revolution, but in the sense of a drastic, rapid, and painful redistribution such as accompanied the French or Russian revolutions" (pp. 119-20).

[40]The following discussion is based on the section of Chap. 2 of DEVELOPMENT THROUGH REVOLUTION entitled "The Structure of Scientific Revolutions," pp. 61-75. This is the title of the much-heralded book by Thomas Kuhn (Chicago: University of Chicago Press, 1966).

[41]IBID., pp. 77-78.

[42]IBID., p. 254.

[43]See Gutierrez, "Liberation Movements and Theology," CONCILIUM 93 (1974): 138-39. Concerning the German theology of revolution, Gutierrez gives reference to the works collected by E. Feil and R. Weth, DISKUSSION ZUR "THEOLOGIE DER REVOLUTION" (Mainz: Matthias-Grunewald; Munchen: Chr. Kaiser, 1971).

[44]Assmann, THEOLOGY FOR A NOMAD CHURCH, Paul Burns, trans., and Frederick Herzog, intro. (Maryknoll, New York: Orbis Books, 1976), p. 92. Echoing Gutierrez's position, but with his usual passion, Assmann claims that European Christians, and especially German intellectuals, tied as they are into the one-dimensional consumer societies, project their own contemporary needs onto the Latin-American scene. He says they are prone to these traumas because "the political implications of the Englightenment have still not been realized and that until now revolutions have always been

frustrated in the country that has produced most writing on the subject of revolution; and in the almost congenital tendency to order and obedience that reached its culmination in the Third Reich" (p. 88).

[45]Calvez, POLITICS AND SOCIETY IN THE THIRD WORLD, see Introduction, pp. 1-3.

[46]IBID., pp. 255-57 Calvez notes that this situation stands in stark contrast to European development in the nineteenth century when the States, with few exceptions, were onlookers, refusing to intervene.

[47]IBID., p. 257. Calvez states that in the developing countries the political class that today is getting the developmental process started will soon be replaced (p. 2).

[48]Calvez gives as an example the contrast, yet similarities, between "socialist" Guinea and Mali and the "capitalist" Ivory Coast. A further discussion on "what kind" of capitalism or "what kind" of socialism will be found in Chapter Six.

[49]This is similar to what van Leeuwen has said, "Mild men will not ride the tigers of development." He sees, rather, an attempt by those with authoritarian power to "impose" development on the ordinary people. Van Leeuwen predicts that because governments can speed development only to a degree, the rising level of frustration will have to be channeled into directions other than that of economic expectations. Therefore, a deliberately heightened nationalism, a carefully planned ideological fervor, and even military adventures are likely by-products of development (DEVELOPMENT THROUGH REVOLUTION, p. 120).

[50]Calvez, POLITICS AND SOCIETY, p. 264. Gunnar Myrdal, one of the great proponents of development

planning, claims that such planning and intervention are what a state needs and what politics is
about. He defines the project as follows: "A
macro-plan for inducing changes simultaneously in
a great number of conditions, not only the economic, and doing it in such a way so as to coordinate
all these changes in order to reach a maximum development effect of efforts and sacrifices"
(CHALLENGE OF WORLD POVERTY, p. 21). He rightly
points out in his ASIAN DRAMA, Vol. 1, p. 115ff,
that the intellectual elite in developing countries are, on the one hand, the vehicles for modernization ideals, but on the other hand, belong
or have numerous ties to privileged groups that
have vested interests in the institutional status
quo. While many of them realize that planning for
development requires radical social change, unless
they are willing to adopt totalitarian methods,
they must be satisfied with cautious measures
which upset as little as possible the inherited
traditional social setting.

[51]See RELIGION, REVOLUTION AND THE FUTURE, p.
218. For a discussion on why Metz selected the
term "political" for this theological enterprise
as well as the principal criticisms leveled
against its use and his own defense, see Chap. 1
of Marcel Xhaufflaire, LA "THEOLOGIE POLITIQUE":
INTRODUCTION A LA THEOLOGIE POLITIQUE DE J. B.
METZ, Vol. 1 (Paris: Les editions du Cerf, 1972),
pp. 17-26. Also see Helmut Peukert, ed.,
DISKUSSION ZUR "POLITISCHE THEOLOGIE" (Munchen:
Chr. Kaiser; Mainz: Matthias-Grunewald, 1969) and
David Kelly's Introduction to Metz's essay, "Prophetic Authority," in RELIGION AND POLITICAL SO-
CIETY. Herbert Richardson, in an essay in the same
volume, "What Makes a Society Political?" discusses politics more in an Anglo-American context--
what I have designated the "third perspective" on
politics. "Politics," according to Richardson,
"allows persons and groups that have differing
aspirations to live together in relative peace and
to cooperate in limited ways for the sake of spe-

cific finite benefits." He adds, "Whenever politics seeks to be more than this, it must inevitably become far less" (p. 120).

[52]THEOLOGY OF THE WORLD, W. Glen-Doepel, trans. (New York: Herder and Herder, 1969), p. 143. Also see Metz's article, "Political Theology," in SACRAMENTUM MUNDI Vol. 5. Metz's recent work, FAITH IH HISTORY AND SOCIETY (New York: Seabury Press, 1980, original German 1977), presents his thought in a more systematic form.

[53]Moltmann, "Political Theology," THEOLOGY TODAY 28 (April 1971): 6.

[54]See Claude Geffre, "Recent Developments in Fundamental Theology: An Interpretation," CONCILIUM 46 (1969): 5-28. Metz states in "The Church's Social Function in the Light of a 'Political Theology,'" CONCILIUM 36 (1968): 9, that his intention in political theology is "to lay bare...a basic feature within theological awareness at large." Indeed Metz subtitles his FAITH IN HISTORY AND SOCIETY, "Toward a Practical Fundamental Theology."

[55]Metz, THEOLOGY OF THE WORLD, p. 107.

[56]For a summary of the discussions surrounding this matter, see Xhaufflaire, LA "THEOLOGIE POLITIQUE," Chap. 1, esp. pp. 22-25. Also see the discussion by Hans Kung, ON BEING A CHRISTIAN, pp. 556-57.

[57]Metz develops the distinction between "state" and "society" in "Politische Theologie in der Diskussion," in DISKUSSION ZUR "POLITISCHEN THEOLOGIE," pp. 267-301. Metz states that he believes that this historical distinction is important if democracy is not to succumb to apolitical forms of social order (p. 290). Also see Xhaufflaire, LA "THEOLOGIE POLITIQUE," p. 27.

[58]Xhaufflaire, LA "THEOLOGIE POLITIQUE," pp. 28-31.

[59]See Metz, "The Future in the Memory of Suffering," CONCILIUM 76 (1972): 10-11. Also see Metz, "Prophetic Authority," in RELIGION AND POLTICAL SOCIETY, pp. 177-209.

[60]ON BEING A CHRISTIAN, pp. 556-57.

[61]THEOLOGY OF THE WORLD, pp. 109-10. Metz is reacting to the position exemplified in the following excerpt from Rudolf Bultmann, HISTORY AND ESCHATOLOGY (New York: Harpers, 1967), p. 36: "The consciousness of being the eschatological community is at the same time the consciousness of being taken out of the still existing world. The world is the sphere of uncleanness and sin, it is a foreign country for the Christians whose commonwealth is in heaven (Phil. iii. 20). Therefore neither the Christian community nor the individuals within it have any responsibility for the present world and its orders, for the tasks of society and the state."

[62]THEOLOGY AND LIBERATION, p. 225.

[63]Kraemer, CHRISTIAN MESSAGE IN A NON-CHRISTIAN WORLD, p. 148ff. Also see E. Bolaji Idowu, AFRICAN TRADITIONAL RELIGION (Maryknoll, New York: Orbis Books, 1974). Concerning the Latin-American situation, see Jose Miguez Bonino, "Popular Piety in Latin-America," CONCILIUM 96 (1974): 148-57. Mydral, CHALLENGE OF WORLD POVERTY, p. 59, states that popular religion, distinguished from the intellectualized and abstruse forms in which it exists in sacred literature and learned religions teachings, acts as a tremendous force for social inertia and therefore supports any degree of social and economic inequality that is inherited. Also see Calvez, POLITICS AND SOCIETY, Chap. 12, "Traditional Religions and Underdevelopment," pp. 165-79. Calvez examines traditional Catholicism

in Latin America and Islam in other Third World countries. Concerning the former, he distinguishes between the simplistic kind of providentialism--in extreme forms superstition which is common among the lower social classes--and the dualistic emphasis on "eternal life" instead of this world, which is typical of the upper classes. Both, Calvez insists, are unpropitious to development. Drawing on a work edited by Jacques Austruy, ISLAM ET DEVELOPEMENT ECONOMIQUE, Calvez notes that Islam found incompatible the individualism of capitalist enterprise, but it is not opposed to collective risk. The aspect of Islam that is regarded as most favorable to development today is the feeling for the collectivity, the idea of the community of believers which transcends political frontiers (pp. 173-174). All of these examples point to the inapplicability of political theology of the German bent to the question of Third World development.

[64]See Gutierrez, THEOLOGY OF LIBERATION, p. 245, n. 80. Also see Rubem Alves, A THEOLOGY OF HUMAN HOPE (Washington, D.C.: Corpus Books, 1969). Alves is especially critical of Moltmann's emphasis on God's promise as something which pulls history forward from the future.

[65]Answering the criticism of Trutz Rendtorff, "Politische Ethik oder 'politisch Theologie'?" in DIKUSSION ZUR "POLITISCHE THEOLOGIE," Metz admits the need of a political ethic to mediate between theory and practice. Metz sees a need for a new association between politics and morals, but his new association must be one that refuses to be content with the affluent-society morality in which morals is relegated to the realm of the private. He calls for a radical democratization of the social infrastructure and a nourishing from below of freedom and effective responsibility. One thing above all must be avoided, according to Metz: "the dissolution of political imagination and political action into the pure business of

planning." See "The Future in the Memory of Suffering," CONCILIUM 76 (1972): 11-13. Metz draws on Pannenberg, who has stated that a Christian ethic is, and ought to be, an ethic not only of "order" but of "change." This essay appears in adapted form in Metz's FAITH IN HISTORY AND SOCIETY.

Moltmann approaches this problem of the relationship between religion and politics or theory and practice by redefining the concept of hermeneutic. Hermeneutic cannot be simply a matter of understanding, but rather, it is itself performative--an action directed toward the transformation of the world. M. Douglas Meeks, ORIGINS OF THE THEOLOGY OF HOPE (Philadelphia: Fortress Press, 1974) says that Moltmann's new understanding of hermeneutic is one of the most significant contributions he has made to contemporary theology (pp. 140-45). Moltmann employs this political hermeneutic in the final chapter of THE CRUCIFIED GOD--but not to the satisfaction of the liberationists.

[66]See Hugo Assmann, PRACTICAL THEOLOGY OF LIBERATION, E. Cardenal, pref., G. Gutierrez, intro., P. Burns, trans. (London: Search Press, 1975), pp. 92-96. Also see Gutierrez, THEOLOGY OF LIBERATION, p. 245, n. 80.

[67]DOING THEOLOGY IN A REVOLUTIONARY SITUATION (Philadelphia: Fortress Press - Confrontation Books, 1975), pp. 145-59.

[68]THEOLOGY OF LIBERATION, p. 48.

[69]IBID., p. 49

THE THEOLOGIES OF REVOLUTION AND LIBERATION:

A CRITIQUE

THE THEOLOGY OF REVOLUTION:
ITS CONTEMPORARY CONTEXT

That which makes the discussion of any concept specifically theological - be it revolution, liberation, politics or development - is the introduction into the discussion of the question of revelation. The reality, availability and intentionality of God in relation to the meaning of the goals of the human family provide the essence of theology. The particular understanding of revelation, as well as the eschatological stance adopted, will determine the principal thrust of any theological undertaking. The place and purpose of the Church within such a system will be determined by the prior understanding of revelation and eschatology.

Because Richard Shaull is commonly regarded as one of the principal initiators of the contemporary theology of revolution, as well as its best representative, I shall center my critique of the theology of revolution on his position. Shaull, however, is a student of Paul Lehmann and writes out of what could be called Lehmann's reformed, ecumenical "contextual/koinonia" ethical and theological perspective. Rubem Alves, one of the liberation theologians we shall examine, is a student of Shaull and also reflects Lehmann's perspective. Indeed Lehmann, who has long been a student of Latin-American affairs, has also had a notable effect on Roman Catholic liberation theologians in Latin America. By giving a brief outline of Lehmann's approach, we shall have a model against which to reflect the similarities and differences in the theology of the authors we are going to critique. Moreover, Lehmann's position, which has been strongly influenced by Karl Barth's biblical christocentric approach, but united with a theology of secularization, will serve as a counterpoint to my own position elaborated in Chapter Six.

1. A BACKGROUND MODEL:
PAUL LEHMANN'S
CONTEXTUAL/KOINONIA METHOD

Lehmann believes that the Christian's policies of action should be determined not just by the immediate situation, as for example, Joseph Fletcher would claim, but by the wider context of what God is doing in the world. The difficulty, of course, is determining what God is doing in the world. It is, in the context of the present thesis, the question of revelation.

Sensitive Christians may be able to agree in a general way about God's action in the world, but when it comes down to particular and complex situations, agreement is not arrived at easily. For Lehmann, the clue for identifying this divine activity is God's political work to "make and keep human life human."[1] True humanity for Lehmann is defined as "mature manhood," which is found in the New Testament and is to be tested by being set against the "measure of fullness of Christ." We find in Lehmann, therefore, this definite christocentric orientation.

This point of departure for ethical reflection on the part of Christians is the existing Christian fellowship, the koinonia. It is within the koinonia that the Christian confesses that God is most fundamentally apprehended, God's will is discerned, and strength and encouragement are given the Christian to carry out God's program. Lehmann

works out the rationale for this position by examining the close affinity between ethics and ethos.
He traces the word "ethos" to the Greek verb
meaning "to be accustomed to." He states, "The
idea is that what one is accustomed to gives stability to the human situation and thus makes conduct possible and meaningful."[2]

In the course of history, according to
Lehmann, a distinction became drawn between "morality" and "ethics." Morality became associated
with behavior according to custom...ethos. Ethics,
on the other hand, implied reason and reflective
analysis. Lehmann is willing to admit that ethics
is, in some sense, a social product, and, therefore, he does not see the need to make the sharp
distinction between ethos and ethics. Christian
ethics is generally reflective, but such reflection must be intimately connected with the ethos
of Christians. But Christian ethos cannot be
found in the individual Christian. Rather, it is
found in the Christian fellowship, the Church, the
koinonia. This leads Lehmann to define Christian
ethics as "the disciplined reflection upon the
question, and its answer: what am I as a believer
in Jesus Christ, and as a member of his Church, to
do?"[3] Because Lehmann has a social understanding
of the human self--that is, there is a necessary
relationship between the internal society of God
and self and the external, embodied society, the
Church, because the community contributes to the
"shaping" of the selfhood of its members--he can
answer his own question on Christian ethics with:
"I am to do what I am."[4]

Lehmann speaks of the community contributing
to the shaping of the selfhood in terms of conscience. He states, "It is the conscience--theo-
nomously understood--which forges the link between
what God is doing in the world and man's free obedience to that authority."[5] This conscience is
shaped by God in the koinonia and becomes sensi-
tized to God's humanizing work to achieve a new
humanity, the maturity of men and women.

Concerning the Christian's specific conduct, Lehmann's standard judgment for a particular action is, does it make human life more human? He stresses, however, that the answer to this question can never be learned as a rational principle, but rather in each case as a content-filled relationship within the koinonia:

Here, in an ongoing experiment in the concrete reality and possibility of man's interrelatedness and openness for man, the human ethos acquires a framework of meaning and a pattern of action which undergird the diversity and complexity of the concrete ethical situation with vitality and purpose.[6]

Lehmann's theological/ethical stance has been succinctly summarized by Carl-Henric Grenholm:[7]

(1) An action is right if, and only if, it concurs with the will of God.
(2) The will of God is known only through knowledge of how God acts in history.
(3) Knowledge of how God acts in history is only given to us as members of the Christian congregation, the koinonia.
(4) Knowledge of how God acts in history is only given to us in the current situation and cannot be generalized in rules for action.

A question which arises immediately upon examination of Lehmann's position is what about those outside the koinonia? Lehmann recognizes the problem; whether or not his solution is satisfactory, is another question. He writes that when Jesus says, "I have other sheep, that are not of this fold...they will heed my voice," this means that the Holy Spirit also acts outside the Church and can guide the actions of non-Christians also.[8] Like Barth, on the basis of the doctrine of the Lordship of Christ, he tries to give an explanation of the fact that certain non-Christians sometimes have the same moral conceptions as those within the <u>koinonia</u>. The difference is that those who are members of the <u>koinonia</u> have acquired knowledge of God's action, while those outside are only unconsciously involved in this. But like Barth, it seems that Lehmann must say non-Christians (those outside the <u>koinonia</u>) are incapable of <u>conscious</u> moral decisions.

Once Lehmann's position has been outlined, the importance of what I have called the three pivotal concepts in theology should be apparent: Revelation for Lehmann has been formulated in the question, "Where is God most active in history?" Lehmann's answer to that question: "Within the <u>koinonia</u>," is the question of ecclesiology. Certainly with the emphasis Lehmann places on the Church, some description of eschatology surfaces in the question of what the Christian and the community are to do to participate in God's work of bringing the human family to maturity.

In the following critique, the way certain representative authors of the theologies of revolution and liberation handle these specific questions will be examined and criticized in light of the definitions of revelation, eschatology and ecclesiology which I have worked out in Chapter Two. What follows is not a comprehensive critique of these theologians, but rather a sustained probe into those fundamental presuppositions underlying their theology, namely, their understanding of revelation, eschatology and ecclesiology. We shall turn now to Richard Shaull and the theology of revolution.

2. THE THEOLOGY OF REVOLUTION: RICHARD SHAULL

On the question of revelation, Shaull appears to accept the theological method of correlation which has been described earlier. He states that an effort must be made "to keep going the difficult but not impossible running conversation between the full biblical and theological tradition and the contemporary human situation."9 Shaull embraces the general outlines of Moltmann's theology of hope, and agrees with Moltmann and Metz that any theology which takes the future seriously must be concerned with the political realm. Christian symbols point to a God who goes ahead of us and who is bringing the new future into being. God's Word is a word of promise which radically calls into question the established social order and frees one to hope for and to serve the things that are to come.

Shaull adds a further dimension to the position of Moltmann and Metz, however, which radically temporalizes his eschatological outlook. Shaull notes that "biblical symbols and images stress discontinuity, judgment, the end of the world and the emergence of the radically new." He is convinced that Christians' own inward experience of death and resurrection equips them to let the old die when its time has come, and frees them to give form to the new possibilities open before them. According to Shaull, the Christian faith can provide the resources necessary for people to become authentic revolutionaries--something, he insists, the world badly needs. He states:

> Our Western world needs cadres of men and women who are as seriously concerned as the Marxists in China or earlier in Eastern Europe, to bury the dead, violate the old and create the new. When such a moment arrives, the distinctiveness of the Christian witness does not lie in its emphasis upon the values to be preserved from the past, but rather in the freedom it offers to bury without remorse, to create the new in response to the future rather than in reaction against the past,

and to preserve an iconoclastic attitude throughout the revolution.[10]

It is not a new theological language that is needed, according to Shaull (and in contrast to Rubem Alves, as we shall see later), but a new involvement "in those places in the world where God is most dynamically at work."[11] This statement has caught the attention of the theological community, but also brought Shaull some severe criticism. How does one determine that God is "dynamically at work" in any particular situation? Shaull relies heavily on biblical parallels which he claims pinpoint God's action in revolutionary situations. The danger in this is that revelation is apt to become nothing but a self-reflection of a group's momentary actions, ramified by select biblical texts. The temptation is to forget the fleeting and illusive nature of God's self-disclosure as discernible by men and women in human actions in the enthusism for a particular revolutionary project.

Actually, as Shaull has developed his thought on this matter, it turns out that "those places in the world where God is most dynamically at work" are very specific. Knowledge of how and where God acts in the world can be known only by those who are in the midst of the revolutionary struggle. Shaull says, "God's action in the world creates an ongoing process of social change, and consequently our faithfulness to him requires that we be involved at the cutting edge of change."[12] The "faithful ones" are those who make up the koinonia, the Church--as Shaull understands it. True theology is the result of a collective enterprise carried on by those within the koinonia.[13] The implication of this is that God is not available to those outside the Christian community. This will become clearer when we examine Shaull's understanding of the Christian community, the koinonia or Church.

Finally, in the underlying argument as to why a Christian must choose a revolutionary strategy for social change rather than a reformist one, Shaull displays his uncritical use of the Bible. Based on the New Testament's "paradigm of death and resurrection," Shaull argues that history develops not in a continuous but, rather, discontinuous manner; therefore, Christians must choose the revolutionary path--a complete break with the old, a turning to the totally new. All of this has prompted Trutz Rendtorff to declare that Shaull's theology is a notably ambivalent union of political radicality and uncritical Bible theology.[14] Because of the latter, Carl-Henric Grenholm places Shaull in the Barthian tradition.[15]

From this point of view of eschatology, the theology of revolution poses the dilemma of attempting to advance the coming kingdom of peace, of shalom, by violent means. Michael Novak has summarized this dilemma well when he writes:

> People who make revolution in the name of humanity come face to face with the major ethical dilemma of all such revolutionaries in our century: Is it right to kill a human being in the name of his own and one's own humanity? If you turn to armed violence, are you any better than those whose policies have outraged your own moral sensitivities?"[16]

Shaull states his own position on the use of violence in this way:

> What is important is not whether violence is outlawed, but whether its use, when absolutely necessary, is geared to a strategy of constant struggle for limited changes in society, or is set in the context, as so often in the past, of total warfare and the total overthrow of the social order.[17]

Gustavo Gutierrez claims that theologies of revolution, including Shaull's, tended to belittle the theological and political questions involved. As noted earlier, Gutierrez says:

> They...ran the risk--notwithstanding the intention of their initiators--of 'baptizing' and in the long run impeding the revolution and counter-violence, because they furnished an ad hoc Christian ideology and ignored the level of political analysis at which these options are in the first instance being exercised.[18]

Significant implications flowing from Shaull's position are reflected in his understanding of the role of the Church in society. His position can be clarified by contrasting it with that of Moltmann and Metz. Both of the latter theologians see the Church as "an institution of freedom that is critical of society." Prophetic denunciation--"this must change!"--rather than any direct program of social and political action, is the proper role for the Church. Only indirectly, by holding to the conviction that building up a more human world is genuinely possible because of the promise made in Jesus' death and resurrection, does the Church involve itself in political matters.

Shaull, on the other hand, is convinced that his "new strategy for revolution" must involve small groups of dedicated Christians who engage in a type of "guerrilla warfare."[19] Christians must rediscover the meaning of sects--small groups of dissenters who are in but not of the established order. In the West, those "who are convinced that they can work for the future of man only if they enter into a total struggle with the system" should enter into solidarity with "those in Asia, Africa and Latin America, who struggle against the same system on the periphery of it." According to Shaull, the vanguard of the revolution are those who, victimized by the present system, reject what exists now and dedicate themselves to a changed future.[20]

Shaull expects little from the institutional Church in the revolutionary struggle. He does not think the Church should expect to be a power structure working for a radical change, nor even a creator of revolutionary movements.[21] But the mission he envisions for the revolutionary sects is broad and ambitious, if not indeed unrealistic. He admits that Christian communities have no special insights into this revolutionary action and, therefore, he suggests that they cooperate with others in study and experimentation along the lines of what could be called resistance and subversion. The revolutionary groups resist by developing new bases for power, by forming pressure groups and organizing various movements "of eventual political significance." They subvert by discovering how to use established institutions for their own transformation in spite of themselves. Shaull says:

> if modern bureaucracy tends to solve all minor problems but to overlook more basic ones, and to stifle initiative and creativity, it is essential now to develop, within institutions, small groups of people committed to constantly upsetting their stability, taking new initiatives and launching new experiments--and willing to pay the price of such subversive acts..."[22]

The specifically Christian justification for this resistance and subversion seems to be Shaull's assurance that Christ himself was so subversive that the political and religious leaders of his time put him to death. We have here another example of Shaull's dependence on superficial biblical parallels.

When Shaull's description of the mission of the Church--Church here meaning small revolutionary sects--is coupled with his view that "there may be some situations in which only the threat or use of violence can set the process of change in motion," it is easy to imagine that others, less astute and less willing to make the qualifications and distinctions that Shaull does, would be apt to adopt this theological endeavor as their revolutionary ideology.[23] They would be tempted to declare that the place that God is most dynamically at work in the world is in their own revolutionary movement; their revolution is God's revolution.

Latin-American liberation theologians are anxious to disassociate themselves from such a theology of revolution. Even one of their more radical proponents, Hugo Assmann, who admits that in their writings talk of God and Christ does appear in the context of strategy and tactics, denies liberation theologians are trying to find theological justifications for particular actions before they are undertaken. He says, "Mentioning God in the context of particular levels of action is a proper feature of the process language of practice...."[24] But, unlike the theologians of revolution, liberation theologians insist they do not attempt to elaborate a theory of revolution on the basis of theology apart from a social analysis of a particular revolutionary situation. Instead they confine themselves to critical reflection on revolutionary action. Assmann summarizes his criticism of the theology of revolution in this way.

If one takes an explicit theology of revolution as an attempt to:

(a) define the revolution to come, what it will be and should be, on the basis of theological categories;
(b) seek theoretical permission, a divine license, a legitimating and sacralizing cloak for revolutionaries;

(c) use the theoretical instrument of theology to provide the concrete constituent elements of a revolutionary ideology;

(d) further use the theology to provide the basis for a revolutionary strategy and the tactical steps composing it; then I think it necessary to approach such a theology in an extremely critical spirit.[25]

Whether or not all of these elements are evident in Shaull's theology of revolution is debatable. Luis Segundo, for example has accused Shaull of speaking "two different languages"--one which is intensely committed and revolutionary when he is talking about the historical realm, but another much more reserved and inhibited when he tries to translate all that into theological terms. He quotes Shaull to illustrate the latter point.

> The Kingdom of God always stands over against every social and political order, thus exposing its dehumanizing elements and judging it. At the same time the Kingdom is a dynamic reality; it is "coming" through the work of him who is restoring the nations....[26]

In the first phrase of the quote, according to Segundo, Shaull relativizes all historical realities with the result that "far from being dynamic, they become the mere object of static contemplation." In an attempt to correct this, Shaull introduces the word "dynamic" into the next sentence and then adds that the Kingdom is coming. But, Segundo asks, "Through whom or what?" "Alas," Segundo continues, "the turn of Shaull's remarks can only produce despair in Latin America. No human being, no human group, no human ideology, no human process of change is responsible--only God alone."[27] This refusal on the part of Shaull to opt for anyone or anything in concrete history stems, Segundo argues, from the influence of the

Reformation teaching of justification by faith alone. This preoccupation on the part of Segundo with the justification by faith theme will be examined more closely in our discussion of his theology, but his comments here do indicate that at least for one of the liberation theologians Shaull's theology is not revolutionary enough.

Let us return briefly to Assmann to see if his criticism of the theology of revolution is applicable to Richard Shaull. He states in point (a) that he is critical of any theology of revolution that attempts to define the revolution to come--what it will be and should be--on the basis of theological categories. Shaull, indeed, seems to do this when he bases his perspective on history--its discontinuity--on the Christian's inward experience of death and resurrection. The old must be completely destroyed, for the new to be formed.

Concerning Assmann's point (b), that a theoretical permission, a divine license, a legitimating and sacralizing cloak is sought in theology for being a revolutionary, Shaull does say that the Christian faith can provide the resources necessary for people to become revolutionaries. The specifically Christian justification for revolutionary resistance and subversion is, according to Shaull, the biblical testimony of Christ as a subversive revolutionary. Criticism (c), according to Assmann, is that the theoretical instrument of theology is used to provide the concrete constituent elements of a revolutionary ideology. In this case, Shaull's advocation of a resurrection of the theology of the sectarian movement as a basis for his "new strategy for revolution" could be interpreted as a concrete constituent element of a revolutionary ideology. Following from this, and concerning Assmann's point (d) that theology is used to provide the basis for revolutionary strategy and the tactical steps composing it, Shaull argues that from within these small Christian groups a godly type of guerrilla warfare can be staged against the "system."

In summary, if we take Shaull's language at face value, Assmann's criticisms seem to apply; Shaull's theology could easily be construed as an ideological justification of violent revolution.

From the point of view of revelation, it can be said that Shaull's theology of revolution, while outwardly adopting the method of correlation, has a dangerous tendency of localizing too readily God's revelation in some revolutionary project. Although neither revolution nor violence can be ruled out absolutely by theology, any more than absolute pacificism can be insisted upon, still the illusiveness of God's presence in human actions, especially violent ones, can never be overlooked. The risk of faith, which is there because of the prior risk involved in identifying God's revelation, carries over as the risk of every theological enterprise. Shaull and those formulating a theology of revolution seem to have forgotten this. They appear too sure of themselves in pinpointing just where God is most dynamically at work in the world. They seem too ready to admit that violence will bring about God's Kingdom.

Concerning the Church, the theology of revolution, by its very nature, brackets that aspect of the Church's mission which insists on dialogue and reconciliation. Guillermo Blanco, in a book entitled THE GOSPEL ACCORDING TO JUDAS, ridicules the revolutionary position with scathing irony:

Forward!
Go and teach to use the machine gun;
Resist evil, smite the foolish one on both
    cheeks;
If you forgive men their faults, you will
    slow down the historical process;
Pray for your enemies only once you have
    efficiently killed them off;
Take your gun and follow me....[28]

Defining the Church as small revolutionary sects dedicated to resistance and subversion fails to do justice to that aspect of its mission which calls it to demonstrate to those outside what the coming Kingdom may be like--an open, hopeful, and therefore joyfully celebrating community. In the theology of revolution even the Church's service to the rest of the world, its dedication to development, is narrowed to the revolutionary transformation of the institutions of society through resistance and subversion.

THE THEOLOGY OF LIBERATION: FOUR AUTHORS AND THEIR WORK

1. RENE LAURENTIN: LIBERATION, DEVELOPMENT AND SALVATION[29]

Laurentin's work offers a good starting place for this critique of liberation theology. Although we are examining it under the theology of liberation, it could be discussed, and perhaps more properly so, as a theology of development. In fact, when the book was first published in French in 1969, it was entitled DEVELOPPEMENT ET SALUT. Three years later when it was translated into English, Laurentin added the word liberation to the title. Laurentin did not make this change just to be relevant, although that motive cannot be ruled out altogether. I suggest that the fundamental reason why Laurentin made the addition was because his theological method called for it. As we shall see in our examination of Laurentin's position, his theological method is extremely positivistic. Theology for him is a reflection upon official sources. Once the term liberation appeared in official Church documents--in this case, in the documents of the Conference of the Latin-American Bishops in Medellin--it became the proper, and necessary, object for theological elaboration.

In the preface to the English edition, Laurentin gives two reasons why the word development is being replaced more and more by the term liberation: First, it is becoming apparent that there can be no development until there is liberation from a system that maintains underdevelopment; and secondly, liberation reflects an extremely rich biblical notion.[30] Both of these arguments have been discussed in the preceding chapter.

Concerning the question of revelation, Laurentin maintains a position that might be called magisterial-biblical. Revelation, for Laurentin, is a thing of the past. Although the origin or impulse for world development can be identified with the Holy Spirit whose action is within the body of Christ, still this action never should be conceived as new revelation, "for revelation was completed at the end of the apostolic times."[31] In their search for liberation, however, men and women cannot rid themselves of their past. They cannot, as Laurentin puts it, "forget revelation" as they seek to construct a world of justice and human fellowship.[32]

Laurentin proposes the question, "Can there be a theology of development?" For him it is clear that there is a theology of God and a theology of the person in his or her inseparable relationship with God the creator and redeemer. It is clear that people are divinized through grace.[33] Such "clarity" is possible because of Laurentin's understanding of the "data" or the "facts" of revelation. For him, they are readily available for our examination in the "sources of revelation." In other words, there is no "question" about the reality and availability of God, about the meaning of redemption, salvation, sanctification or eternal life. We have been given the "facts" about these. As far as a theology of development or liberation is concerned, we must search the "sources" to see if there is a legitimate basis for such a theology. These sources are the Scriptures and the magisterial pronouncements of the Church.

Laurentin examines these sources in great detail and concludes that the modern notion of development is alien to Scripture; it is not the "object of revelation from on high." He does, however, detect in the precept of love, especially as formulated in the judgment scene of Matthew 25, a basic theme relevant to development. He then ties in this precept of love with the law of nature--"that profound law written on the hearts of men" (Romans 2:14-16). These relevant themes are fortified by the traditions of the Church Fathers and reach their culmination in Vatican II's document THE CHURCH IN THE MODERN WORLD. In the latter, the Church teaches that the Gospel message is in harmony with the loftier strivings of the human race.[34] So it is in Scripture interpreted by the Church that the meaning of the person and the meaning of charity are revealed as a divine and human exigency. It is by this process that we find the basis for a theology of development and liberation.

Laurentin admits that cultural change calls theology to new research in twofold fidelity to the revelation of God and the problems of the human family. Still it is clear from Laurentin's viewpoint that God will not be revealed within the daily experiences and problems of humankind. God's revelation has been completed. Laurentin carefully employs the past tense when speaking about revelation: "God himself encountered men in history, in that very specialized human condition in which he gave to men the universal message of the Gospel." Laurentin's view of revelation--and we may presume that means, for him, Scripture authoritatively interpreted by the Church--is summed up in his statement: "May revelation once again inspire a great plan encompassing the whole of mankind!"[35]

With such a positivistic understanding of revelation, a theology of development or liberation based on it can apply to the present in only an extrinsic way. What took place in the past and cannot be forgotten must be brought up to date and applied to the contemporary problems of development or liberation.

Concerning the question of eschatology, which here is basically the question of the meaning of history, Laurentin discusses two options: an eschatology of continuity and an eschatology of discontinuity.[36] The choice between one or the other intimately affects a theology of development. The former, Laurentin identifies as the Teilhardian option. It stresses theological involvement in the world. Salvation is achieved in the very fabric of the world. In this view, eschatology means the fulfillment of the plan of progress which of itself tends toward the omega point, Jesus Christ. As Laurentin expresses it:

> Pushed to its limits this view enables us to have a theology of development, for man's fulfillment comes through total human development, rooted in the material and temporal, both economic and cultural. Man fulfills himself through structures which intrinsically affect his relationship with God and his salvation in the full sense of the word.[37]

The eschatology of discontinuity, Laurentin labels the Pascalian view. In this option human history is conceived as unfolding horizontally. Salvation is the vertical dimension in this scheme. It is of a completely different order than that affected by technical, scientific or cultural progress. Development from this eschatological stance "appears as a more or less commendable human option, with merely an extrinsic relationship to salvation."[38]

To close the gap between the two eschatological options, Laurentin says we must turn to a study of the data of revelation [emphasis mine]. He combs Scripture, examines biblical and traditional doctrines on the rights of the poor, the ownership and use of property, and the relationship between material prosperity and men's and women's supernatural destiny. He concludes that the earth is the place where men and women learn to possess together a heritage which is already a sign of the reality of our everlasting heritage.[39] His final answer he finds in Article 39 of THE CHURCH IN THE MODERN WORLD: "Earthly progress must be carefully distinguished from the growth of Christ's Kingdom. Nevertheless, to the extent that the former can contribute to the better ordering of human society, it is of vital concern to the Kingdom of God."

Laurentin says that neither of the eschatological options can be reached authentically except in correlation with the other. This duality stems from a structural condition of the human intellect, from its limitations when faced with the complexity of the world. The human being grasps reality through complementary sides of the same thing. He gives examples of nature and grace, the mercy and the justice of God, service of the world and missionary activity, corporal and spiritual, temporal and eternal. Evident in Laurentin's position is the very dualism that I am attempting to avoid in this thesis by my elaboration of the "theological shift" reflected, for example, in Maurice Blondel's "method of immanence." Further, contrary to my position, Laurentin sees commitment to development, not of the essence of Christian mission, but rather a valid theological option. He seems to waver, however, between development as necessary or optional. He sees the option for development as a particularly favorable way for realizing divine love, agape, in today's world, but in much stronger terms he adds, "...there is no salvation without the upbuilding of the world, and still less so if we scorn the task."[40]

I agree wholeheartedly with Laurentin's final
statement concerning a commitment to development,
but I cannot agree with the theological rationale
or method behind it. Turning to the question of
ecclesiology, we find Laurentin stating in a very
straightforward way that the Church's "prime responsibility is to face up to a salvation that is
to be realized on earth."[41] But when we look deeper, we find that for Laurentin development has no
place in the Church's essential mission. He admits
that evangelizing and civilizing--which he inter-
changes with mission and development--are not conflicting tasks; still evangelization is "primordial." Evangelization explains the meaning of salvation; it "directs man to the objective means of
the same salvation to which he is called."[42]

Civilization, which Laurentin calls "the fruit
of development," is the "organic state in which
salvation is accomplished." Authentic Christians
foster civilization or the flowering of the "human
values" which have the nature of an evangelical
preparation or evangelical virtualities [emphasis
mine]. It is in the individual Christian, therefore, that evangelizing and civilizing or·mission
and development coincide. The Church as Church
has no real part in it. Furthermore, when all is
said and done, development for Laurentin amounts
to pre-evangelization.

Laurentin sees revelation as a thing of the
past rather than as the continuous self-disclosure
of God in the midst of human experience; he maintains the polarities of the continuous and discontinuous views of eschatology. He likewise maintains the division between the Church's "essential
task" of evangelization and the Christian's obligation to participate in development. Although he
speaks of convergences and reconciliations between
the "data of revelation" and contemporary problems, between building the world and awaiting salvation, between preaching to pagans and overall
human development, a basic dichotomy remains.

Laurentin calls for a reconversion of ecclesiology so the Church can become once again a sign for mankind of the possible future of God. This means the Church must move from a closed to an open society, from a static to a dynamic, from the juridical to the vital, from the ecclesiastical to the cosmic. Yet despite this, development has no essential part in the Church's mission. The essential mission of the Church is to evangelize and, according to Laurentin, "The essential object of evangelization is to save by releasing the yearning for love which God has placed in the heart of man who is created in his image."[43]

2. RUBEM ALVES: A THEOLOGY OF HUMAN HOPE AND TOMORROW'S CHILD[44]

Rubem Alves is a Latin-American theologian, a Protestant, whose THEOLOGY OF HUMAN HOPE was hailed as a milestone a few years ago. Prepared first as a doctrinal dissertation under the direction of Richard Shaull, it reveals obvious traces of Shaull's influence. This is evident in its acceptance of violent revolution, its frequent appeal to biblical parallels, and in the minimal role that the institutional Church is depicted as playing in the liberation struggle. What is significant, from the point of view of the present critique, is that Alves has done an about-face in his eschatological stance from the time of this first work in 1969 to the time of his later book, TOMORROW'S CHILD, written in 1972. He supports both his original and revised eschatological positions unhesitantly with biblical parallels. Before examining this eschatological switch, we will look at Alves' understanding of revelation.

Alves states at the outset of A THEOLOGY OF HUMAN HOPE that his theological explorations are intended to be "nothing more than an expression of participation in a community of Christians who are struggling to discover how to speak faithfully the language of faith in the context of their commitment to the historical liberation of man."[45] Because words carry intelligibility and therefore power, the Christian community must look for a new language which can enable "messianic humanism" (what Alves is attempting to promote) to answer the challenge of "humanistic messianism" (Marxism) or political humanism. In his project, Alves tries hard to define revelation as history, but as will be shown in this analysis, he is basically tied to a biblical understanding of revelation.

In light of the claims of political humanism, which Alves says must be taken seriously, he makes a critique of the language of major theological schools of thought and finds them all wanting. Existentialism, whether of Kierkegaard or of Bultmann, will not take the world seriously enough for a new tomorrow; language becomes a category for the purely subjective.[46] Barth, according to Alves' critique, takes election very seriously, but not history. When pushed to the wall, Barth must affirm in fact that history is over. [I made a similar criticism of Barth's eschatological view in Chapter Three.] Humanization becomes a function of the right hearing of the Word, and not the critical transformation of history. And yet, without a seriousness about history, one can never understand the aspirations of political humanism.[47]

Moltmann's analysis of the biblical community of faith, while closely related to the ideas of political humanism on some points, still, according to Alves, ends up close to Bultmann and Barth. What makes life human in the world--namely, transcendence--is mediated in Moltmann's theology by an act of consciousness as it looks back to a certain event of the past. The only mode of God's presence in the world would be the word of promise, the word that points to the elusiveness of God, to God's future. If this is true, then action which genuinely relates people to transcendence is, according to Alves, once again the preaching and the hearing of the Word. In this understanding, men and women are not the creators of this new future, but rather, they act "in light of the promised future that is to come." Action becomes imitation. Somehow our present is supposed to "correspond" to the future which revelation brings to us. But according to Alves, the only present political attitude which could "correspond" to that future would be pacifism. Conflict and struggle could not "correspond" to the future. Alves concluded that Moltmann's _primum movens_, which pulls history into the future, has in fact no dimension in the present.[48]

The basic conflict between the language of political humanism (a new consciousness which Alves believes is emerging in the Third World) and the language of hope suggested by Moltmann is this: Political humanism understands that the negation of the inhuman in "what is," plus the hope which grows outs of transcendence informed by suffering, and the creation of the new future, all begin from the present condition of men and women and their insertion into history. The language of hope, on the other hand, sees the present situation without possibilities unless people are confronted with a nonhistorical and transcendent reality that does not have any dimension in the present, being only mediated by the Word. This, for Alves, is not enough. It does not meet the challenge of political humanism which places its hopes for the creation of the new future within the present condition of the human family.

The task of theology, therefore, according to Alves, is to create a new language that will take seriously in its own formulation the critique of political humanism and add something real to its aspirations and program. This "something real" which is added means that the achievement of humanization comes about by the reality and power of a deliverance which occurs in history and yet from beyond history. Insisting that revelation is history, Alves goes back to the experience of the biblical communities and points out that what brought them to liberation was neither their determination to be free nor the particular historical circumstances in which they found themselves. Rather, they were "forced" to be free.[49] On what basis Alves makes this judgment he does not say, but it would seem that he merely accepts it on the apparent word of the Bible.

Biblical language, according to Alves, arose out of the experience of this historical efficacy, not as a result of the power of humans, but as given to them—efficacy as grace; efficacy "in spite of." The people came to understand this as an act of power from beyond history, as an act of God. [I would suggest, rather, that the people came to <u>presume</u> this as an act of power from beyond history, as the act of God.] Alves insists that this language about God, because it told of events of liberating power in the past, offers a ground of hope in the present. The past, in Alves' view, becomes the clue for understanding the possibilities of liberation in the context of the present.

Contemporary biblical communities, Alves argues, because of their unique understanding of history, extrapolate the past experience of human liberation into the present and future and find in this historical context the answer to the question which Lehmann has posed, "What is necessary to make and to keep human life human in the world?" To remember the past, however, is not an attempt to become "contemporaneous with the fulfilled time of past revelation." According to Alves, this attempt at "transtemporalization," which has been so central for Protestant theology, is no longer relevant for a language that speaks about God as the presence of the future.[50]

In spite of his claim that revelation is history, it still seems that Alves does not speak about God's availability in contemporary human experience. If God is revealed in the present, then this revelation can be recognized only through the clue of the biblical experience. This becomes evident when Alves states that it is obvious that others beside those in the community of faith have the ability to hope for the future. The power to project is intrinsic to the will, part of the very spirit of man. And yet, "this power of transcendence over the hypnotizing grasp of the given facts of the present" can be nothing more than wish fulfillment if it is not controlled by the language of faith. With the language of faith, on the other hand, the power to project is controlled by the memory of the historical dialectics of liberation--that is, revelation. Alves criticizes Moltmann for building this theology on the elusive word of promise which looks back on a certain event of the past. But Alves himself depends on the memory of what he calls the historical dialectics of liberation. Moreover, to be able to perceive in this "history" the acts of God demands no less an elusive act of faith!

For Alves, then, revelation is history, but history that can be read correctly only through biblical eyes. Messianic humanism believes in the humanizing determination of the transcendent, but that belief is based not on the present, but rather, past experience. When Alves says the new language he is searching for does not mediate a transcendent reality to men and women, but rather, provides them a critical reading of the newspapers [echoes of Barth!], he still does not say that in reading the newspaper one might encounter signs of the transcendent. An understanding of revelation, mediated through history but interpreted only through the Bible, is still positivistic. The "source" of revelation as history is still the Bible, and with this source the risk is taken out of theology. The consequences of this method will be seen as we turn to examine the stance that Alves takes on the question of eschatology.

In his THEOLOGY OF HUMAN HOPE, Alves radically historicizes eschatology. The new language of faith which he is seeking to develop is to be totally historical. Everything that does not refer to the world of men and women and their hope for liberation, is rejected. The language of the community of faith "floats on the everchanging flux of history." There is no glimpse of eternity, stability, the "wholly other" or the "eternal now." These things, according to Alves, destroy the spirit of men and women. Rather, transcendence is in the midst of life and takes shape in the permanent relativizing of the present. This continually opens the present for new possibilities; it makes possible the dialectics of freedom.

For Alves, even the language of the community of faith is secondary to the ongoing dialectics of freedom or politics of liberation. Alves elaborates his dialectics of freedom by using the biblical model of God as the "suffering slave." The slave is a man without a future, without a right to hope. But the condition of the slave contains the secret of freedom. That secret, in the scheme worked out by Alves, consists of this: The "what is" must be negated for the sake of liberation. Now the slave does not always have the will and the power to freedom. When the community of faith identified its God with the slave, it was thereby indicating that the secret of freedom, which the condition of the slave contains, is united in God with the will and power of liberation. God, the suffering slave, therefore, is the one on whom liberation depends. But to liberate the oppressed, the slave must become a warrior. God's presence in the world is like a bomb, Alves claims, to be set exactly under the powers of old. The use of violence in the politics of the Messiah is an instrument to liberate not only the slave but also the master against whom it is used.[51] Love, according to Alves, takes shape as an activity that aims at the destruction of the objective and subjective conditions of slavery here and now.

At this point, Alves is advocating violent revolution in the name of the "warrior slave" who is present in the world "like a bomb." Later we shall see how Alves tempers this position considerably.

In another context and in less biblical language, Alves describes his eschatological stance as radical utopianism.[52] By this term, Alves seems to mean that he maintains a radical conception of men and women and their world. The radical view of the world rejects what he calls "technologism." This term is similar to what other liberation theologians have called developmentalism. Both presuppose that underdevelopment is essentially an economic and scientific problem that has little relationship to qualitative and value questions. Technologism implies that a highly technical elite can solve the world's problems without, as Alves puts it, the "dysfunctional emotional element" of the majority of people. The utopia to which this technologism supposedly leads is one that is entirely functional, but also one from which has been eliminated the elements of imagination, creativity and freedom. Any system which destroys these elements is enslaving. Imagination entails being able to name things that are absent. This, in turn, breaks the spell of the things present and opens the way to a creative future. Alves rejects technologism and insists that human beings, rather than being mere consumers in the development system, are creators of development practice. "It is not enough that man eats bread," Alves states. "Bread must be eaten as 'sacrament,' symbol of a meaningful world."

Alves' conception of the human person is also radical, not only because the person is the end and purpose of development, but also because people themselves are "in process." This means that they find their destiny not in a utopian end point, but in the process of creating a new world. "Man is human when he creates," Alves says. "Therefore it is amidst the process that man finds his true humanity." The radical utopia that Alves envisions, therefore, "aims at no utopia but at a society which remains permanently open and unfinished." As a radical utopia its future is not a day or a place but a permanent horizon, a point of reference which both invites and informs that the task is permanently unfinished.

Alves, in placing the human family's ultimate concern completely in the "process" of liberation, ends up with a type of Sisyphean understanding of the Kingdom of God. Our struggle for it is never-ending because the Kingdom is located in the struggle itself. How enthusiasm for the struggle is to be maintained is not clear; it would seem that a certain passivity could creep in when fervor wanes. Indeed, this can be detected in what we have described as Alves' about-face in eschatological stance.

In his work, TOMORROW'S CHILD, Alves admits that for now the dominant powers are so organized and, thanks to science, so invulnerable, that one can no longer maintain any hope of overthrowing them.[53] Neither can captivity be abolished by wishing it away. That is the way of the magician, the child, the prophet, the visionary, the artist. They live by the revolution which has already taken place in their consciousness. The danger in this, which Alves calls the "politics of consciousness," is that it proclaims that one can enjoy now, in all its fullness, something that does not yet exist. "It announces redemption of an unredeemed world, celebration when life is still groaning in travail, play in a world built on war."[54]

The solution to this dark dilemma Alves once again finds in the Bible--this time in the character of Jeremiah. We must learn from Jeremiah, who was neither a prophet of revolution nor a priest of the status quo, how to "sing a song in exile." We must plant a fig tree which we know will not bear fruit until the time of our grandchildren. [One is tempted to say, using Alves' earlier imagery, that God, present in the world as a bomb, has been equipped with a long and slow burning fuse!] Like Jeremiah, we must reject both the revolutionaries' illusions of quick delivery and the despair of those who no longer see any future. We must keep hope alive--"the <u>presentiment</u> that <u>imagination is more real</u> and <u>reality less real</u> than it looks."[55] For Alves, the Bible does not tell <u>how</u> delivery will come, but <u>that</u> it will come:

> It [the Bible] acknowledges that the creative event erupts in history and assumes a social form, but it does not have any formula for duplicating it....
> Our task is thus simply to be able to recognize the social mark of the creative event.[56]

Alves calls for a disciplined love like that which has given prophets, revolutionaries, and saints the courage to die for the future they envisaged. For, he states:

> This is not the moment of birth. It is not the moment of political confrontation. But if we are sowing something really new, it is inevitable that the community of faith and the existing order are on collison course. Persecution will come....
> If our child was aborted, let us lay eggs which will be hatched long after we are dead.[57]

Alves has thus arrived at an eschatological posture that is reminiscent of the "patient expectation" evident in Luther's Two Kingdoms theory: "Our task is thus simply to be able to recognize the social marks of the creative event." He states further, "We are not saved by works: we cannot produce the creative event. We are saved by grace. The creative event simply takes place and offers itself to us.... The only thing that we can do is to join it."[58] This seems to be a long way from becoming "warrior slaves" with the "God bomb" in our hands! Indeed, his fellow liberationist, Segundo, accuses Alves of a basic Lutheran posture in this regard.[59] Alves' position probably can be explained more accurately in light of the contextual/koinonia theology of Lehmann and Shaull: Men and women are called upon to "join in" the transforming work of God in history. The initiative is always God's; our participation in the work does not guarantee there will be no suffering and setbacks, but the final victory, because of God's action in Christ, is assured.

It cannot be denied, however, that Alves' revolutionary enthusiasm has been dampened and that in his language there are shades of passivity and patient expectation. But whatever position Alves assumes, he assures us that it is the one that most fits the biblical model; it is the biblical answer.

Alves gives very little attention to the institutional Church as such. He speaks, rather, about the biblical community or the community of faith. The Church, for Alves, is where the Spirit of God is groaning in the human community. His ecclesiological position is similar to that of Baum and Stackhouse, as discussed earlier.[60] He argues that the institutional Church has not been the midwife of the future, and he is especially critical of Moltmann's position that where the Church has not preached the Word there is no history and no hope. On the contrary, Alves asserts, many of

the movements that today display the deepest concern for the creation of a new tomorrow for the
human family operate within the limits of a purely
secular and humanist assessment of the situation.[61]

Although Alves may be correct in his assertion
that the institutional Church has not been the
"midwife of the future," and that purely secular
and humanist movements are more deeply concerned
about the "creation of a tomorrow" than the
Church, still the solution hardly comes from
broadening the understanding of Church by mere
definition to "where the Spirit of God is groaning
in the human community." Moreover, this seems to
contradict Alves' concept of communities of faith
as biblical communities. One cannot have it both
ways.

The biblical understanding of revelation which
Alves holds enables him to switch positions on key
theological concepts, i.e., eschatology, and support each position with ample biblical references.
The weakness in this method should be apparent.

3. JUAN LUIS SEGUNDO:
A THEOLOGY FOR ARTISANS OF A NEW HUMANITY[62]

Juan Luis Segundo is one of the best-known
liberation theologians. His five-volume work, A
THEOLOGY FOR ARTISANS OF A NEW HUMANITY, has been
widely publicized and generally well received in
this country. Some of the volumes are even being
used as texts in seminary classrooms. But as we
shall see in the following critique, Segundo
builds his theology on some very questionable
theological presuppositions. Again, we will in-
vestigate his understanding of those critical issues, revelation, eschatology, and ecclesiology.

For Segundo, revelation is knowledge--knowledge of the "mystery," knowledge of the divine plan. All humankind is called to participate in God's redemption through his Son, but only certain ones are chosen to know the "game plan:"

> We not only know in some vague way that God has a salvation plan. We also know how this plan works itself out. This in summary form, is the faith of the Church, which is the mystery of Christ.... It is in summary form the 'whole' mystery--not just part of it.... The Church is the consciousness of humanity, as it were.[63]

How are we to be so confident, so sure of all this? Segundo maintains that we not only have knowledge about God through the Old Testament and rational understanding--knowledge from outside, he calls it--but we have knowledge of God from within. Does it come, perhaps, through present experience? No, indeed, it is knowledge of God which only the incarnate God himself can communicate to us. How do we become aware of this knowledge? By reading the Gospel. John's First Epistle tells us that the revelation of the Word can be summed up in the clear expression, God is Love.

If, indeed, all this knowledge comes to us in packaged form, what about those who have not been given this revelatory knowledge? Within non-Christian religions is God being revealed in some way? According to Segundo, in light of full revelation in Christ, all other religions, including the religion of Israel, involve idolatry. This does not mean that every attempt to enter into a relationship with God outside "positive revelation" [the phrase is Segundo's] is condemned to failure. But it does mean that the possibility of such a relationship is not realized precisely through the religions themselves, but through other pathways. These other pathways are traced in the Bible. One of these is love which prepares the way for faith. Once again, this love is not fostered through the religious element in non-Christian religions as such, but rather it must come through something that transcends the religious aspect and passes judgment on it.[64]

The second pathway which leads to a relationship with God is human experience. According to Segundo, any pathway toward authenticity in our being and life is a preparation for the gospel; every profound experience is an opportunity for "precatechesis," for "pre-evangelization."[65] This means that a "human happening" is not just an "occasion" for the believer to exercise his or her "charity" or to interject his or her "doctrine;" such happenings or experiences possess an interior act of grace and therefore own proper summons to the Gospel.[66] This summons is not, however, revelation. For, although people will not encounter God "in the skies or in the beyond," but only "in man, in his history," still God "does not surface from history." Rather, "revelation is a light shed on history, a word spoken somewhere about history." Clearly indicating that, for him, revelation is a phenomenon that took place only in the past, Segundo states:

> Now this light and this word are not intemporal or of the present day. They come to us from a past.
> The Church...should unceasingly be about the work of creatively translating this message...in terms of the problems that are posed today by human beings who are subjects of history.[67]

Segundo cautions that, although Christianity is a "revealed message" [the terminology is Segundo's] and because of this there is something unalterable and untouchable in Christian doctrine, still this should not be a hindrance to dialogue.

The reason for this is twofold: "What has been revealed is not something capable of modifying real-
life experience" [in other words, it is just
information], and this revealed message is not "a
recipe book of solutions for concrete problems."
That is to say, a Christian can never be sure that
"a given solution is 'the' Christian solution."
Therefore, a Christian can enter dialogue with an
attitude of sincere searching for "the world has
much to teach him about God."[68]

Certainly, revelation is not "a recipe book of
solutions for concrete problems." But neither is
it a "revealed message," that is, some type of
privileged information. Rather, it is our presumed
perception of God's presence in everyday experience and, in an ultimate way, in Jesus of Nazareth
--in his very person, his life, death and resurrection, in addition to his teaching. Even then,
his teaching added no "new information" from some
extrinsic source. Indeed, Christians can never be
sure that a "given solution is 'the' Christian solution" because Jesus Christ did not come as some
information-bearing problem-solver, but as one who
demonstrated by his life--or so we claim--that
there is something more than meets the eye, in him
and in life itself. If we risk opening ourselves
to the invitation of this "something more," fullness of human life is possible. We enter into
dialogue, not with some revealed information that
others do not possess, but with the faith conviction that Jesus clarified and personifies in an
ultimate way that which is available to everyone.
One wonders when Segundo says that "the world has
much to teach him [the Christian] about God," if
he believes the Christian has some other or additional "revealed message," and if so, how he or
she acquired it.

From this outline of Segundo's understanding
of revelation and the corner into which he draws
himself because of his extreme intellectualistic
and positivisitic approach--revelation is infor-

mation available in sources from the past—one might ask just how liberating his theology actually is. As we shall see presently, Segundo, in working out his eschatological position, seems to forget his own qualification that a Christian can never be sure that "a given solution is 'the' Christian solution" to a concrete problem. He insists upon a single option for the Christian in order to establish the Kingdom of God.

Segundo's views on eschatology are presented in scattered bits throughout his five-volume work, but the essence of his position comes to the fore clearly and, in a sense, startlingly, in an article in CONCILIUM entitled "Capitalism—Socialism: A Theological Crux."[69] We shall deal extensively with Segundo's eschatological outlook both in this article and in his five-volume work, because, as he admits, it represents the general view of many of the liberation theologians. I am convinced that an analysis of Segundo's position will expose some serious weaknesses.

In GRACE AND THE HUMAN CONDITION, volume 2 of his larger work, Segundo draws upon the thought of St. Paul in developing his eschatological posture. He admits that in the part of the New Testament which most faithfully reflects the environment in which Christianity was born, Christ's message—with the exception of a few shadings—is translated into a salvation context which accords with the last stage of Old Testament thought. There, salvation is conceived of as being extraterrestrial and as depending fundamentally on the free performance of religious and moral duties during this life. But Segundo turns to St. Paul who, he claims, picks up on the "few shadings" of an earlier Old Testament position and elaborates an original idiom that is more appropriate for expressing the Christian conception of salvation. Although Segundo admits that Paul still maintains some tension between that which is "already received in part" and that which is "still to come

in part," basically salvation has to do with liberty now. Segundo contends: "The eschatological
element is radically temporal; for Christian
eschatology, far from threatening liberty as it
might seem to do on the surface, is actually the
eschatology of liberty." He sees this position,
which he identifies with that of St. Paul, summed
up in the words of Paul Lehmann: "In short, maturity is salvation."[70]

From the thought of Teilhard de Chardin,
Segundo develops his argument on the value and
meaning of human activity.[71] The Second Vatican
Council, in its document THE CHURCH IN THE MODERN
WORLD, reflects this same train of thought, but
Segundo claims its teaching on the establishment
of the Kingdom contains seeming contradictions. He
argues in this way: If, as the Council states,
the Kingdom is already present in mystery and will
be brought into full flower when the Lord returns,
then it follows logically that "the expectation of
a new earth must not weaken but rather stimulate
our concern for cultivating this one. For here
grows the body of a new human family...." Segundo,
quoting from the Council document, makes an eli-
sion at this point and thereby deletes an important qualifying phrase: "...a body which even now
is able to give some kind of foreshadowing of the
new age to come." [Emphasis mine.] Segundo continues his argument: "But this statement makes it
difficult to explain the one which follows almost
immediately: 'Earthly progress must be carefully
distinguished from the growth of Christ's
Kingdom.'"[72]

It seems clear that Segundo is determined
here, as he did in his treatment of St. Paul, to
eliminate the tension between human endeavor and
the coming Kingdom of God. According to him, we
establish, build, create the Kingdom here and now.
In another context in discussing various theologies of liberation, he states: "There is something
common and basic for all of them--the view that

men, on a political as well as individual basis, <u>construct the Kingdom of God</u> from within history now." [Emphasis mine.] He then gives reference to Gustavo Gutierrez and Hugo Assmann among others.[73]

The manner is which Segundo overcomes what he calls a seeming contradiction in the conciliar text is questionable, from my point of view, although consistent with his theological method in general. Instead of examining the obvious tensions arising from divergent theological viewpoints of those who drafted and approved the document, instead of looking into what might be called the "politics" of the document, Segundo appeals to a traditional principle of exegesis--<u>lectio diffi-cilior</u>. Basically, the principle operates in this manner: If two texts of a given work do not agree, all other things being equal, one should prefer the more difficult reading, the <u>lectio diffi-cilior</u>. It should be kept in mind that for Segundo the task of theology is to translate documents to fit current problems. Applying the principle of <u>lecto difficilior</u> to the Council documents, Segundo says:

> In transmitting the Christian message, the Council could certainly have allowed certain things, hallowed by custom, to slip by without paying attention to them. But when we are clearly and obviously faced with a statement that rectifies what the Church had been saying and thinking habitually in recent times, then we can be sure that deep reflection and a clear intent is at work."[74]

Although there is an underlying truth in what Segundo is saying--that the seemingly new and the divergent provide insights into the direction in which theology is moving, still the method here seems primarily employed to justify his own purpose. Segundo wants to rectify the "contradiction" in the Council's teaching by eliminating the tension between the Kingdom of God and the strivings of the human family. I maintain that the Council stated what had to be stated, namely, that between human endeavor and the coming Kingdom there is an intimate relationship, but one cannot be identified with the other. The difficulties which Segundo's position entails will become apparent as we continue this critique.

Segundo claims that, although all the volumes in his THEOLOGY FOR ARTISANS OF A NEW HUMANITY constitute a "political" theology, volume 5, EVOLUTION AND GUILT, traces the main lines of what could be called a "theology of politics." He equates this with a moral theology.[75] It is here that the consequences of his understanding of revelation and eschatology will become evident. He states:

> A moral doctrine that proceeds from divine revelation is also a moral doctrine that takes due account of what has been revealed: i.e, God's plan for the universe. And this plan is strictly social.... The only destiny that still retains the character of a goal for humanity...is the goal of a society in which each person directs his creative potentialities toward the common good.[76]

For Segundo, the discovery of the inescapable political interpretation of the Gospel is the logical and fruitful end result of a humanity that has become conscious of humanity as a universal phenomenon. Humanity has not only become conscious of itself but has accepted the challenge of directing it toward the future. Although Segundo warns that a "politicized morality" should not be reduced to "solutions of mechanical, mass-level sort," we shall see that he is convinced it can and must decide on certain acute problems which face society today.

As suggested at the beginning of this chapter, it is in a very revealing article, "Capitalism-- Socialism: A Theological Crux," that the culmination of Segundo's theological position comes into focus. He begins the article by making a claim for liberation theology which lacks a certain humility, if not realism: "It [liberation theology] is theology seen from...the one standpoint indicated by Christian sources as the authentic, privileged one for the right understanding of divine revelation in Jesus Christ."[77] Segundo does not even make such a definitive statement as this in his discussion of Christian dialogue with non-Christian religions! It should be noted, moreover, that liberation theology receives its privileged position by an appeal to Christian "sources." By the end of the article, Segundo is proclaiming that there is no way, theologically, that the Church can leave open the option between capitalism and socialism. His argument proceeds as follows:

First, the question is posed whether it is legitimate to ask theology to make an option between two socioeconomic or sociopolitical systems. Segundo examines various answers which have been proposed in the past. He dismisses the traditional Catholic answer because, he says, it is based on questionable theological assumptions. That position maintains that theology can make such a decision, but it must say "no" to socialism because it does not recognize the natural right of man to private ownership. He then turns to consider two negative answers to the question--one pragmatic, the other theoretical. The negative pragmatic answer to the question whether theology can choose capitalism or socialism is based on the proposition that the Church must remain apolitical in the world. The Church deals in absolute values, those pertaining to salvation, and it could never make a judgment concerning the relative values involved in the preference of one system of political life over another. Segundo sees in this answer a danger of absolutizing the Church, claiming its objects, words, gestures and authorities form a vertical link between the faithful and God. In this scheme the Church is considered the autonomous center of salvation.

In contrast to this position, Segundo wants to absolutize human society. He suggests that "human life in society, liberated as far as possible from alienations, constitutes the absolute value, and...all religious institutions, all dogmas, all sacraments, and all the ecclesiastical authorities have only a relative, that is, a functional value."[78] I would not disagree with the second part of this statement, nor the first, if "human life in community, liberated as far as possible from alienations" were looked upon as a glimpse of the Kingdom, but even then ambiguities remain and there is a danger of absolutizing the life of this particular society or community. Why relativize human life in the Church only to absolutize it in society, or why relativize the Church and absolutize the community? Segundo still has not been liberated from an "absolutist" position, be it Church or community, socialism or capitalism, human striving or God's gift.

The negative theoretical answer to the question posed by Segundo comes, he claims, from German political theology and the theology of revolution. This position absolutizes not the Church, but that which the Church serves--the eschatological Kingdom of God. Segundo quotes and criticizes the position of Metz and Moltmann. According to Metz: "What distinguishes 'Christian eschatology' from the ideologies of the future in the East and West is not that it knows more, but that it knows less about that future which mankind is trying to discern, and that it persists in its lack of knowledge." This means, according to Metz, that the Church "must institutionalize that eschatological reserve by establishing itself as an instance of critical liberty in the face of social development in order to reject the tendency of the latter to present itself as absolute."[79] Moltmann represents basically this same position. The functionality of the Church is to prevent "premature and inopportune" anticipations of the Kingdom of God, be they false universalism or absolutism of the Church or any other historical projects. Political theology de-absolutizes both the existing order and any projected order.[80]

Segundo notes that German political theology and those writing on the theology of revolution choose with utmost care the terms which indicate the relationship between the relative political order and the absolute eschatological order. Moltmann uses anticipation to describe the relationship; Metz uses outline or design. Weth, who has written on the theology of revolution, uses analogy or image. "But," asks Segundo, "who consecrates his life to an 'analogy'? Who dies for an 'outline'? Who moves a human mass, a whole people, in the name of an 'anticipation'?" Latin-American liberation theologians, in contrast, are set on constructing the Kingdom of God from within history now. Because of this, they agree in principle to some causality between all political parties and the definitive Kingdom. Segundo accuses recent political theology in Europe, both Catholic and Protestant, of retreating once again to the Reformation principle of justification by faith alone.[81]

In his book, THE LIBERATION OF THEOLOGY, Segundo amplifies this contention. German political theology is, according to Segundo, "markedly dependent on the Lutheran theology of justification." Because of this, it systemically attempts to eliminate from theologico-political language any terms that might suggest causal relationship between historical activity and the construction of the eschatological Kingdom. Segundo attributes this to the disappearance of merit from Protestant theology from the time of the Reformation. This disappearance, Segundo claims, "seems to have undermined the possibility of any theology of history in Protestant thought." He states:

> In Catholic theology the only thing that united the plane of human activity in history with the plane of God's eternal Kingdom was the notion of merit, that is, the eternal worth of human effort and right intention. But even this tie was cut in the Protestant theology of salvation by faith alone: i.e., salvation by virtue of Christ's merit alone.[82]

Segundo continues his argument by asserting that the doctrine of justification by faith alone and the key notion that glory belongs to God alone (soli Deo gloria) are intimately related to the other central theme of Lutheran theology, the doctrine of the two kingdoms. The result of this, Segundo asserts, is the "eschatological relativization of any and every existing historical reality," the "desacralization of any and every political regime." He admits that this relativization has an initial liberating character, but that it ends up being a "politically neutral theology." This basic Catholic/Lutheran dichotomy is summarized by Segundo as follows:

> In short, it has much to do with something that Karl Barth stressed once again shortly before his death: i.e., the rejection of the Catholic attempt to connect God 'and' man, faith 'and' good works. Thus the Lutheran rejection of this 'and' in the problem of justification turns faith into the confident but essentially passive acceptance of God's fixed plan for human destiny and the construction of his eschatological Kingdom.[83]

Segundo, as was mentioned earlier, lays this same charge against his fellow Latin-American the-

ologian, Rubem Alves. He characteries Alves' conception of the whole process of change as "radically pessimistic." The Kingdom of God can be
fashioned only by someone who is free from sin;
every change prompted by men and women cannot help
but lose out to the "world-dominating" sin; therefore, efforts of humans are useless and God must
operate alone. He quotes from Alves:

> That is why messianic humanism refuses to
> draw its hope from the slave's faithful-
> ness to the protest that is intrinsic to
> his condition as slave. Its historical
> experience shows that those who once were
> the negative slaves, and therefore the
> bearers of freedom, become, once they
> achieve their freedom, dominated by con-
> cern for the preservation of their pres-
> ent and are infected with the sin of
> their masters.... The structure of op-
> pression, accordingly, is able to create
> a man in its image and likeness, a man
> whose consciousness is as unfree as that
> of his master.... His will to freedom
> becomes will to domestication. The his-
> tory of freedom, therefore, cannot be
> based on the powers of <u>man</u> <u>alone</u>.[84]

Segundo then asks, "Is Alves suggesting that
there is a better chance for success when man
works <u>with</u> God?" He answers for Alves: "The question is offbase, for the reason we cited earlier:
a theology derived from Luther finds it very difficult to conceive of any collaboration."

I suggest that Segundo's analysis of Alves'
position does not take adequate account of the
later Calvinist Reformed tradition out of which
Alves--following Shaull and Lehmann--is writing.
Alves does not see the actions of men and women as
useless; indeed, men and women are called to participate with God who acts in history to bring
about the liberation and salvation--maturity--of

the human family. In the ecumenical climate today, few theologians, even among the liberationists, would contribute to the strivings of men and women the cause of the coming Kingdom. The Second Vatican Council carefully avoided this inference, as was pointed out earlier. This preoccupation with the question of causation is, I suggest, Segundo's problem and it could easily lead to a dangerous overemphasis of human achievement, a forgetfulness of the ambiguity of the human situation--in theological terms the problem is sin--a tendency to reduce theology to an ideology. As Langdon Gilkey has stated it,

> ...men and women remain ambiguous, still haunted by the inward problems of self-love, still, therefore, unable to control themselves morally, to be just to their neighbor and to curb their own infinite concupiscence to consume the world--still determined, whatever their intentions, by their bondage to their own security, fulfillment and glory.[85]

While I do not agree with Segundo's basic criticism of Alves, nor his contention that the problem essentially stems from the doctrine of salvation by faith alone, I do insist, as I did in my own critique of Alves, that at times his language would seem to justify Segundo's contention that Alves gives no ultimate worth to people's strivings. For example, Alves states:

> The normal unfolding of the politics of the old cannot give birth to the new. The new is here nothing more than the old under a different form, a different mask. It regenerates itself, thereby perpetuating the old world of unfreedom under a different guise. But because God's politics negates the natural unfolding of the old, room is made for the new. And one can truly say that it is created ex

nihilo, since the new cannot be explained
in terms of the logic of natural causality.[86]

I believe that Alves is correct on the matter of
"natural causality," as I indicated above, but it
is difficult to interpret the statement that liberation of the human family is created ex nihilo
as anything but an expression of passivity.

In spite of the difference in eschatological
approach between Segundo and Alves--which I suggest is not so great as Segundo claims--I see a
strong influence of the same radical Reformed
thought, typified by Lehmann, in the writings of
Segundo. Indeed, after his severe criticism of the
"Protestant" strain in the theological views of
Alves, Moltmann and Metz, he adds without qualm,
"Let us adopt Paul Lehmann's assumption that God's
policy is to make human existence human and maintain it as such."[87] My criticism of him, therefore, with certain change of emphasis, will be
similar to my criticism of Alves and Shaull--the
too facile and narrow identification of revelation
(God's action in history) with a specific group,
the too positivistic verification of that revelation through an appeal to Scripture or doctrine,
and the too ideologically determined parameters of
the Church. The last-mentioned criticism will
become clearer as we proceed.

We return now to Segundo's essay on capitalism
and socialism. After rejecting the traditional
affirmative answer as to whether theology can pronounce on socialism or capitalism, as well as the
pragmatic and theoretical negative answers, he
turns to his own reconstruction. He claims that
he is looking for a positive or negative relationship between theology and socialism, not on the
level of morals, but on the basis of dogma.
Segundo, true to his biblical understanding of
revelation, turns to the prophets. Because of
their vision of the "divine present," he claims
they built a project for the future which was his-

toric and human. It was, according to Segundo, a "political" project which the prophets did not "eschatologize." The conclusion which he draws from this rather nebulous analysis of the prophets as builders of the future is this:

> Every theology which refuses to make a theological judgment, that is, to invoke the word of God, about a political reality, on the pretext that science cannot demonstrate that the future will beyond a doubt be better, draws further away from the prophetic function.[88]

Segundo then jumps to the New Testament and the "theology of Jesus." He finds that Jesus "absolutizes imprudently" during the course of his cures and conversions. According to Segundo, Jesus gives these instances the most absolute name in theology of the time: salvation. "Just as he called cures of uncertain consequence the 'arrival of the Kingdom', so he calls a momentary, ambiguous, still unrealized decision of Zacchaeus 'entry to salvation.'"[89] The conclusion Segundo arrives at is that there is no reason why theology cannot pronounce on political alternatives exactly parallel to the alternatives that were the object of the theology of Jesus throughout his preaching. Furthermore, Latin-American theologians should no more have to put forward a project for a socialist society which will guarantee in advance that the evident defects of known socialist systems will be avoided, than Jesus should have been required, before telling the sick man, "Your faith has saved you," to give a guarantee that "the cure will not be followed by even a greater sickness." We have here an example of what Segundo apparently means by "translating" the Word of God to fit the problems of contemporary men and women. One wonders, however, what has happened to the hard sociological analysis of the situation, upon which Segundo insists theology must be constructed.

Segundo's critique of capitalism and his theological decision for socialism apparently comes down to the following:

> Historical sensibility to hunger and illiteracy, for example, calls for a society where competition and profit will not be the law and where provision of basic food and culture to an underdeveloped people will be regarded as liberation.[90]

In summarizing his position, Segundo claims that the eschatological aspect of all Christian theology does not relativize the present, but binds it to the absolute. But at the same time, he maintains that the eschatological element forestalls the possibility of degeneration into inhuman rigidity or stagnation as well as the tendency to sacralize the existing order merely because it is there. One might question how Segundo can have it both ways. Moltmann has taken him to task for this equivocacy, as will be pointed out later. In fact, it seems that Segundo wants to relativize the existing order so the absolute social order--a socialist society, liberated as far as possible from alienations--can be constructed. Given his understanding of revelation as God's message which contains God's plan for the world, and given his understanding of eschatology that it is up to human beings to construct the Kingdom here and now, it is not difficult to see how Segundo would insist upon socialism as the only Christian option. Although he makes some concessions to the ambiguous nature of all endeavors, as is evident in the following quote, still his basic option is predetermined:

> The relationship with a liberating event, no matter how ambiguous and provisional (as in the examples from the gospel), derives from the strength of God himself who promotes it, a genuinely causal character with respect to the def-

inite Kingdom of God. This causality is partial, fragile, often erroneous and having to be remade, but it is something very different from anticipations, outlines, or analogies of the Kingdom. In the face of options between racial separation and full community of rights, free international demand and supply and a balanced market (with an eye to the underprivileged countries) or capitalism and socialism, what is at stake is no mere analogy of the Kingdom. What is at stake, in a fragmentary fashion if you like, is the eschatological Kingdom itself whose realization and revelation are awaited with anguish by the whole universe.[91]

Moltmann criticizes Segundo for this last statement, saying that he, Segundo, rejects the critical expression used by Metz and himself for describing the relationship between the present situation and the future Kingdom, namely, "anticipation," "outline," or "analogy," and replacing it with an equally relativizing expression--"fragment."[92] As I pointed out earlier, Segundo seems to want it both ways. One might say that he gingerly brings in the back door what he boisterously pushed out the front.

Turning to the question of ecclesiology, we find that Segundo's understanding of revelation directly affects his conception of the Church. Revelation, the message of God's plan for the world, is entrusted to the Church. The Church, in turn, must translate this message and apply it to every situation, confident that in doing so some who are "implicit" Christians may become "explicit" ones. Segundo still maintains the natural/supernatural distinction. He bases this on what he calls the two lines of salvation revealed in the Gospel. The supernatural approach is found in Mark 16, 15-16: "Go into the whole world and pro-

claim the Good News to all creation. The man who
believes in it and accepts baptism will be saved;
the man who refuses to believe in it will be condemned." The natural approach, according to
Segundo, is found in Matthew 25, 31-46: "I was
hungry and you gave me to eat..., etc." In the
Christian, these two approaches converge, because
the Christian is the one who knows beforehand
God's plan at the time of judgment. In a startling
statement, for which there seems to be no New
Testament justification, Segundo states that the
thing which distinguishes the Christian at the
last judgment is

> ...the Christian will not be surprised by
> the criterion used to judge all men. He
> will not ask the Lord: 'When did I see
> you?' For if he is a believer, he is so
> precisely because he has accepted the
> revelation of this universal plan which
> culminates in the last judgment. The
> Christian is he who already knows.[93]

In light of Segundo's overall position, this
statement implies, it seems, that the Lord at the
final judgment will have employed the same "scientific social analysis" as did the liberation theologians.

The Church, then, according to Segundo, is the
community that knows. And yet it does not know
for its own sake. It must be not only the community of faith, but also the community of sacraments. This means it must be a sign to others of
the revealed message: God is love. All men travel
the same road, unless they deliberately turn
aside, and that is the road of self-giving love.
The only thing is, some know what relates to all.
Election is not a privilege but a responsibility.
Furthermore, the Church is absolutely necessary
for salvation--Segundo accepts this as a Church
dogma--for those who know. This dogma is not meant
to concentrate on the boundaries of the Church,

according to Segundo, but is to highlight the universal mediatory role of the Church. In the midst of the human race there must be people who know the mystery of love.[94]

The fundamental mission of the Church, then, is to transmit the faith. That faith proclaims that the Kingdom is already in our midst. Because the Church is a sacrament, the clarity and transparency of its sign function for those outside is its primary concern. There is no advantage for the Church to seek to bring within its boundaries the masses, if this would mean the purity of its sign function would be affected. For the Church only aids those who belong to it when their membership corresponds with the function the Church is called to exercise. Segundo is emphatic when he states that the Church must be purified of superstitious practices and beliefs with which much of the religion of masses is tainted. Membership must be based on a personal explicit adherence to faith. He realizes this might be seen as reducing membership to an elite group, but for Segundo it is the only solution. The Church must guide between the temptation of becoming a sect, on the one hand, and stressing the universal aspect to the point where it is synonymous with the surrounding culture, on the other. Segundo suggests a minority Church composed of communities of historical engagement with a sacramental practice related to this engagement. He refers to the "reflected" action of these elite communities as serving the masses and opening the paths for them to higher and more human levels.

Segundo claims that the eschatological element in Christian theology does not define the function of the ecclesial community in the midst of the society around it. In other words, he opposes the position that political theology maintains that the Church must relativize every historical project which attempts to absolutize itself. Rather, he is convinced that the Church must take a stand on vital issues facing the human family, at least opting for the overall structure within which these issues will be solved--i.e., a socialist rather than a capitalist society. When it comes to particular projects, however, Segundo is hesitant about legitimizing the Church's involvement. He is aware that the institutional Church has used its political power in the past for selfish as well as unselfish purposes. In what is perhaps his most significant contribution to the discussion of the relationship between the Church and society, Segundo develops a "theory of substitution" to guide the Church in its involvement in particular projects. It will be discussed in more detail in the following chapter, but in essence it consists of the following:

The Church's role in particular projects must be "substitutive." This means that the Church as Church may take an active role in projects within the political realm when other institutions in society are at the time unable or unwilling to carry them out. Even then, Segundo outlines a series of restrictions on entering and remaining in certain projects. In doing this he still gives evidence of making a clear distinction between the laity and hierarchy in the Church.

Segundo says the Church as a sacramental community could be faithful to her essence and mission if she "evinced a clear commitment to collaborate in the work of authentic human development, without getting mixed up in the political government of the state; or even if she reacted strongly against political regimes that violate man." But Segundo says that this aspect of the Church's mission will be appreciated more clearly and concretely "if people see Christians, as individuals and fellow citizens, assuming personal responsibility in this area; if they see them supporting regimes that foster human betterment and rebelling against those which do the opposite.[95]

Considering the radical eschatological stance which Segundo has adopted--men and women construct the Kingdom of God from within history--and his understanding of revelation as the "known plan" for the Kindgom, it is surprising that his ecclesiology is not more revolutionary. The Church can and must opt for socialism, but beyond that it seems that Segundo's Church--elite communities historically engaged--must be a sign to those outside that God is love and that the socialist society they advocate will be, in some fragmentary fashion, the eschatological Kingdom itself.

Segundo's understanding of revelation is extremely intellectualistic and positivistic; his eschatological stance is radical on the surface, but ambiguous when closely scrutinized. Concerning the Church, Segundo's ecclesiology tends to be by his own admission narrow and elitist. He stresses the demonstrative aspect of the Church's mission, but only hesitantly integrates the Church's obligation to work for human development into its essential mission.

4. GUSTAVO GUTIERREZ:
A THEOLOGY OF LIBERATION[96]

Gustavo Gutierrez has formulated the most thorough Latin-American liberation theology to date. He outlines the radical position the Church must take in hastening the social transformation in Latin America. For the Church to turn in on itself, to fail to place itself squarely within the revolutionary process, would be its greatest "o-mission," according to Gutierrez. Liberation theology offers not only a new theme for theological reflection, but, Gutierrez insists, a new way of doing theology. It is a committed theology , a reflection on praxis which attempts to assimilate itself into the very process through which Latin-American society is being transformed.

Although, like Segundo, Gutierrez claims his theology grows out of a scientific social analysis of the unique Latin-American situation, still the argument upon which A THEOLOGY OF LIBERATION rests can hardly be called Latin American. He actually presents the process of liberation as the continuation and culmination of the European history of freedom. As Moltmann says of Gutierrez's otherwise "magnificent" book:

> One gets a glimpse into this history of freedom by being enlightened about Kant and Hegel, Rousseau and Feuerbach, Marx and Freud. The 'secularization process' is portrayed in detail through the work of Gogarten, Bonhoeffer, Cox and Metz. This is all worked through independently and offers many new insights--but precisely only in the framework of Europe's history, scarcely in the history of Latin America. Gutierrez has written an invaluable contribution to European theology. But where is Latin America in it all?[97]

Although Moltmann's criticism is well taken, the purpose of the present critique is to determine Gutierrez's understanding of the concepts of revelation and eschatology and how this understanding affects his perspective on the mission of the Church.

Direct discussion of Gutierrez's understanding of revelation is limited. The phrase which occurs again and again is "the Word of God," or "in light of the Word of God." One might reasonably suspect, especially with key references to Barth, that we are faced with another relatively narrow biblical understanding of revelation: "The Bible presents liberation--salvation--in Christ as the total gift...; it gives the whole process of liberation its deepest meaning and its complete and unforeseeable fulfillment."[98] Further, Gutierrez admits that today "there is a greater sensitivity to the anthropological aspects of revelation.... In revealing God to us, the Gospel message reveals us to ourselves in our situation before the Lord and other men." He then quotes Barth's famous comment concerning Christian anthropocentrism: "Man is the measure of all things, since God became man."[99]

But Gutierrez also quotes Congar with approval: "Instead of using only revelation and tradition as starting points, as classical theology has generally done, it must start with facts and questions derived from the world and from history." This sounds like the method of correlation outlined in Chapter Three. Gutierrez cautions, however, that "by pointing to the sources of revelation" [emphasis mine], pastoral activity in the world can be protected from activism and immediatism. The "sources" here would appear to refer to the Bible and tradition embodied in Church dogmas. On the other hand, Gutierrez says: "A theology which has as its points of reference only 'truths' which have been established once and for all--and not Truth which is also the Way--can only be static and, in the long run, sterile."[100]

We begin to detect the ambiguous pattern of Gutierrez's employment of the concept of revelation. There are "sources" of revelation: "We must search the Gospel message for the answer to what, according to Camus, constitutes the most important question facing all people: 'To decide whether life deserves to be lived or not.'" On the other hand, there is human experience: Gutierrez declares that only through participation in the process of liberation will nuances of the Word of God be heard which are imperceptible in other existential situations and without which there can be no authentic faithfulness to the Lord.[101]

In discussing the universal call to salvation, which would imply the universal availability or revelation of God, Gutierrez traces Rahner's "su-

pernatural existential" and Blondel's "transnatur-
al state of man," and then states, "Historically
and concretely we know man only as actually called
to meet God." This historical point of view enables us to see with more biblical eyes that men
and women are called to meet the Lord insofar as
they constitute a community. A "convocation" reaffirms the possibility of the presence of grace,
that is, of the acceptance of a personal relationship with the Lord, in all people, whether they
are conscious of it or not. This leads to a consideration of "anonymous Christianity," which
Gutierrez admits is a poor phrase and one that
must be refined, but it does point to "a reality
which is itself indisputable; all men are in
Christ efficaciously called to communion with
God.[102] On what basis is such a reality "indisputable?" On the basis of the Word of God, would
be Gutierrez's undoubted response. This position
is consistent with his statement that there is
only one history--a "Christo-finalized history."
He illustrates and ratifies this latter claim by
the study of two great biblical themes, creation
and salvation.

And yet, against this rather positivistic view
of revelation we find Gutierrez saying, "The modes
of God's presence determine the forms of our encounter with him. If...each man is the living
temple of God, we meet God in our encounter with
men, in the commitment to the historical process
of mankind...." Quoting from Scripture, "To know
God is to do justice," he adds, "the God of biblical revelation is known through interhuman justice."[103] My position, as presented in Chapter
Three, is more cautious. Knowledge of God revealed
in interhuman justice can be clarified by the reflection on revelation found in the Bible. At
times Gutierrez says basically the same thing, but
always with qualification. For example:

In human love there is a depth which man
does not suspect: it is through it that

man encounters God. If utopia humanizes
economic, social, and political liberation, this humanness--in light of the
Gospel--reveals God [emphasis mine]. If
doing justice leads us to a knowledge of
God, to find him is in turn a necessary
consequence."104

We find in Gutierrez a hesitancy about admitting that God can be found in the depth of human
experience, in human encounters and action even
without the Gospel illumination. On the other
hand, when he speaks about liberation theology as
an understanding of faith conducted from a commitment to solidarity with the oppressed classes and
starting from their world, he seems to limit the
availability of God to the oppressed and those
struggling for them. The danger of an understanding of revelation which would attempt to limit the
freedom of God's self-disclosure should be apparent. We shall follow this train of Gutierrez's
thought further.

Gutierrez claims again and again that in contrast to theologies of development and revolution
--which he says merely apply a certain process of
theological thought to certain aspects of the political world--the theology of liberation is based
on a "new kind of apprehension of faith." The new
kind of apprehension of faith results from a different kind of reasoning and a demanding spiritual
experience. It depends on a commitment to the
process of liberation among the exploited classes
and peripheral people of society, and it leads to
a "new way of being a man." Because there can be
no faith without revelation, that is, there can be
no response to God until God has made known to men
and women that the invitation is there, this new
kind of apprehension of faith involves a particular understanding of revelation. Gutierrez is saying that among the "exploited class" is the place
where God is available to people today.105

Gutierrez says that exploited lower classes, oppressed cultures, and races subject to discrimination are beginning to make their own voices heard and are gradually becoming subjects of their own history. They are forging a radically different society. They experience this new awareness from within the historical process of liberation which, according to Gutierrez, seeks to build a truly egalitarian, fraternal and just society. Because there are "whole peoples who are suffering poverty and despoliation..., who scarcely know they are men," Christians in growing numbers are joining into solidarity with them in an effort to raise their consciousness. "This gives rise to a new way of being a man and a believer, of living and thinking the faith, of being called together in an ecclesia."[106]

Turning to the Christian concept of love of neighbor, Gutierrez, seeming to forget that "religious imperialism" of an earlier day based on the passage in Luke's Gospel, "Go out into the highways and byways and force them to come in" (14,23), proclaims that "my neighbor" is the man "in whose path I deliberately place myself." My neighbor is "the man I seek out in streets and squares, in factories and marginal barrios, in the fields and mines." And the purpose of placing oneself in the path of these creatures is to let them know that they are "a by-product of a system...for which we are responsible.... They are the oppressed, the exploited, the workers cheated of the fruit of their work, stripped of their being as men."[107]

The assumption made by Gutierrez and other liberation theologians that the poor and exploited classes are "scarcely aware they are men," or "stripped of their being as men," has brought severe criticism from the sociologist, Peter Berger.[108] He points out some highly questionable assumptions on which this method of "consciousness raising" is based. According to Berger, it in-

volves philosophical error and political irony.
The philosophical error is that it assumes the
"hierarchical view of consciousness." The "masses"
do not understand their own situation and must be
enlightened by selected higher-class individuals.
The "enlightenment" does not have to do with
levels of information on specific topics, but with
levels of freedom and therefore of humanity.

The political irony in this outlook is, according to Berger, that those who embrace the
method usually see themselves as genuine demo-
crats, close to "the masses" and emphatically
"antielitist." They delude themselves in not
recognizing their "cognitive imperialism." They
should be called "missionaries," says Berger, because "a peculiar mixture of arrogance ('I know
the truth') and benevolence ('I want to serve
you') has always been the chief psychological
hallmark of missionary activity." Berger concludes
that no one is "more conscious" than anyone else:
different individuals are conscious of different
things, and the peasant knows his world far better
than any outsider ever can.

At first reading it might appear that Berger
is proposing a wholesale "hands-off, let the happy
natives continue being poor in their own mythic
world." But I suggest that is not the case.
Rather, it is a call to liberationists for modesty
and honesty. If one admits that "raising consciousness" has to do with the levels of information on specific topics, that is one thing, but if
it is insisted upon that this "enlightenment" is
going to produce "new men" out of those who are
"scarcely aware they are men," we are dealing with
a matter much more fundamental--the change of the
very being of the individual person. A certain
modesty is lacking in this second approach and
that element, vital for dialogue--"you can teach
me something even as I teach you"--seems to be
overlooked. Moreover, those who claim to be speaking on behalf of the "masses" should recognize

that they may be putting more words into the
mouths of the peasants--often one political option
which is purported to be the scientific truth--
than they are reflecting the honest hopes and aspirations of the masses. This is what Berger calls
"cognitive imperialism."

Gutierrez insists, however, that being in
solidarity with the exploited classes not only
leads to a new way of being human, and therefore,
to a new apprehension of faith, but leads away
from any type of collaboration with the oppressors
and their structures of exploitation. He states:

> One cannot be for the poor and oppressed
> if one is not against all that gives rise
> to man's exploitation of man. For this
> same reason, solidarity cannot limit it-
> self to just saying 'no' to the way
> things are arranged.... It must be an ef-
> fort to forge a new society in which the
> worker is not subordinated to the owner
> of the means of production, a society in
> which assumption of social responsibility
> for political affairs will include social
> responsibility for real liberty and will
> lead to the emergence of a new social
> consciousness.[109]

Elsewhere, Gutierrez states that this rejection of the existing situation "does not produce
an escapist attitude, but rather a will to revolution."[110]

Following Gutierrez, step by step, through
this presentation leads one to the conclusion that
in order to experience the presence of God today,
or to be able to theologize, one must first be
committed in a concrete way to the liberation of
the exploited class. The exploited class, of
course, is identified "scientifically" by a Marxist-Leninist analysis of the economic and political situation. Only when the individual is com-

mitted completely to the liberation of the exploited class, which commitment includes by necessity that one join in the project of constructing
a qualitatively new social order in which the
means of production will be in the hands of the
"people," only then can that individual become a
new person and thereby open himself or herself to
a new kind of apprehension of faith. Only then can
one theologize, that is, reflect on liberating
praxis in the light of the Word of God. The parameters of revelation, of God's disclosure in every-
day human experience, are limited by a prior commitment to a particular project arrived at by a
particular type of social analysis. As Gutierrez
states, "This is what it is all about, life in the
presence of the Lord at the heart of political
activity with the full realization of all this entails in terms of conflicts and the demand for
scientific rationale."[111] Gutierrez leaves himself open for criticism here, for it appears that
he considers it self-evident that a Marxist or
neo-Marxist social, economic and political analysis is the correct one for Latin America. But such
an assumption needs defense. As Ronald Preston
states:

> It can hardly be a _theological_ judgment
> that Marxism is _the_ 'scientific' politi-
> cal and social analysis. Therefore it
> must be argued out in political and so-
> cial terms.... The Marxist theories all
> embody useful insights, but each one tak-
> en separately, and the whole lot taken
> together, are sufficiently defective as a
> basis for prediction (which is the point
> of claiming to be a scientific theory) to
> provide a very unsafe ground for action.
> This is not least because Marxism is
> clearly related to the nineteenth-century
> state of British and West European
> thought and society out of which it grew

(aware of conditioning factors in all other thought except its own).[112]

Preston states further that Gutierrez writes of the need for a "scientific" approach in order to discover laws proper to the political world which will give revolutionary activity effectiveness, and assumes he has found that approach in Marxism. Moltmann concurs with this criticism of Gutierrez and other liberationists when he states, "One is called upon to opt, in a moral alternative, for the oppressed against the oppressors and to accept Marxism as the right prophecy of the situation."[113]

Gutierrez denies that liberation theology originates in an effort to justify this commitment. Rather, it attempts to make participation in liberating praxis more creative and critical. He further admits that such an approach "enables it to re-read theological views of the past and select critically anything these have to contribute." This "re-reading" and "selecting critically" is possible because of a different way of knowing. Knowledge, in turn, is linked with transformation. History is known only by transforming it and transforming oneself. Truth must be verified (veri-fied)--literally, truth must be made.[114]

Because of this intimate link between knowledge and transformation, between theory and practice, the Gospel, too, not only can but must be re-read. This will perhaps lead to rediscovery of something forgotten or neglected in its implications by scriptural hermeneutics. For Gutierrez, the Gospel truth is something that we have to work at. But in a typical qualification, Gutierrez adds,

> This does not mean a mechanical correspondence with modern insistence on linking knowledge and transformation and on living a truth which is being verified.

But the cultural world in which we live offers a starting point and shows the way ahead for the advance of theological thought along a new road, yet with continued and necessary references to its own sources.[115]

How such a statement coincides with Gutierrez's persistent use of "entirely new" and "a complete break with the past" to describe his theological enterprise is difficult to see. Indeed, Gutierrez's "different kind of knowing" and "different kind of apprehension of faith" which lead to a "new way of being a man" seem to contradict his reference to theology's own sources--presumably Scripture and tradition.

From one aspect of Gutierrez's thought, we could expect an eschatological stance similar to that of Segundo--the Kingdom of God is to be constructed by us here and now. But again, Gutierrez will not commit himself completely, and, I believe, rightly so in this instance. He states:

The growth of the Kingdom of God occurs historically in political liberation, in so far as this allows man to realize himself more fully. But it goes beyond this. The Kingdom of God condemns from within historical instances of liberation, their limitations and ambiguities, proclaims their complete fulfillment and impels them effectively towards total communion.... Without liberating historical events there is no growth of the Kingdom, but the process of liberation will not overcome the root causes of oppression and of man's exploitation by man, until the coming of the Kingdom, which is, above all, a gift of the Lord.[116]

With qualification upon qualification, Gutierrez states that "The Kingdom is realized in a society of brotherhood and justice." However, "The Kingdom must not be confused with the establishment of a just society." On the other hand, "This does not mean that it is indifferent to this society. Nor does it mean that this just society consititutes a 'necessary condition' for the arrival of the Kingdom nor that they are closely linked, nor that they converge." One might ask at this point just what it does mean. Gutierrez's way of explaining it is this: "The political is grafted into the eternal."[117] Whatever the precise meaning of Gutierrez's statements might be, it does not seem to correspond to the position of Segundo who sees a definite causal relationship between human endeavor and the coming Kingdom.

The position of Gutierrez can perhaps be clarified by looking briefly at his use of utopia as the mediating factor between the present situation and the future Kingdom. Although he states that he is following the thought of his fellow Latin American, Paulo Freire, at this point, an underlying dependence on Karl Mannheim and Ernst Bloch is apparent. Gutierrez states that utopian thinking involves action in the present under two aspects--denunciation and annunciation. Utopia necessarily involves a denunciation of the existing order because the existing order is oppressive and unjust. Utopian thinking is completely revolutionary in its approach, not reformist. Utopia is also annunciation of what is not yet, and yet what will be. It is the field of creative imagination, a forecast of a different order of things, a new society. The time between the denunciation and the annunciation is the time for building, the time for historical praxis.

Utopia, unlike ideology, belongs to the rational order, according to Gutierrez. Ideology does not offer an adequate or scientific knowledge of reality. Utopia, on the other hand, leads to an authentic and scientific knowledge or reality and to a praxis which transforms what exists.

Following the thought of Paulo Freire, Gutierrez declares, "In today's world it is only the oppressed person, the oppressed class, the oppressed peoples that can denounce and announce. Only they are capable of working out revolutionary utopias and not conservative or reformist ideologies.[118]

One wonders how realistic it is to expect oppressed peoples to work out "revolutionary utopias." As we have seen earlier, Calvez, in his analysis of Third World societies, claims that in fact the thrust for development--call it revolutionary utopias if you like--is not being shouldered by the "people" but by a small, elite group. Gutierrez would include among the oppressed, of course, those who have pledged solidarity with them, but the possibility and danger of "cognitive imperialism" as Berger has pointed out should not be overlooked.

For Gutierrez, utopia takes the place of any social ethic or moral guidelines for directing the liberation process. He insists that it is not ideology because it is based on scientific analysis of existing conditions in Latin America. Moltmann challenges the liberation theologians on this very point. He charges that, for all their claims, they are not basing their theology on a thorough scientific analysis of the history of their own people. Instead, they "make declamations of seminar-Marxism as a world view."[119] A statement such as the following by Gutierrez is probably what Moltmann had in mind:

> The historical plan, the utopia of liberation as creation of a new social consciousness and as a social appropriation not only of the means of production, but also of the political process, and, definitively, of freedom, is the proper arena for the cultural revolution. That is to say, it is the arena of the permanent creation of a new man in a different society characterized by solidarity.

Therefore, that creation is the place of encounter between political liberation and the communion of all men with God.[120]

One may properly question whether any utopia or utopian thinking can be based completely on scientific analysis or, more fundamentally, whether any scientific analysis can be completely objective, that is, absolutely free from any ideological overtones. On the contrary, utopian thinking, if it is to unite and move people toward a particular goal, is bound to have elements of the mythic, the dream, or the leap of faith. The important thing is to be aware of it.[121]

Gutierrez admits that the Gospel does not provide a utopia for us; this is a human work. Utopia prevents the historical task of liberation from falling into an idealism or evasion, and at the same time "keeps us from any confusion of the Kingdom with any one historical stage, from any idolatry toward unavoidably ambiguous human achievement, from absolutizing of revolution."[122] The question which remains unanswered in Gutierrez's scheme is "how?" How does the mediation of utopia prevent and ensure all of these things? It all sounds so excellent when the discussion is on the level of the liberation of all of humankind from alienation and injustice, but what about particular cases involving violent struggle, questionable possibilities for success, etc? Is every cause which calls itself a movement for liberation, by its very nature, an instrument of the Kingdom?

Within the political movements for liberation, Gregory Baum notes that the Church "will have to play a critical role, examine the means that are adopted and evaluate the ideals of human life that are being proposed."[123] But it is questionable in Gutierrez's liberation theology--which is not interested in social ethics or moral theology--whether utopian thinking as a means of mediating between theory and practice, between religion and politics, can, in specific cases, adequately "examine the means that are adopted" and "evaluate the ideals of human life that are being proposed."

Moreover, there is a danger that utopian thinking, with its challenge to "dream forward" and its presentation of impossibilities as possibilities, will lead to the refusal to pay attention to evidence and the precise goals of the present. It can lead to anti-intellectualism and stereotyped judgments. If liberation movements, based on utopian thinking, are successful, there is the danger they will lead to tyranny because of their claim to embody a greater perfection than the facts warrant.[124]

Finally, I would agree with Preston when he states that the utopian element in a theology of social change such as Gutierrez's is closely related to his preoccupation with the Marxist analysis. He states:

> In Marxism two elements are curiously related. One is the claim to be a 'scientific' theory of social change...; the other is its utopian horizon in its picture of the coming classless society. Related to these is the curious tension in it between the 'scientific' theories which purport to uncover the dialectical power struggles through which social change will inevitably proceed until the classless society is reached, and the view that men should create for themselves and seize revolutionary opportunities to push the process on.[125]

Gutierrez, I suggest, accepts too readily the Marxist claim to be scientific, and at the same time says that Christianity and Marxism are congenial because both drive us, through utopian thinking, to take hold of our future.

The same ambiguity which runs through all of Gutierrez's theology that we have examined appears also in his understanding of the Church. There is no question about the importance of the Church in the theology of Gutierrez. For him, the very life of the Church becomes the locus theologicus. Gutierrez places the Church in the service of the Kingdom. By its preaching, its sacraments and by the charity of its members, the Church proclaims and "shelters" the Kingdom of God. By taking this position, Gutierrez dismisses the mentality of "Christendom" in which temporalities lack autonomy and the mission of the Church is directed inwardly. But he also dismisses the "New Christendom" response of Jacques Maritain. Maritain's position, which granted autonomy to the temporal sphere, still suffered from a certain "ecclesiastical narcissism." That is, the Church was still considered the center of salvation, and the purpose of creating a just and democratic society was to achieve conditions favorable to the activity of the Church in the world.[126]

According to Gutierrez's analysis, there developed from Maritain's position a more refined response to the question of the relationship between the Church and the rest of the world. By emphasizing a definite "distinction of planes," theologians were able to elaborate a response which would grant the world its autonomy not only wiht regard to ecclesiastical authority, but with regard to the Church's mission itself. Building up the earthly city is an endeavor which exists in its own right. This meant that the Church's mission had two aspects--evangelization and the inspiration of the temporal sphere. The Church was not to interfere, as an institution, in temporal affairs except indirectly through the mediation of the conscience of the individual Christian.

According to this understanding, therefore, the Church has no responsibility for "constructing the world." The institutional Church, understood

here as being synonymous with the hierarchy, betrayed its function if it interfered directly in
political affairs. Laypeople, on the other hand,
had the obligation to build both the Church and
the world.

Gutierrez argues that such a position is
untenable. It cannot be honestly said that the
Church does not interfere in the temporal sphere.
Here he disagrees with those who claim that society has become completely secularized. Dominant
groups have always used the Church to maintain and
legitimize their position. Now, when the poor and
exploited classes are making their voices heard
within the Church, it is not surprising that the
privileged classes would call for the Church to
return to its "purely religious function," which
means, of course, legitimizing the status quo.[127]

Gutierrez sees the Church in Latin America as
being sharply divided. In a capitalistic society
there is bound to be the sharp division with one
class against the other. The Church cannot ignore
this same division among its members--Christians
who suffer from injustice and exploitation, and
those who benefit from the established order. The
Church must, in light of this situation, place
itself squarely within the process of revolution,
amidst violence which is present in various ways,
but always on the side of the exploited classes.
It is useless to argue that such a commitment
would cause division in the Church; the division
already exists. Although the Church must work for
reconciliation, there can be no reconciliation
until the present unjust order is destroyed and a
new society, qualitatively different, is established. Because the Church often is the only
voice that can make itself heard on behalf of the
exploited classes, it has no choice but to throw
its social weight and resources behind the revolutionary transformation that is in process.[128]

All of this puts the Church in a very radical position; one wonders what the revolutionary plan is. But once again, Gutierrez stops short of spelling this out. After all this revolutionary rhetoric, we find Gutierrez declaring:

> The primary task of the Church...is to celebrate with joy the salvific action of the Lord in history. In the creation of brotherhood implied and signified by this celebration, the Church--taken as a whole--plays a role which is unique, but varies according to historical circumstances.[129]

The unique contribution which the Church makes seems to come, according to Gutierrez's position, in the politicizing and conscienticizing aspects of evangelization. The preaching of the Gospel, insofar as it is a message of total love, has an inescapable political dimension because it is addressed to people who live within a fabric of social relationships. In the Latin-American situation, these social relationships keep people in a subhuman condition. The consciousness-raising dimension of preaching of the Gospel makes these people capable of challenging the privileged oppressors.[130]

How this activity differ .- from the "indirect influence through the conscience of individual Christians" in the "distinction of planes" model is difficult to see. Unlike Segundo, for example, Gutierrez provides no specifications as to how and when the Church as Church should involve itself in specific projects of liberation and development. In the end, one is forced to agree with the comment of Richard Neuhaus that there almost seems to be two Gutierrezes--one the revolutionary trumpeting "the new man in the new society," and the other the more cautious theologian positioning his arguments in relation to the larger theological and political discourse, both of the past and of

the international community.131   My criticism, as
a result of the present critique, is that this
"cautious theologian positioning his arguments in
relation to the larger theological...discourse,"
is extremely difficult to pin down on an understanding of revelation, eschatology and the specific mission of the Church. He sounds the trumpet
for attack, but the principles upon which the
battle is to be waged remain ambiguous.

BLACK THEOLOGY AND WOMEN'S LIBERATION:
A THEOLOGICAL PROBE

The principal focus of the foregoing critique
has been the Church's mission in the Third World.
Liberation theology has been primarily a Latin-
American phenomenon and the crisis in the Church's
mission is especially evident there.   But there
have been continual calls from minority and oppressed groups within both the First and the Third
World that they should cooperate and encourage one
another in the common cause of liberation. Especially in the United States, a theology of black
liberation has grown out of the struggles of the
black community to gain freedom and equality, to
throw off the oppression of racism which is mediated by the culture and religion of the nation.
Women also have been reflecting from the theological perspective on their efforts to uncover and
overcome the ancient oppression of sexism.   With
the common quest for liberation, many felt these
various groups and communities should meet for
discussion and dialogue.

In August of 1975 in Detroit a conference,
"Theology in the Americas," was held. It brought
together spokespersons for Latin-American Liberation, blacks, women and other minority groups.
Although there was an underlying faith that the
world was changeable--and must be changed--still
the diverse perspectives on the source or object

of oppression were so pronounced that solidarity
was impossible. The Latin-American theologians
were insistent on identifying, by means of social
analysis, economic imperialism of the Northern nations as the principal enemy. Blacks, identifying
racism as the source of oppression, were accused
by the Latins of not facing the class division
within their own community. The blacks, on the
other hand, insisted that class analysis can never
be separated from the analysis of race, the latter
being the more universal problem. Women, for their
part, claimed that although sexism, that is, the
subjugation of women as women, is historically
interrelated with economic and racial oppressions
and hence can never be found in pure form, still
it is an oppression sui generis. The women charged
that published works on Latin-American liberation
theology and U.S. American black theology do not
mention the subjugation of women at all. They noted that this is especially relevant for Latin
America, where an oppressive machismo dominates
the entire culture.[132]

At the end of a week of what were at times
heated discussions, the summary report states: "At
the present time our solidarity is tenuous. It is
preferable to suffer for some time with our present consciousness of the difference which we have
just begun to explore and not try to contrive
solidarity."[133]

My purpose in underlining the present incom-
patibility among various groups that are attempting to theologize on their experience of the
struggle for liberation is not to minimize their
efforts nor the need for continual dialogue, but
to emphasize the discretion required in discussing
various liberation theologies. In other words,
moving from Latin-American liberation theology to
the theology of black liberation or women's liberation involves more than merely changing certain
words. In the critique being undertaken here,
however, I feel justified in making a theological

probe into the theologies of black liberation and women's liberation, with the understanding that it is a limited critique, not so much concerned with the social context out of which these theologies arose, as with those basic theological presuppositions involved in an understanding of revelation and eschatology and the impact of that understanding on the particular theologian's conception of the Church and its mission. Our probe will take us first into the theology of James Cone and then into certain aspects of the theology of women's liberation.

1. JAMES CONE:
A BLACK THEOLOGY OF LIBERATION
AND GOD OF THE OPPRESSED[134]

James Cone has become the chief spokesperson for theologians who are attempting to reflect on the experience of black people, especially in the United States, in their struggle for liberation. A forceful and at times angry writer, Cone has attracted the attention of the white community and the criticism of his fellow black theologians. In his first work, BLACK THEOLOGY AND BLACK POWER,[135] Cone attempted to explain the religious significance of the black struggle. A year later, in A BLACK THEOLOGY OF LIBERATION, he insisted that Christian theology must be black theology because Christianity is a religion of liberation for the oppressed and the blacks in America are the oppressed of today. THE SPIRITUALS AND THE BLUES[136] delved into the theological and social significance of the music of the blacks in their struggle for survival. In his more recent book, GOD OF THE OPPRESSED, Cone attempts to bring into synthesis his earlier thoughts and answer the criticism of his colleagues. As we shall see in this present critique, which will focus on the BLACK THEOLOGY OF LIBERATION and GOD OF THE OPPRESSED, Cone's undertaking of revelation has remained essentially

Barthian, his eschatological stance has been greatly tempered and his ecclesiology remains narrow, sketchy and incomplete.

Black theology, according to Cone, is an attempt by the black community itself to define what the knowledge of God means for its existence in a white racist society. To ask how the black community knows that its assertions about God are valid is to ask the question about revelation. Revelation, Cone says, "is the epistemological justification of a community's claims about ontological reality." The theologian's task is to make intelligible the community's view of God and man by making "a rational analysis of revelation so that the presuppositional character of Christian theology will be clear from the outset."[137]

After an amazing exercise in eclectics in which Cone says black theology will take certain elements from a variety of positions concerning the understanding of revelation--positions ranging from the "so-called Barthian school" to general revelation--we find that the basic presupposition in black theology is the reality of the biblical God.[138] This is in spite of the fact that earlier Cone says black theology agrees with contemporary theology, that divine revelation is not the rational discovery of God's attributes or assent to infallible biblical propositions, nor yet an aspect of human self-consciousness. Rather, revelation has to do with God--with God's personal relationship with men and women, with God's divine will in history.

The interesting thing about Cone's approach from the point of view of this critique of revelation as the foundation of theology, is the way he claims to define revelation "on the one hand retaining the essence of the biblical emphasis, and on the other hand being relevant to the situation of oppressed black people."[139] Indeed, at times it would seem that Cone had adopted the correla-

tive method of understanding revelation. The main
thesis of his GOD OF THE OPPRESSED is, he claims,
to point out that "one's social and historical
context decides not only the questions we address
to God but also the mode or form of the answers
given to the questions."[140]   Because racists can
agree with revelation as God's self-disclosure,
blacks must understand it as God's self-disclosure
to the oppressed of the land.   Blacks today are
the oppressed of the land and, therefore, the contemporary equivalent of the oppressed or poor of
the Bible.   Because God's self-disclosure has become known in the history of the oppressed of
Israel and decisively in the Oppressed One, Jesus
Christ, it is impossible to say anything about
Christ without seeing him as being involved in the
contemporary liberation of all oppressed people.
There can be no revelation without a condition of
oppression, which in turn opens to the possibility
of liberation.   The God of black theology is the
God of and for the oppressed of the land; this God
is available to the oppressed through the process
of liberation.   As Cone puts it, "God not only reveals to the oppressed their divine right to break
the chains [of oppression] by any means necessary,
but also assures them that their work in their own
liberation is God's own work."[141]

Whether or not there is knowledge of God independent of the Bible is for Cone a nonquestion. He
deals with it in the same way he deals with his
absolute identification of black with the oppressed and white with the oppressor: The theologian cannot deal with the "what if;" he can be
concerned only with the "what is."   "It is not his
task to settle logical problems unrelated to the
affairs of men.   It is his task to speak to his
times, pointing to God's revelation in the events
around him." In the same way that, in fact, whites
are the oppressors and blacks are the oppressed,
so general revelation primarily applies to oppressed people; whether it applies to others, according to Cone, is not important. To the extent

that blacks rebel against ungodly treatment, God has made himself known. There is no need to read the Bible to know that human enslavement is ungodly.[142]

Cone tried hard, especially in GOD OF THE OPPRESSED to bring together black experience and the Bible as the key sources of black theology. He also admits that the tradition and history of Western Christianity cannot be ignored. He makes the following qualification, however: "...Our study of that tradition must be done in the light of the Word disclosed in Scripture as interpreted by black people."[143] Ultimately, study of black experience, for Cone, would have to come under the same qualification. For example the black theologian, J. Deotis Roberts, claims that Cone's Barthianism curtails any meaningful dialogue with African theologians who are taking seriously their precolonial religious tradition; in light of this criticism, Cone makes a gesture toward admitting universal revelation. But it is only a gesture and he quickly draws back again within his christocentric and biblically oriented understanding of revelation.[144]

Black experience and Scripture find their union in affirming a transcendent reality which prevents black theology from becoming a mere cultural history of black people. Cone states, "For black people that transcendent reality is none other than Jesus Christ, of whom Scripture speaks. The Bible is the witness of God's self-disclosure in Jesus Christ. Thus the black experience requires that Scripture be a source of black theology."[145]

Cone makes a distinction between Scripture as a source of black theology and Jesus as its content. He then identifies Jesus as "the eternal event of liberation in the divine person who makes freedom a constituent of human existence." From this emerges "the interdependence of Jesus and the black experience." The conclusion Cone draws from

all of this is: "Truly to speak of the black experience is to speak of Jesus." He even goes so
far as to say, "The convergence of Jesus Christ
and black experience is the meaning of the
Incarnation." Cone's reasoning is as follows:

> Because God became man in Jesus Christ,
> he disclosed the divine will to be with
> humanity in our wretchedness. And because
> we blacks accept his presence in Jesus as
> the true definition of our humanity,
> blackness and divinity are dialectically
> bound together as one reality. This is
> the theological meaning of the paradoxi-
> cal assertion about the primacy of the
> black experience and Jesus Christ as wit-
> nessed in Scripture.[146]

For all his claims about black experience,
Cone ends up with a positivistic biblical understanding of revelation--this time with a polemic
twist. Before leaving the question of revelation,
some mention should be made about God's identification of black with the oppressed and white with
the oppressor, and his limiting of God's self-
disclosure to the oppressed. One might think that
blackness is a metaphor for the universal humanity
available to all people, but when Cone states that
the black man's sin was that of having tried to
love the white man on his own terms when what he
should have done was kill him, one senses a strong
racial identity.[147]

Rosemary Ruether criticizes Cone's simplistic
identification of whites with oppressors and
blacks with the oppressed in this way:

> Cone's oppressor/oppressed dialectic of-
> fers no comparable concept of fidelity of
> the elect people to an intrinsic standard
> of righteousness, which would judge them-
> selves, and not merely judge others.
> Rather, the righteousness of the black

man becomes automatic, inherent in the
situation of oppression as an 'inalien-
able right.' The white man becomes the
unself-critical 'righteous one.'[148]

The same criticism leveled against the Latin-
American liberation theologians would hold concerning Cone's limiting God's availability to a
particular group. The only difference is that Cone
identifies them by class, employing scientific social analysis. Cone's views on possible reconciliation will be examined in light of his eschatological position.

Cone's eschatological stance follows logically
from his positivistic and polemical understanding
of revelation. Rightly, Cone points out that no
eschatological perspective is sufficient that does
not challenge the present order. Black theology
suggests that when people really believe in the
resurrection of Christ and take seriously the
promise revealed through him, they cannot be satisfied with the present reality of injustice that
reconciles the oppressed to unjust treatment. Not
to fight this evil is to deny the resurrection.
In his BLACK THEOLOGY OF LIBERATION, Cone claims
that blacks now believe that they can do something
to change the world and they are determined to do
so. He says that blacks have had their fill of
singing about pearly gates, golden streets and
long white robes. Their voices are hoarse from
singing songs about heaven, but their poverty and
misery are still with them.[149] The question is,
what is to be done?

Cone insists that liberation is more than the
recognition that iron shackles are inhuman; it is
also the willingness to do what is necessary to
break the chains. It is self-determination in
history and laying claim to that which rightfully
belongs to humanity. And yet, Cone cautions, it
is not limited to what is possible in history.[150]
Therefore, "It does not matter that white people

have all the guns and that militarily speaking, we
have no chance of winning," says Cone. Those "who
die for freedom have not died in vain; they will
see the Kingdom of God."[151]

We can see in Cone an eschatological switch
similar to the one we detected in Rubem Alves.
From the radical "the mistake the black man made
was that he tried to love the white man on his own
terms, when what he should have done was kill
him," we find Cone saying in the GOD OF THE
OPPRESSED:

> Indeed what can the oppressed blacks to-
> day do in order to break the power of the
> Pentagon? Of course, we may 'play' revo-
> lutionary and delude ourselves that we
> can do battle against the atomic bomb.
> Usually when the reality of the political
> situation dawns upon the oppressed, those
> who have no vision from another world
> tend to give up in despair. But those
> who have heard about the coming of the
> Lord Jesus and have a vision of crossing
> on the other side of Jordan, are not ter-
> ribly disturbed about what happens in
> Washington D.C..... Black people can
> struggle because they truly believe that
> one day they will be taken out of their
> misery.[152]

Cone denies that such a position as this,
expressed so often in the songs and sermons of
black people, was an "opiate." Rather, "it was
black people's vision of a new identity for themselves.... This vision of Jesus as the Coming One
who will take them back to heaven held people together mentally as they struggled physically to
make real the future in their present."[153] The
final victory will take place with the Second Coming of Christ. In the meantime Christians, according to Cone, are called to suffer with God in the
fight against evil. "This vocation," he insists

again, "is not a passive endurance of injustice but, rather, a political and social praxis of liberation in the world, relieving the suffering of the little ones and proclaiming that God has freed them to struggle for the fulfillment of humanity."154 Cone admits that the continued existence of black suffering offers a serious challenge to the biblical and black faith, but it does not negate it. And yet, in all of this the hope for a better world here and now seems very remote. The future breaks into the present, but only to assure those suffering that the future Kingdom will be possessed. Especially when this perspective is combined with the rigid restrictions which Cone places on any black/white reconciliation, the outlook for liberation and human development here and now seems next to impossible. Concerning reconciliation, Cone states:

> When whites undergo the true experience of conversion wherein they die to whiteness and are reborn anew in order to struggle against whiteness and for liberation of the oppressed, there is a place for them in the black struggle of freedom.... But it must be made absolutely clear that it is the black community that decides both the authenticity of white conversion and also the place these converts will play in the black struggle for freedom.... White converts, if there are any to be found, must be made to realize that they are like babies who have barely learned how to walk and talk.155

Cone says that white conversion must be looked upon as God's gift of blackness made possible through the presence of the divine in the social context of black existence. It is God's gift and yet Cone warns that a word about reconciliation too soon or at the wrong time only grants whites more power to oppress black people.156 So even God's gift is rigidly controlled by the black community.

Alves says the oppressed must plant a tree;
Cone says they must bite the bullet--or point the
bullet at the white man's head. As for the Kingdom, Cone, using the Exodus model, sees God's people being led from the slavery of whiteness,
through a path of suffering, to the Promised Land
of reborn humanity. But the God of the Bible not
only leads his people out of whiteness, he comes
to destroy whiteness, to abolish its works and
pomps and overthrow its evil dominion so that the
true Kingdom may arise. The resurrection to blackness is enjoyed, first of all, by the black-skin-
ned Chosen People, but through them it is extended
to the gentiles, the white-skinned oppressors,
who, through the black Israel may find their false
selves overthrown in order to receive through the
black man a resurrection and restored humanity.157
This is the Kingdom of God, according to Cone. We
must now look at the Church's role in this theological scheme.

Although Cone asserts that what he writes as
black theology is what he believes to be the faith
of the black church community, and therefore black
theology is Church theology, still he has not
worked out an ecclesiology in any detail. Consistent with his Barthian view, the Church is the
place where the Word of God is preached. In his
early writings, Cone could see little room in the
black church for the black liberation struggle. He
suggested that, in political matters, it would be
well for black Christians to turn from theology to
those ideologies and movements in the cause of
black liberation which offer direction and definite programs. He even states that the "real sin
of the black church and its leaders is that they
even convinced themselves that they were doing the
right thing by advocating the obedience to white
oppression as a means of entering at death the
future age of heavenly bliss."158 Later he wrote
that the black church taught survival, that is, "a
way of remaining physically alive in a situation
of oppression without losing one's dignity."159

In GOD OF THE OPPRESSED, Cone outlines the requirements for the Church to be the true Church of Jesus Christ. The faith it verbalizes is not enough. It must live in the world on the basis of what it proclaims. He states:

> ... The mission of the Church is defined by its proclamation, and the proclamation is authenticated by the mission. For the sake of the mission of the Church in the world, we must continually ask, What actions deny the Truth disclosed in Jesus Christ? Where should the line be drawn? Can the Church of Jesus Christ be racist and Christian at the same time? Can the Church of Jesus Christ be politically, socially, and economically identified with the structures of oppression and also be a servant of Christ? Can the Church of Jesus Christ fail to make liberation of the poor the center of its message and work, and still remain faithful to its Lord.[160]

The answers to these questions are, of course, obvious. The response that Cone proposes I cannot disagree with: "Any interpretation of the gospel in any historical period that fails to see Jesus as the Liberator of the oppressed is heretical. Any view of the gospel that fails to understand the Church as that community of the oppressed is not Christian and is thus heretical." But in determining the parameters of the oppressed in a simplistic way, I cannot agree with. Furthermore, although Cone speaks about the need of the Church to be politically, socially and economically dissociated from the structures of oppression, he offers little on how the Church as Church should make its influence felt in the process and project of liberation and development.

Except for passing reference to the need for black brothers and sisters who have suffered the pain of a broken community to seek reconciliation with one another, Cone gives little emphasis to the Church's mission to demonstrate to those outside what the Kingdom of justice and love and reconciliation is all about.[161] Furthermore, he is extremely critical of his black colleagues when they speak of such things.[162] Finally, as might be expected, Cone gives no recognition to the Church as a sacramental community celebrating the Eucharist, not only as a sign and pledge of unity and reconciliation, but as a means of achieving them here and now.

After this critique of Cone, it would appear that our initial suggestion is in fact the case: Cone's understanding of revelation is basically Barthian--positivistically biblical; his eschatological position has been tempered in a manner similar to that of Alves from violence to passivity, and his ecclesiology remains sketchy and incomplete.

2. THE THEOLOGY OF WOMEN'S LIBERATION: AN EXPLANATORY NOTE

In our consideration and critique of various theologies of liberation, there has been no specific discussion of a theology of women's liberation. I suggest that there is no single work dealing with the theology of women's liberation that could be compared in scope and detail to the work of such theologians as Gutierrez or Cone. Rosemary Ruether, Mary Daly and Letty M. Russell, to name but three, have written in the area of liberation, but my initial statement applies as well to their works. A further explanation is in order.

Ruether and Russell have both written theologies of liberation--Ruether, LIBERATION THEOLOGY;[163] Russell, HUMAN LIBERATION IN A FEMINIST PERSPECTIVE - A THEOLOGY.[164] Each, however, deals with the liberation of various groups, not just women. Russell, as the title indicates, claims to be writing from a consciously feminist perspective. Mary Daly's BEYOND GOD THE FATHER: TOWARD A PHILOSOPHY OF WOMEN'S LIBERATION,[165] on the other hand, is a philosophical study rather than a theology, at least theology as it usually is understood.

Ruether's work focuses on human liberation from the situation of the "oppressor-oppressed" relationship as this applies to Christian anti-Semitism, racism, sexism, and colonialism. Therefore, she is not concerned primarily with the theology of women's liberation. Her work fits in more with the general liberationist writings, and I could have included it there except for the following reasons: (1) Ruether relativizes the position of Jesus in her theology as the ultimate revelation of God, as was pointed out in Chapter Three, and therefore places herself at least on the boundary of doing "Christian" theology.[166] (2) Ruether's eschatological stance is so futurist oriented that there is no "time" for a structured Church. Furthermore, her "radical Christianity" is "not interested in ideas of Christ or the Kingdom...or in the church, community, or eucharist except as an expression of man."[167]

The present study admittedly is from the outset an exercise in "Christian" theology with a conscious and particular focus on the "Christian" Church. Although Ruether's LIBERATION THEOLOGY contains many valuable insights and a good critique of other liberation theologies, I feel justified nonetheless in giving a tentative "no" to Ruether's basic theological position. It is for this reason that I have not included her more extensively in my critique of liberation theology.

What is tentative on my part concerning Ruether, is definite in the case of Mary Daly. The basic affirmation of the Christian is that Jesus is Lord, that is, God is revealed in an ultimate, unique and definitive way in Jesus of Nazareth. This does not mean that God is available only in Jesus, as our discussion on present revelation has amply pointed out. But Daly denies that Jesus could be God's unique revelation, because he was male. She states that "...the idea of redemptive incarnation uniquely in the form of a male savior ...is precisely what is impossible."168

As indicated earlier, Daly says her work can accurately be called philosophy. She admits however, that if theology can be torn from its function of "legitimizing patriarchy," then she is attempting to create theology as well as philosophy.169 Indeed, in Daly's work there is evidence of an understanding of revelation, eschatology and ecclesiology. On none of these basic issues is her understanding compatible with the position I have developed in this work. Indeed, from the general tone of her book BEYOND GOD THE FATHER, it seems unlikely that Daly would want to contribute to a reformulation of the Christian Church's mission.

Concerning revelation, continuing what has been mentioned above about the non-uniqueness of God's revelation in Jesus, Daly says that "this is not to deny the charismatic and revelatory power of the personality of Jesus or of other persons." She further suggests that as a uniquely masculine image and language for divinity loses its credibility, "so also the idea of a single divine incarnation in a human being of the male sex may give way in the religious consciousness to an increased awareness of the power of Being in all persons [emphasis mine]."170 This, it appears, is Daly's understanding of revelation--a type of general religious awareness. But when combined with her eschatological stance, a more specified revelation in an Antichrist is envisioned. She states, "In its depth, because it contains a dynamic that drives beyond Christolatry, the women's movement does point to, seek, and constitute the primordial, always present and future Antichrist." She then identifies the Antichrist and the "Second Coming of Women" as synonymous. "This Second Coming is not a return of Christ," she says, "but a new arrival of female presence, once strong and powerful, but enchained since the dawn of patriarchy."[171]

The "kingdom," for Daly, will come about by a "qualitative leap toward psychic androgyny."[172] Only radical feminism can act as "the final cause" in bringing this about, because "of all revolutionary causes it alone opens up human consciousness adequately to the desire for non-hierarchical, nonoppressive society, revealing sexism as the basic model and source of oppression."[173]

Daly's ecclesiology speaks of a sisterhood as a cosmic church which is beyond church.[174] In this new convenant society, women, participating in power of being, hear and speak their own new word while men, who have stolen the power of speech and made all language a system of false words, can learn at least not to dialogue, for it is too soon for that, but listen and hear, knowing that this is how to find their own promise, and to discover at last the way to adequate speech.[175]

From this brief examination of Daly's position on revelation, eschatology and ecclesiology, regardless of what contribution BEYOND GOD THE FATHER may or may not make to women's liberation in general, I suggest it has no part to play in the present reformulation of the Christian Church's missionary responsibility in the areas of of liberation and development. A theology of women's liberation has still to be written.

Concerning Letty Russell's liberation theology, I find many parallels between her work and my own. She attempts to deal in a broadly ecumenical way with the same basic question I have treated, her work under the aegis of liberation and from a feminist perspective, mine under the aegis of development and (inescapably) from a masculine perspective. There is a tendency in her work, as with that of most liberationists, to rely heavily on biblical parallels. Nonetheless, her work, HUMAN LIBERATION IN A FEMINIST PERSPECTIVE, goes beyond a specific theology of women's liberation and could perhaps be considered in a discussion of the theology of liberation in general.

These comments do not minimize the importance of the theology of women's liberation but, rather, point to a need for further elaboration. As is emphasized in this study, there can be no true integral development in a society or church which is sexist. Certainly in carrying out the Church's mission, women have carried and continue to carry more than their share. For interesting reflections on this fact, I suggest Sister Albertus Magnus McGrath's WHAT A MODERN CATHOLIC BELIEVES ABOUT WOMEN, especially Chapter Seven, "Revolutions, Sunday School, Suffrage," and Chapter Eight, "Women as the 'Niggers' of the Church."[176]

SUMMARY OF CHAPTER FIVE

Chapter Five presents a critical analysis of the theological methods employed by leading proponents of the currently popular theological movements--revolution and liberation. The theology of revolution differs from liberation only in degree, being more radical in its approach.

Shaull is taken to represent the theology of revolution; Laurentin, Alves, Segundo, Gutierrez and Cone are chosen to illustrate the theology of liberation. Paul Lehmann's "contextual/koinonia" theological approach is shown to have had considerable influence on these authors, and, like Lehmann, they rely heavily on biblical parallels.

The critical analysis of the theology of these selected authors is directed specifically at their understanding of the concepts of revelation, eschatology and ecclesiology. In both the theologies of liberation and revolution, revelation is understood to be either biblically positivistic or contextually identifiable only within specific movements or groups. In the latter case, God is proposed to be available only to those who are participating actively in some revolutionary activity. In a similar way, their eschatology tends to make the Kingdom the result of radical temporal action associated with the liberation of the oppressed, at one extreme, or completely in God's hand through promised deliverance, at the other. In both revelation and eschatology, Gutierrez, attempting to steer between the extremes, takes a quite radical position on one level of discussion but qualifies it considerably on another level.

In ecclesiology, the majority of these theologians "write off" the institutional Church as being hopelessly identified with the oppressors and, in turn, identify the "true" Church with small, elite groups working for liberation. Unity in the Church at present is impossible because of class conflict. The result of such an approach is an ambivalence that can dangerously confuse theology with ideology.

NOTES ON CHAPTER FIVE

[1]See Lehmann, ETHICS IN A CHRISTIAN CONTEXT (New York: Harper and Row, 1963), pp. 78, 99. See also James B. Nelson, "The Moral Significance of the Church in Contemporary Protestant Contextual

Ethics," JOURNAL OF ECUMENICAL STUDIES 4 (Winter, 1967): 66-91. Much of the following is based on Nelson's discussion of Lehmann.

[2]"The Foundation and Pattern of Christian Behavior," in CHRISTIAN FAITH AND SOCIAL ACTION, J. Hutchinson, ed. (New York: Charles Scribner's Sons, 1953), p. 97. Also see relevant discussion in ETHICS IN CHRISTIAN CONTEXT, pp. 23-25.

[3]ETHICS IN CHRISTIAN CONTEXT, p. 25.

[4]IBID., p. 159. Also see "The Foundation and Pattern of Christian Ethics," p. 107f.

[5]IBID., p. 350. The proper understanding of conscience is of prime importance for Lehmann. He states, "Fundamentally and ultimately, the validity of a Protestant as against a Roman Catholic account of ethics, and of Christian as against philosophical ethics, stands or falls upon the issue: Which account of conscience is correct?" Lehmann's "Protestant versus Catholic" account of ethics appears to be an oversimplification. Many Protestants subscribe to some type of natural law ethics. This is the basic question beneath the current discussion within the World Council of Churches between a theology of revolution and a theology of responsible society. See the study of the question by Carl-Hendric Grenholm. CHRISTIAN SOCIAL ETHICS IN A REVOLUTIONARY AGE: AN ANALYSIS OF THE SOCIAL ETHICS OF JOHN C. BENNETT, HEINZ-DIETRICH WENDLAND AND RICHARD SHAULL (Uppsala: Verbum, 1973).

[6]"The Foundation and Pattern of Christian Ethics," p. 107.

[7]CHRISTIAN SOCIAL ETHICS IN A REVOLUTIONARY AGE, pp. 220-21.

[8]IBID., pp. 154-159. Lehmann discusses this matter in light of criticisms of his position by

John Bennett. My own answer to this question will be presented in Chapter Six.

[9]See "The Revolutionary Challenge to Church and Theology," an Address given at the Geneva Conference on Church and Society, reprinted in THEOLOGY TODAY 23 (January 1967): 479.

[10]"Christian Faith as Scandal in a Technocratic World," in NEW THEOLOGY NO. 6, pp. 130-31. Shaull has been influenced via Lehmann by Herbert Marcuse, THE ONE-DIMENSIONAL MAN (Boston: Beacon Press, 1964), to the effect that technology can contribute to the well being and fulfillment of man only as it is challenged by revolution.

[11]The statement, echoing Lehmann, occurs in "Revolutionary Challenge to the Church," p. 479. Denys Munby asks if the concept is far too vague and general, and if it does not vaguely regard God as identical with the process of history and its crises. See relevant discussion in J. M. Lochman, "Ecumenical Theology of Revolution," NEW THEOLOGY NO. 6, esp. pp. 108-16.

[12]See "Does Religion Demand Social Change?" THEOLOGY TODAY 26 (April 1969): 7.

[13]See "A Theological Perspective on Human Liberation," in WHEN ALL ELSE FAILS, ed. IDOC (Philadelphia: Pilgrim Press, 1970), p. 53. Also see Shaull, "La forma de la Iglesia en la nueve diaspora," CHRISTIANISMO Y SOCIEDAD 2 (1968): 3-17.

[14]See Trutz Rendtorff and Heinz Eduard Todt, THEOLOGIE DER REVOLUTION (Frankfurt am Main: Suhrkamp Verlag, 1968, 1969), p. 67.

[15]See CHRISTIAN SOCIAL ETHICS IN A REVOLUTIONARY AGE, pp. 280-81.

[16]Novak, A THEOLOGY OF RADICAL POLITICS (New York: Herder and Herder, 1969), p. 75.

[17]"The Revolutionary Challenge to Church," p. 475. Also see Peter Berger and Richard Neuhaus, MOVEMENT AND REVOLUTION (Garden City, New York: Doubleday, 1970). Neuhaus attempts to outline a theory of "just revolution" analogous to the classical "just war" theory.

[18]THEOLOGY OF LIBERATION, p. 250, n. 124. Gutierrez distances his own attempt to formulate a theology of liberation from this theology of revolution. Francois Houtart and Andre Rousseau, THE CHURCH AND REVOLUTION, p. 220, claim, however, that Gutierrez has been greatly influenced by Richard Shaull.

[19]"Revolutionary Challenge to Church," p. 475. With little hope for the success of total revolution, Shaull proposes a gradual change of the prevailing system, i.e., "permanent revolution," by concentrated attacks on limited goals within the established social order. For discussion of the ambiguity resulting from the use of the language of guerrilla strategy, see van Leeuwen, DEVELOPMENT THROUGH REVOLUTION, pp. 299-303. Van Leeuwen sees in the "more or less metaphorical" use of the language a translation in which "the violent outlook of guerrilla warfare tends to be veiled and, perhaps, transformed into a number of nonviolent choices."

[20]"Christian Faith as Scandal," pp. 132-33. Because it is within these communities that knowledge of God's action in history comes to light, it is also here that the goals for the revolutionary change can be discerned. Shaull writes, "The shape of the new order becomes most clear, not through the definition of a set of ideals, but in a living community, which expresses and at the same time points to a new reality of social existence, and provides a laboratory in which its diverse aspects can be experimentally worked out." See "Revolution: Heritage and Contemporary Option," in CONTAINMENT AND CHANGE, by Carl Oglesby

and Richard Shaull (New York: Macmillan Co., 1967), p. 246. Shaull's position here, again, is similar to Paul Lehmann's. An action is right if, and only if, it corresponds to God's action in history and that knowledge of how God acts in history, and therefore also of which action is right, can only be given to those who are within the koinonia. John Bennett has pointed out the dilemma in such a position: "If koinonia is a kind of cell group of Christians working together in a revolutionary crisis (as in Shaull's conception), it may be necessary to choose between such groups. This would involve some criteria. If the koinonia is the larger church, it is in continual need of reformation in the light of some criteria." See CHRISTIAN SOCIAL ETHICS IN A CHANGING WORLD, p. 367f.

[21]See "Christian Faith as Scandal," p. 132. Shaull's criticism of the institutional Church goes so far as to suggest establishment of completely independent Christian groups who define their identity over-against the institutional Church. Also see "The Christian World Mission in a Technocratic Era," in THE ECUMENICAL REVIEW 17 (July 1965): 212. Trutz Rendtorff claims the separation from the established or institutional Church is the very starting point of the theology of revolution. See Rendtorff and Todt, THEOLOGIE DER REVOLUTION, p. 61ff. Also see the relevant discussion in Grenholm, CHRISTIAN SOCIAL ETHICS, pp. 251-252.

[22]"Christian Faith as Scandal," p. 134.

[23]A clarification on the term "ideology" is necessary here. I employ it here in the sense defined by Karl Mannheim, IDEOLOGY AND UTOPIA, Louis Wirth and Edward Shils, trans. (New York: Harcourt, Brace, and World, 1966). It is by its nature untruthful, since it entails a "masking" or "veiling" of unavowed and unperceived motives or interests and results in a "false consciousness."

Shaull, on the other hand, sees the task of theology to be that of giving revolutionaries guidance in their social involvement, which means contribution to the formulation of "secular ideologies," which, among other things, contains a conception of goals and nature of history: "Theological reflections on history will be most relevant to the ideological struggle when it is willing to become something of ideology itself." See CONTAINMENT AND CHANGE, p. 226ff. For an analysis of the exact sense in which Shaull uses the concept of "ideology," see Grenholm, CHRISTIAN SOCIAL ETHICS, pp. 225-26. It is clear that Shaull employs the concept in a nonpejorative sense. The possibility of misunderstanding and abuse of the concept seems inherent, however. Gutierrez makes this criticism of theologies of revolution. See "Liberation Movements and Theology," CONCILIUM 93 (1974): 138. The Christians for Socialism Movement in Latin America makes it clear that they believe theology should justify and bolster a particular ideology. See "Final Document" in CHRISTIANS FOR SOCIALISM, John Drury, trans., John Eagleson, ed. (Maryknoll, New York: Orbis Books, 1975), pp. 160-75. Also see Jose Miranda, MARX AND THE BIBLE, John Eagleson, trans. (Maryknoll, New York: Orbis Books, 1974). Miranda argues that through Marx, the "way of thinking" proper to the Bible can finally be recovered. See the critical review of Miranda's work by the biblical scholar John McKenzie, JOURNAL OF BIBLICAL LITERATURE 94 (June 1975): 280-81.

[24]Assmann, THEOLOGY FOR A NOMAD CHURCH, p. 88.

[25]IBID., p. 90.

[26]Segundo, THE LIBERATION OF THEOLOGY, J. Drury, trans. (Maryknoll, New York: Orbis Books, 1976), p. 147. The Shaull quote is from "Revolutionary Change in Theological Perspective," in CHRISTIAN SOCIAL ETHICS IN A CHANGING WORLD, p. 36.

[27]Segundo, LIBERATION OF THEOLOGY, pp. 147-48.

[28]EL EVANGELIO SEGUN JUDAS (Santiago, Chile: Pineda Libros, 1972), p. 86. Quoted by Jose Migues Bonino, DOING THEOLOGY IN A REVOLUTIONARY SITUATION, p. 106.

[29]Charles Underhill Quinn, trans. (Maryknoll, New York: Orbis Books, 1972).

[30]IBID., p. xii. Laurentin is one who maintains that underdevelopment is the by-product of development. "Development...is concentrating wealth and brainpower in a kind of a metropolis-satellite structure which is profitable for the metropolis but deadly for the satellite." (p. x).

[31]IBID., p. 16.

[32]IBID., p. xv.

[33]IBID., p. 54.

[34]IBID., Laurentin examines these various "sources" in detail in Part Three, (Chapters 5, 6, and 7), entitled "Sources for Answering the Question."

[35]IBID., p. 210.

[36]IBID., p. 55. The former is similar to the position I discussed at the beginning of Chapter Four as a "social evolutionary" view; the latter is similar to Shaull's "discontinuous" view of history.

[37]IBID., p.57.

[38]IBID., p. 60.

[39]IBID., p. 101.

[40]IBID., pp. 132-33.

[41]IBID., p. 21.

[42]IBID., pp. 208-209.

[43]IBID., p. 209.

[44]A THEOLOGY OF HUMAN HOPE (Washington, D.C.: Corpus Books, 1969); TOMORROW'S CHILD: IMAGINATION, CREATIVY, AND REBIRTH OF CULTURE (New York: Harper and Row, 1972).

[45]THEOLOGY OF HUMAN HOPE, p. xiii.

[46]IBID., p. 29.

[47]IBID., The following discussion is based on the section of Chapter One entitled, "The Language of the 'Theology of Hope': From a Past that is Rejected to a Future that is Offered," pp. 55-68.

[48]Langdon Gilkey, REAPING THE WHIRLWIND: A CHRISTIAN INTERPRETATION OF HISTORY (New York: Seabury Press, 1976), agrees with Alves on this point and singles him out from among what he calls recent eschatological theologians--theologians of liberation and politics--for his attempt to take the present seriously (pp. 232-33; also pp. 407-08, n. 117).

[49]The following discussion is based on the section of Chapter One entitled, "The Language of Messianic Humanism: Humanization as a Gift," pp. 87-100.

[50]The following discussion is based on Chapter Six, "Theology as a Language of Freedom," pp. 159-168.

[51]IBID., pp. 123-25.

[52]See "Theology and the Liberation of Man," in IN SEARCH OF A THEOLOGY OF DEVELOPMENT (Geneva: SODEPAX, n.d.), pp. 75-92. The following discus-

sion is based on pp. 85-90. Evident in Alves' position, more than in the other liberation theologians' position, is the influence of the thought of Marcuse. It is the technological and repressive society that has emerged from capitalism rather than the capitalist relations of production that is the focus of Alves' critique. Utopian thinking, of course, reflects the thinking of Mannheim and Bloch.

53TOMORROW'S CHILD, pp. 143-44. Alves speaks of the revolutionary mood of the middle and late sixties when "revolutionaries and prophets were born, filled with the confidence that their power was enough to break the old values and create new ones." But their hopes were frustrated: "The creative act was impossible. Why? Because they were powerless." Also see p. 187.

54IBID., pp. 147-48. Alves admits that playing, celebrating, dancing, experiencing wonder, rediscovering the body are all necessary; they are part of the aperitif. Yet they cannot become "substitutive-gratifications" which make the counter-culture community forget about suffering and pain in the world. If the community is to carry out the creative intention to which it has been called, suffering and hope cannot be separated: "Suffering without hope produces resentment and despair. Hope without suffering creates illusions, naivete, and drunkenness" (p. 203). Alves' combining of the two still seems to result only in "patient expectation."

55IBID., pp. 191-94. Again Alves turns to the Bible, for in the biblical world, he claims, "one hopes for the future because one has already seen the creative event taking place in the past" (p. 196).

56IBID., p. 199. Alves places himself in line with Paul Lehmann [and, I would add, Richard Shaull], who, Alves says, is the only contemporary ethical thinker who has perceived clearly that the biblical answer to the ethical question, "What shall I do?" is given in the faith community where "the logic of death and resurrection--or the logic of creativity--has assumed space and time and has determined the style and direction of human inter-relatedness...The question of good is really the question of <u>koinonia</u>, the community which embodies the messianic thrust of the creative intention." Alves adds, "Only the oppressed can be creative." Alves comes very close to Shaull's position, ex-cept that Alves no longer 'sees the Christian as the "revolutionary guerrilla" as Shaull does. Rather, to sow the seeds of highest hope is the only political task now possible for the Christian (p. 197).

[57]IBID., p. 204.

[58]IBID., p. 198. Alves says that the tragedy of revolution was that it lacked the positive vision of a new future for mankind. That freedom follows naturally upon the act of dissolution, cannot be supported by historical evidence. He quotes with approval Pierre Furter, L'IMAGINATION CREATRICE, LA VIOLENCE ET LE CHANGEMENT (Cuerna-vaca, Mexico: CIDOC, 1968), Cuaderno 14: "To imag-ine and believe that the revolutionary act will inaugurate a radically new time implies a magical attitude which does not satisfy the canons of a rigorous reflection, and which is dangerous for a responsible political action." This statement stands in direct contradiction to the position taken by most of the liberation theologians--the "totally new man" in a "totally new society." I suggest that to this extent Alves' liberation the-ology has never been liberated.

[59]Segundo, THE LIBERATION OF THEOLOGY, pp. 145-47. Segundo's criticism of Alves will be examined in detail in our critique of Segundo's own position.

[60]See "Theology and the Liberation of Man," p. 88. Alves holds to a "broad" understanding of Church as I discussed it in Chapter Three. I would have the same criticism of his position as I voiced against that of Baum and Stackhouse.

[61]THEOLOGY OF HUMAN HOPE, p. 66.

[62]Segundo's theological enterprise consists of five volumes in this series. Translated by John Drury (Maryknoll, New York: Orbis Books), the series includes the following titles: Vol. I, THE COMMUNITY CALLED CHURCH (1973); Vol. II, GRACE AND THE HUMAN CONDITION (1973): Vol. III., OUR IDEA OF GOD (1974); Vol. IV., THE SACRAMENTS TODAY (1974); Vol. V., EVOLUTION AND GUILT (1974).

[63]COMMUNITY CALLED CHURCH, p. 29. Segundo admits that although the Christian is not the only one to enter into this plan, he is the one who knows it. He has this knowledge of the plan because "he has received not only redemption but also revelation" (p. 11). "Thanks to the latter revelation, we can say that the community called Church possesses the secret of what is happening in human history, knows its warp and woof, and understands the stakes that are being played out" (p. 25).

[64]IBID., pp. 64-65.

[65]IBID., p. 68.

[66]IBID., p. 125.

[67]OUR IDEA OF GOD, p. 175.

[68]COMMUNITY CALLED CHURCH, pp. 124-15.

[69]CONCILIUM 96 (1974): 105-23.

[70]GRACE AND THE HUMAN CONDITION, pp. 155-58. The quote occurs in Lehmann's ETHICS IN CHRISTIAN CONTEXT, p. 99.

[71]Segundo, IBID., pp. 82-86.

[72]IBID., p. 133. The quote is from Art. 39 of Vatican II's CHURCH IN THE MODERN WORLD.

[73]"Capitalism--Socialism," p. 112. I disagree with Segundo that Gutierrez speaks of construction of the Kingdom by the human family. Gutierrez's position is much more nuanced (or ambiguous), as will become clear when we discuss his work. Assmann's position appears to be much closer to Segundo's. See his "Political Commitment in the Context of the Class Struggle," CONCILIUM 84 (1973): 93-101. Also see his THEOLOGY OF A NOMAD CHURCH, pp. 67-68, and criticism of Assmann by Juan Carlos Scannone, "The Theology of Liberation --Evangelic or Ideological?" CONCILIUM 93 (1974): 150-51.

[74]GRACE AND THE HUMAN CONDITION, p. 136. Gutierrez gives a much more satisfactory explanation of the conciliar statement, "earthly progress must be carefully distinguished from the growth of Christ's Kingdom." See THEOLOGY OF LIBERATION, pp. 168-72. Yet in a note (p. 186, n. 88), Gutierrez refers to an "excellent article" by Segundo, "Evangelizacion y humanizacion," in PERSPECTIVAS PARA EL DIALOGO, No. 41 (March 1970): 9-17. In that article, Segundo proposes three possible interpretations of Art. 39 of CHURCH IN THE MODERN WORLD: 1. The ends of temporal progress and those of the Kingdom are different; 2. the ends of temporal progress and the ends of the Kingdom are the same; 3. the difference being that the Christians "know." The third is distinguished from the second only in the affirmation that the Church also contributes to history "the content of revelation."

[75]EVOLUTION AND GUILT, p. 6. Segundo says that his comments in Vol. 5, along with Vol. 2, represent the basic outline of a Christian moral theology. Vol. 5, however, traces the main lines of

what would be a "theology of politics." In other words," Segundo states, "it is the political version of a theology of grace, dealing with the gift of God coupled with man's effort in history."

76IBID., pp. 110-11.

77"Capitalism--Socialism," p. 105. The following discussion is based on pp. 105-08. Segundo gives reference here, once again, to Gutierrez (and Assmann), yet Gutierrez makes no such sweeping claim for his liberation theology. See his THEOLOGY OF LIBERATION, pp. 3-15.

78IBID., pp. 107-08. Actually, Segundo makes the point in the form of a rhetorical question, but his intention is clear: "Would it not be possible and evangelical to invert his order of values and to declare, with the gospel itself, that the sabbath is made for man and not man for the sabbath? Could this statement not be given the only possible translation, namely that human life in society, liberated as far as possible from alienations, constitutes the absolute value, and that all religious institutions, all dogmas, all the sacraments, and all the ecclesiastical authorities, have only a relative, that is, a functional value?"

79Metz, L'HOMME, ANTHRÔPOCENTRIQUE CHRETIENNE (Paris, 1971), pp. 111, 136. Quoted by Segundo in "Capitalism--Socialism," pp. 110-11.

80Moltmann, "Dieu dans la revolution," in DISCUSSION SUR LA THEOLOGIE DE LA REVOLUTION (Paris, 1972), p. 72. Quoted in Segundo, "Capitalism--Socialism," p. 111.

81"Capitalism--Socialism," p. 112.

82THE LIBERATION OF THEOLOGY, p. 142. The following discussion is based on pp. 142-46.

[83]IBID., p. 143.

[84]IBID., pp. 145-146. Quote is from A THEOLOGY OF HUMAN HOPE, p. 116.

[85]REAPING THE WHIRLWIND, p. 276.

[86]THEOLGY OF HUMAN HOPE, p. 127.   Quoted in LIBERATION OF THEOLOGY, pp. 146-47.

[87]LIBERATION OF THEOLOGY, p. 150.

[88]"Capitalism--Socialism," p. 117.   Jacques Ellul's response to one of the advocates of a theology of revolution who was calling for a new propheticism--"not verbal but a responsible propheticism"--was: "Prophets of what and of whom?   What biblical prophet substituted revolutionary activity for proclamation of the judgment of God?" Every visionary sect, Ellul points out, has pretended to be prophetic--which is a case of confusing prophetism with verbal delirium!"   See VIOLENCE (New York: Seabury Press, 1969), pp. 49-50.

[89]IBID., p. 120.

[90]IBID., p. 121.

[91]IBID., p. 123.

[92]See Moltmann, "An Open Letter to Jose Miguez Bonino," p. 58

[93]COMMUNITY CALLED CHURCH, pp. 10-11.

[94]IBID., pp. 73-76. The following discussion is based on Chapter Four, "Obligation of the Ecclesial Community," pp.78-86.   Also see discussion of Segundo's position by Jose Miguez Bonino, DOING THEOLOGY IN A REVOLUTIONARY SITUATION, pp. 64-65.

[95]IBID., pp. 96-97.

[96]Sister Caridad Inda and John Eagleson, trans. and ed. (Maryknoll, New York: Orbis Books, 1973).

[97]"An Open Letter to Jose Miguez Bonino," p. 59. For a comparison and contrast of the basic tenets of political and liberation theology from one perspective, see "Political Theology and Liberation Theology: An Inquiry into their Fundamental Meaning," by Francis P. Fiorenza in LIBERATION, REVOLUTION AND FREEDOM: THEOLOGICAL PERSPECTIVES, Proceeding of the College Theological Society, Thomas M. McFadden, ed. (New York: Crossroad Books - Seabury Press, 1975), pp. 3-25.

[98]THEOLOGY OF LIBERATION, p. x.

[99]IBID., p. 7. Barth's quote is from AGAINST THE STREAM: SHORTER POST-WAR WRITINGS, 1946-52 (New York: Philosophical Library, 1954).

[100]THEOLOGY OF LIBERATION, p. 12. The Congar quote is from SITUATION ET TACHES PRESENTES DE LA THEOLOGIE (Paris: Les Editions du Cerf, 1967), p. 42.

[101]THEOLOGY OF LIBERATION, pp. 49-50.

[102]IBID., pp. 70-71.

[103]IBID., pp. 194-95.

[104]IBID., p. 238.

[105]See "Liberation Movements and Theology," CONCILIUM 93 (1974): 135-56. I make use of this more recent writing of Gutierrez which clarifies Chap. 10 of the THEOLOGY OF LIBERATION and therefore also clarifies his theological method. I shall also be referring to "Liberation, Theology and Proclamation," CONCILIUM 96 (1974): 57-77.

106"Liberation, Theology and Proclamation," pp. 57-59.

107IBID., p. 59.

108Berger, PYRAMIDS OF SACRIFICE, pp. 112-18. The theory and method of concientizacion, or "consciousness raising," was developed by Paulo Freire as a means by which any oppressed group is taught first to understand their own deprived condition and then (in a unity of theory and practice) to be activated politically for the revolutionary transformation of this condition. See Freire's PEDAGOGY OF THE OPPRESSED (New York: Herder and Herder, 1970).

109"Liberation, Theology and Proclamation," p. 60.

110THEOLOGY OF LIBERATION, p. 174.

111"Liberation Movement," p. 142.

112"Reflections on Theologies of Social Change," in THEOLOGY AND CHANGE: ESSAYS IN MEMORY OF ALAN RICHARDSON, R. H. Preston, ed. (London: SCM Press, 1975), pp. 157-58.

113"An Open Letter," p. 60.

114"Liberation Movements," pp. 139-41.

115IBID., p. 143.

116IBID., p. 144.

117THEOLOGY OF LIBERATION, pp. 231-32.

118IBID., pp. 233-35.

119"An Open Letter," p. 60.

120THEOLOGY OF LIBERATION, p. 237.

121See the comments of Berger on the role of myth in development in PYRAMIDS, pp. 17-31. Berger discusses the myth of growth and modernity or progress that permeates the capitalistic method of development, and the myth of revolution which is strong in the socialist model. Berger states: "The peculiar appeal of Marxism is due in important measure to its capacity for mythological synthesis" (p. 26).

122THEOLOGY OF LIBERATION, p. 238.

123RELIGION AND ALIENATION, p. 289.

124Preston, "Reflection on Theologies," p. 161. Baum, RELIGION AND ALIENATION, p. 289, voices a similar warning: "Especially if the liberation movement becomes successful and takes over the rule in a particular country, the church must remain watchful that the utopia of social justice does not turn into an ideology of the victors and defend the new establishment against the reasonable demands of the poor and the marginal."

125Preston, "Reflection on Theologies," p. 162.

126THEOLOGY OF LIBERATION. See Gutierrez' Chapter Four, "Different Responses," for a discussion of these various positions (pp. 53-58).

127IBID. See Chapter Five, "Crisis of the Distinction of Planes Model," pp. 63-73.

128IBID. See the section, "Christian Brotherhood and Class Struggle," pp. 272-79.

129IBID., p. 265.

130IBID., p. 269.

131Neuhaus, "Liberation Theology and the Captivities of Jesus," WORLDVIEW 16 (June 1973): 47.

132For a detailed presentation of preparatory
documents and correspondence, the presentations at
the conference, and an after-conference evaluation, see THEOLOGY IN THE AMERICAS, S. Torres and
J. Eagleson, eds. (Maryknoll, New York: Orbis
Books, 1976). See pp. 397-98 of this same work
for a list of articles on the conference appearing
in various periodicals. Gregory Baum's "The Christian Left at Detroit," THE ECUMENIST (September-
October, 1975) is included in the present volume,
as well as a "Preface and a Conclusion" by Robert
McAffee Brown. For an additional report by Brown,
as well as one by Beverly Wildung Harrison, see
CHRISTIANITY AND CRISIS 35 (October 17, 1975).

133Quoted by Baum in "The Christian Left at
Detroit," THEOLOGIES OF THE AMERICAS, pp. 400-01.

134A BLACK THEOLOGY OF LIBERATION (Philadelphia: J. B. Lippincott, 1970); GOD OF THE
OPPRESSED (New York: Seabury, 1975).

135(New York: Seabury Press, 1969).

136(New York: Seabury Press, 1972).

137BLACK THEOLOGY OF LIBERATION, pp. 85-86.

138IBID., p. 107.

139IBID., pp. 90-91.

140GOD OF THE OPPRESSED, p. 15.

141BLACK THEOLOGY OF LIBERATION, pp. 91-92.

142IBID., pp. 98-99.

143GOD OF THE OPPRESSED

144See Cone's defense of his own position--
often in the form of a counterattack--which appears primarily in the Notes of GOD OF THE

OPPRESSED. Concerning revelation, see p. 252, n. 38. J. Deotis Roberts, A BLACK POLITICAL THEOLOGY (Philadelphia, Westminster, 1974), in his criticism of Cone's persistent Barthianism, states: "Thus Cone's outline of the meaning of revelation --which he considers to be one his strongest points--turns out to be a most inadequate position. Black theology requires an understanding of revelation sufficiently comprehensive to deal with the pan-African context of the black religious experience.... What would be helpful is an understanding of revelation of God as manifest in all creation and all history as measured by the supreme revelation of God in the incarnation." (p. 20).

[145]GOD OF THE OPPRESSED, p. 31.

[146]IBID., pp. 34-36.

[147]BLACK THEOLOGY OF LIBERATION, pp. 100-01.

[148]Ruether, LIBERATION THEOLOGY (New York: Paulist Press, 1972), p. 138. In GOD OF THE OPPRESSED, p. 225, Cone continues this identification: "God has chosen what is black in America to shame the whites. In a society where white is equated with good and black is defined as bad, humanity and divinity mean an unqualified identification with blackness. The divine election of the oppresssed means that black people are given the power of judgment over the high and mighty whites. What else can a Christian ethic say than that the oppressed in the struggle are the concrete signs of God's presence with us today?"

[149]BLACK THEOLOGY OF LIBERATION, p. 241.

[150]GOD OF THE OPPRESSED, pp. 156-57.

[151]BLACK THEOLOGY OF LIBERATION, p. 248.

[152]GOD OF THE OPPRESSED, p. 132.

[153]IBID., p. 130,

[154]IBID., p. 177.

[155]IBID., p. 242.

[156]IBID., p. 243. Cone is especially critical of the position of Roberts' LIBERATION AND RECONCILIATION: A BLACK THEOLOGY (Philadelphia: Westminster Press, 1971). Cone states: "Roberts said what should not have been said, because he should have known that, despite his honest intention to face the truth of the gospel, white oppressors are not prepared to hear the truth, much less do it, because truth would condemn them" (p. 243).

[157]See "God in Black Theology," Chap. 4 of BLACK THEOLOGY OF LIBERATION, esp. pp. 129-50. See also Ruether's discussion of Cone in her LIBERATION THEOLOGY, esp. pp. 134-35.

[158]BLACK THEOLOGY AND BLACK POWER, p. 107.

[159]"Theological Reflections on Reconciliation," CHRISTIANITY AND CRISIS 32 (January 22, 1973): 303.

[160]GOD OF THE OPPRESSED, p. 37.

[161]IBID., p. 245. Cone states: "Therefore as black theologians, we must begin to ask, not about black people's reconciliation with white oppressors, but about our reconciliation with each other." Cone adds, "For unless we can get together with our African brothers and sisters for shaping of our future, then white capitalists in America and Europe will destroy us." It is interesting that Cone admits that in this context reconciliation precedes liberation: "For unless we are reconciled with each other and begin to join hands in the struggle for black freedom, we black people will not be able to survive." The basis for this dialogue and reconciliation among blacks is for

Cone a foregone conclusion: "Clearly there is a basis for speaking across cultural lines, namely, the Bible" (p. 37). Not all black theologians would agree.

162See note 156 above. Cone says, for example, that because Roberts' book, LIBERATION AND RECON-CILIATION, was well received among the white church establishment, it should be obvious that he is on the wrong theological track (GOD OF THE OPPRESSED, pp. 243-44). Cone dismisses Roberts' A BLACK POLITICAL THEOLOGY, in which Roberts "revis-its" the theme of liberation and reconciliation, by saying that Roberts still fails to grasp the depth of the problem. (p. 275, n. 17).

163(New York: Paulist Press, 1972).

164(Philadelphia: Westminster Press, 1974).

165(Boston: Beacon Press, 1973).

166See in Chapter Three of the present study, comments about Ruether's theological position by McBrien, Dulles, and Baum, p. 95.

167"A New Church?" COMMONWEAL 90 (1969): 66.

168BEYOND GOD THE FATHER, p. 96.

169IBID., p. 6. With specific reference to Daly, Russell makes the following comment: "In the women's liberation movement there has been a lot of rejection of the Bible as the basis for theol-ogy because of the patriarchal, cultural attitudes that it reveals. Yet those who would do Christian theology cannot abandon the story of Jesus of Nazareth." See HUMAN LIBERATION IN A FEMINIST PERSPECTIVE, p. 58.

170BEYOND GOD THE FATHER, pp. 70-71.

171IBID., p. 96.

[172]IBID., p. 97.

[173]IBID., p. 190.

[174]IBID., p. 155. Daly states that while she was tempted to call Chapter Six "Sisterhood as Cosmic Church" instead of "Sisterhood as Cosmic Covenant," she changed her mind because of the negative reaction among her feminist friends. She does employ the term church within the chapter, however, and therefore I believe I am justified in so designating her ecclesiology as I have.

[175]IBID., pp. 173-74.

[176](Chicago: Thomas More Press, 1972). Concerning the specific contribution of women to the missionary movement of the nineteenth century, both Protestant and Catholic, Sister McGrath suggests that such a history still remains to be written. She notes that "It is in the mission fields that women have been free to take initiatives and to probe abilities in evangelization, in the care of souls, and in ecclesiastical administration which would have been forbidden to them, and are still forbidden to them, in the fully developed home "churches" (pp. 98-90).

PART THREE: REFORMULATION AND ITS IMPLICATIONS

CHAPTER SIX

MISSIONARY THEOLOGY AS A THEOLOGY OF DEVELOPMENT

THE PRESENT SITUATION:
A POLITICAL AND THEOLOGICAL SHIFT

It has been argued in the preceding chapters
that the "crisis of missions" stems from a change
in the status of many former "missionary lands"
and from a shift in the theological rationale behind the missionary endeavor of the Church.   The
complex decolonization of Third World nations was
accompanied by a decolonization process in the
Christian Church itself.   As newly independent
states began to make their voices heard indivi-
dually and as the Third World bloc on the international scene, especially at the United Nations,
Christian leaders from former missionary lands
began to speak out at regional and international
religious   forums--at   the   World   Council   of
Churches, the Second Vatican Council, and subsequent Synods of Bishops as well as at regional
conferences.

This common demand of Third World churches and
states to be recognized and listened to by the
rest of the world represents what could be called,
in the broad sense of the term, a "political"
shift. Both nations and churches, indeed the family of nations and the family of churches, were
affected.   A new reading of the "signs of the
times" has become necessary; a rethinking of the
Church's role in the world and a refocus of its
mission become imminent. As Thomas Kuhn would say,
a new "paradigm" has emerged on the political
scene in both nations and churches.[1]

Accompanying this "political shift" is what I have described as a shift in theology. The latter did not arise merely as a result of the political shift, but rather developed in correlation with it. In this theological shift, revelation becomes freed from a narrow biblical or doctrinal understanding. A positivistic approach to theology, one in which written "sources" are merely searched, sorted and applied, no longer suffices. Current theology, rather, recognizes that in the deepest yearnings and actions of individuals and societies for meaning and fulfillment they are invited to some type of encounter with the transcendent, with the "something more" in their midst, with God. As Karl Rahner aptly states:

> Christian hope, without relying on the present world considered as separate from God, is also a hope <u>for</u> this world, the hope that we are those who achieve the final consummation when we respond to the creative task God lays upon us even in this world in a spirit of justice, love and obedience, and so become the completers of his creation.[2]

Hope for this world, as Rahner points out, depends on our response. John Cobb emphasizes this when he writes, "The immanence of God in the world <u>is</u> a ground for hope. But whether we will respond to God's persuasive lure to move forward to the realization of new forms of existence or will lose what we now prize as freedom, imagination and love, depends on human response."[3]

Current theology admits, therefore, that in the decisions of individuals and groups the possibility always exists that they will say "no" to the invitation--to the "lure" to move forward to the more fully human, the inviting and hoped-for future. It sees in the multitude of decisions of men and women in the world a choice for or against liberation, integral human development, salvation.

God is available to humankind in ordinary, every-day experience; all creation is "graced." But this does not mean that progress is inevitable. The ambiguity of the human situation always remains. This "available" God is always mediated and therefore in need of discernment and interpretation. Furthermore, any presumed perception of God in human experience must be tested within the community of faith. From the Christian perspective, this community must always be in dialogue with its privileged writings--the New Testament and the writings received from the Jewish community--as well as later tradition.

Christians constitute that community within graced humanity which clarifies and interprets what it presumes to be God's present revelation in and through its faith in Jesus Christ. In him, they believe that God has been manifest in a unique and ultimate way. They believe that in and with Jesus of Nazareth the Kingdom of God has pierced and permeated creation in an ultimate, although as yet mysterious, way. They believe that through his life, death and resurrection we have reason to hope that the powers of evil in individuals and in institutions and structures that societies have fashioned will not prevail.

Christians feel compelled to share this hope-filled "Good News" that gives meaning and direction to their lives. Conscious, however, that God is available to every individual and to all peoples, Christians are convinced that in today's world they can best make known their understanding of God effecting salvation through Jesus Christ, and at the same time purify and deepen their own perception of this mystery, by open and honest dialogue. They realize that they must demonstrate by their life in community that they are taking their side of the dialogue seriously by celebrating and acting out their beliefs. If, indeed, the coming Kingdom will bring in its fullness that "shalom" for which humankind yearns, then a glimpse, a foretaste, a sign of that shalom must be evident in the community which claims that its founder and sustainer embodied that very Kingdom. It must demonstrate the meaning of its claim to be the salt of the earth and the light of the world.

In this new theological "paradigm" it has been pointed out that the Christian's call or election to membership in the Church is not one of privilege but of responsibility. All are called to the Kingdom; some are called to the Church. Those called to membership and mission in the Church take upon themselves the responsibility of continuing and extending the saving and liberating work of Jesus Christ. Membership and participation in the mission of the Church can and should be a joyous, transforming experience. Christians should enthusiastically encourage and welcome those who, as a result of what they hear, observe and experience of the Christian way of life, are moved to seek membership in the Church and to share in its saving mission.

To labor for the Kingdom is to work unceasingly to remove those obstacles which stand in the way of a more just, peaceful, reconciling and mutually sharing human community. The diaconal aspect of the Church's mission calls it to participate in the integral development of each individual and of all humankind. In doing this, it joins and cooperates with all other individuals and groups who are laboring in just ways for the liberation and humanization of the universe.

Because of the political and theological shift that has taken place, the Church must refocus its missionary endeavor. The energy and resources which formerly were employed to convert and keep as many people as possible within the Church so their souls might be saved, must now be directed to the integral development of individuals and societies. The seemingly endless debate on the primacy of either evangelization or social action, evidenced in Pope Paul's apostolic exhortation ON EVANGELIZATION IN THE MODERN WORLD and the World Council of Churches' Assembly in Nairobi, leads to no solution. As Moltmann has pointed out, evangelization and humanization in Christian terms are not alternatives. Nor, he insists, is inner repentance an alternative to social change; nor is the "vertical dimension" of faith replaceable merely by the "horizontal dimension" of love for one's neighbor. Likewise, the humanity of Jesus cannot be used to eclipse his divinity. Both dimensions, Moltmann insists, coincide in Jesus' death on the cross, and separating them "enforces alternatives and calls for a parting of ways, in dividing the unity of God and man in the person, the imitation and the future of Christ."[4]

Those who claim the primacy of changing the individual (assuming that circumstances will take care of themselves), forget that the causes of misery are found not only in the attitudes of men and women, but in the institutionalized structure of societies as well. On the other hand, structures which hold people in misery can be broken down, but there is no guarantee that they then will be happy. Rather than either/or, or first/second, both must be done at the same time. As described by Moltmann:

> Personal, inner change without a change in circumstances and structures is an idealist illusion, as though man were only a soul and not a body as well. But a change in external circumstances without inner renewal is a materialist illusion, as though man were only a product of his social circumstances and nothing else.... If the title 'Christ' refers to the redeemer and liberator, then practical 'Christian' action can only be directed towards the liberation of man from his inhumanity. Consequently the 'coin-

cidence' of the change of circumstances and of human activity as a change in man himself applies to Christian practice to an eminent degree.[5]

It has been argued in the previous chapters that the term development is the most comprehensive and suitable concept under which to approach the question of humanization and redemption because of its broad acceptance in the non-religious world and, at the same time, its adaptability to theological interpretation and elaboration. Furthermore, we have critiqued alternative attempts to elaborate a theological position vis-a-vis the current world situation and found in them serious theological shortcomings. In the theologies of revolution and liberation, we found an understanding of revelation which ranged from a biblically or doctrinally positivistic position (Laurentin, Segundo, Cone, and to a certain extent Alves) to a contextual understanding which would limit discernment of God's action in the world to a specific group, be they identified by their revolutionary commitment and activity (Shaull, Alves) or, by purportedly strict scientific analysis, as the oppressed (Gutierrez).

The eschatological stance adopted by the various theologians examined shows a strong inclination toward an understanding of the Kingdom of God as something that humankind can build here and now through revolutionary action (Segundo, Shaull, early Alves, early Cone). The liberated "new man" would live in a qualitatively different "new society." It would be completely egalitarian in structure, with the ownership of the means of production in the hands of the workers (Segundo, Gutierrez). However, once the revolutionary fervor subsides, there is a tendency to make an "about-face" in their eschatological stance. Suffering for the sake of succeeding generations becomes the acceptable posture, either through painful yet hopeful waiting (Alves) or through

deliberate seeking of martyrdom with the confidence that the next world will be better (Cone).

The position taken here is that a theology of
development can embrace the best in these theologies and still avoid their theological shortcomings.   Earlier,   it   was   shown   that   although
development can be conceived exclusively as a part
of the diaconal or service aspect of the Church's
mission, it can also be explained in such a way--
somewhat analogous to Blondel's use of the concept
"action"--to include not only "doing" but also
"dialoguing" and "demonstrating." That is, integral human development includes <u>kerygma</u> and <u>koin-
onia</u> and therefore is suitable for an elaboration
of the Church's overall mission. Encompassing the
threefold mission of the Church, and yet with an
obvious emphasis on the servant aspect of the
Church, development becomes a suitable aegis under
which to reformulate missionary theology. Following Christ involves a change in the person and a
change in the circumstances in which the person
lives.   This is, likewise, the goal of integral
human development. We must elaborate.

PRESENT REVELATION AND DEVELOPMENT:
POSITIVE AND NEGATIVE INDICATORS

Once again our discussion will center on the
basic theological concepts of revelation and
eschatology. In the Prospectus (Chapter Seven), I
will attempt to outline an ecumenical ecclesiology
that will facilitate this formulation of the
Church's missionary theology as a theology of
development.

The Christian believes that God is redemptively present in human history, in ordinary human
experience.   Because of this, the Christian sees
in the strivings of individuals and groups for a
more just, equitable, forgiving and loving society, glimpses--admittedly never completely unambig-
uous--of God's activity in the world. "Sneak pre-

views," one might call these glimpses, or, to speak in more biblical language, "Now we see indistinctly, as in a mirror" (1 Cor. 13, 12). With this understanding of revelation, the Church can offer humankind what Pope Paul VI, in his encyclical ON THE DEVELOPMENT OF PEOPLES, suggests is her characteristic attribute: "a global vision of man and of the human race." Indeed, from the specifically Christian point of view, the ultimate revelation of God in the man Jesus, has ennobled humankind and sanctified the very "stuff" of the universe. Because of this, Christians should be able to express a fervor, a dedication, a passion for every individual and the world itself which would point to God's own love expressed in creation--a love that reached its climax in Jesus "in whom God was reconciling the world to himself" (2 Cor. 5, 19). As Bas van Iersel has stated, "The Gospel provides only one fundamental element for a normative view of man, and that is the model of man's absolute involvement with his fellowman in need, the model of human solidarity."6

Even from the christocentric point of view, however, the "risk" element in all identification of God's revelation must not be forgotten. Andre Bieler reminds us of this when he writes:

> Considering on the one hand the permanent mystery inherent in the knowledge of the living Christ, and on the other the dynamic renewing power this same Christ communicated to man, to society and to the whole world, it is obvious that the knowledge of Christ's presence, action and will in the world can never be gained once and for all. There is always such a distance between Christ and his creation in perpetual movement that no Church can claim to describe what truth is without a constant influx of power from Christ and his Holy Spirit, without the renewing force of historical realism.7

Admitting the problematical aspect of all theological endeavors, Christians can, nevertheless, by building on the belief that God is redemptively present in all striving for meaningful human development, find a theological basis for entering into dialogue and cooperation with all men and women of good will who seek this common goal. More will be said about formulating this goal in the next section. The point here is that the understanding of revelation suggested makes possible, from a theological point of view, a common striving for development. Christians will always be in dialogue with the privileged, foundational literature of their community in clarifying what they presume to be God's persuasive lure into the more human future.

It can be stated further that God is not only present in the strivings for development, but also in a prophetic way in those instances where people become aware of their "underdevelopment." The "shock of underdevelopment," as Denis Goulet calls it, cuts across both rich and poor nations and peoples.[8] This phrase seems more suitable than "conscientization" or "the raising of consciousness," because it does not specify the particular way that this process takes place, nor does it carry with it the negative overtones of intellectual imperialism present in the concept of conscientization, as pointed out by Berger.[9]

For those who are poor, the shock of underdevelopment comes when they realize, by whatever means, that things could be different; that, as individuals and societies, they should have input into decisions affecting their future; that they and cultural life of their society; that a share in the world's resources is rightfully theirs. Later we shall examine the Church's role vis-a-vis the shock of underdevelopment among the poor.

For the rich, the shock of underdevelopment may occur on several levels. First, one could speak about the level of "bad conscience." Either by personal or vicarious experience, individuals and groups within the rich countries come to an awareness that they cannot continue to maintain their integrity and self-respect in our shrinking world when two-thirds of its inhabitants are undernourished, unhealthy, and generally lack the opportunities of sharing in and contributing to the development of the human family. The citizens and governments in rich countries, and, indeed, those pockets of rich within Third World countries cannot continue to live with bad consciences over a long period of time once they have been "shocked" into the realization of the plight of the poor. Pope Paul VI has warned that the continued greed of rich countries "will certainly call down upon them the judgment of God and the wrath of the poor, with consequences no one can foretell." Pope John Paul II forcefully reiterated this theme in his address to the United Nations in October of 1979.[10] THE STATEMENT OF THE BEIRUT CONFERENCE (The Conference on World Cooperation for Development, 1968) notes that the majority of Christians live in the developed North and if this area is wealthy far beyond the general level of world society, they profit from this unbalanced prosperity and must in consequence account for their stewardship.[11]

Retrospectively, certain events of recent history could be pointed to as possible moments of "revelation" when the shock of underdevelopment raised the consciousness of a considerable number of people to a new level and facilitated, if not demanded, action on behalf of justice. For example, television coverage of the civil rights march in Birmingham, Alabama, showing club-swinging mounted policemen and vicious police dogs turned brutally on a crowd of black men, women and children, caused numerous citizens of the United States to reassess seriously their position on the rights of blacks. The Christmas Eve bombings of North Vietnam cities, the unlawful bombing in

Cambodia, the My Lai massacre, the killing of students at Kent State during a protest against Vietnam, the startling pictures of thousands upon thousands of people starving in the Sahel area of Africa, and more recently in Cambodia, the "Saturday night massacre" in the Watergate scandal, in different ways and to various degrees shocked the people of the United States into a new awareness of their own underdevelopment.

A second level on which the shock of underdevelopment can affect the rich is on the level of survival--at least survival of the level of living to which they have become accustomed. The material wealth of the industrialized West had convinced them that they knew both the goals of development and the means to achieve those goals. They operated on a technological and economic ethos that there were no limits on expansion and no problems that could not eventually be solved by technology. For the Third World, this meant the pie was always getting bigger; nations need only to get in line and be patient.

THE LIMITS OF GROWTH, a study sponsored by the Club of Rome and produced by the Massachusetts Institute of Technology, was published in 1972. The study postulated that, with the rapid exhaustion of known resources and the energy needed to process them on the one hand, and the limited carrying power of the world ecological system on the other, there is little basis for the optimistic models of development that assumed almost limitless growth. The study insisted that indeed there are limits to growth and they are not so far in the future as some people would like to think. Furthermore, they will radically alter the lifestyle, especially of richer countries.[12]

According to Richard Dickinson, "All the talk about 'dehumanizing technology and materialism' which was convincing too few people, was suddenly converted from a moral and spiritual issue into a question of survival or at least a loss of a way of life."[13]

The shock of underdevelopment in this case comes when the rich nations are forced to admit that their concern for justice in the use of the world's goods came, not as a result of the cries of the poor, but in the abrupt realization that their own style of life might be threatened. It did, however, force the question of social justice into the world arena once again. How could five percent of the world's population arrogate to itself almost one-half of the world's annual use of nonrenewable resources? It forced a reexamination of development objectives in terms of human and communitarian values and of people's participation in the social process. The question emerged, not only development, but development with what and for what?

It is not surprising that some Third World countries saw this sudden concern for natural resources and ecology as another way of diverting attention away from the concerns of the Third World and actually curtailing their development. Others questioned why they could not exploit their resources and those of the ocean now, even as the industrialized world had been doing for years. Whatever the reaction of the Third World countries or the industrialized West, it is certain that the limits-of-growth debate shocked everyone into examining more deeply the meaning and the dimensions of development.

Because limits of growth is a human concern, it is a Christian concern. Charles Birch, speaking at the World Council of Churches Assembly in Nairobi, suggested that "ecology is part of evangelism." One of the respondents to Birch's address, Kosuke Koyama, concurred: "If we do not come to nature sacramentally and covenantally we will not treat our neighbors sacramentally and covenantally."[14] Birch challenged the churches:

If we are to break the poverty barrier for almost two-thirds of the earth's people, if we are to continue to inhabit the earth, there has to be a revolution in the relationship of human beings to each other. The churches of the world have now to choose whether or not they become part of that revolution.[15]

Later in his address, Birch states succinctly, "The rich must live more simply, that the poor may simply live."

If the limits-of-growth debate shocked rich countries into the realization that their model of development based on continuous expansion was wanting, the 1973 oil embargo by the Organization of Petroleum Exporting Countries (OPEC) came as a psychological shock to their presumed world dominance. Although the poorest of the poor nations undoubtedly suffered the greatest because of the oil price increase that resulted from the embargo, it did give new impetus to the Group of 77 (a bloc of less-developed countries which now numbers about 110) to push for a new international economic order. Although they did not get a clear commitment on their attempt at the fourth meeting of the United Nations Conference on Trade and Development (UNCTAD IV) to secure a common fund that would hopefully stablize world prices for various raw materials, they have shocked rich countries into the realization that global economic interdependence is no longer a mere topic for speculation, but a reality that must be faced.[16]

Finally, the shock of underdevelopment can affect rich individuals and nations on the level of human values. Some of the authentic humanizing values that people in less-developed nations have been able to maintain and cultivate jar the rich into a realization that their worship of wealth, of power and of domination brings with it dehumanization. Family and community loyalty, respect for the elderly, reverence for nature, pride in handicraft and folk art are only a few of the values that certain Third World peoples have preserved. The richness and diversity of non-Western cultures can shock the industrialized world into seeing their own cultural and humanizing underdevelopment.[17] The Church, confident that God is available to every person--the rich are no exception--must present the opportunities for this shock of underdevelopment to reach the rich as well as the poor by development education.[18] The rich nations, especially, must be prodded to consider if the collective structures and policies under which they prosper serve not to alleviate but to perpetuate the conditions of the less-developed countries.

The shock of underdevelopment, therefore, can be experienced by both the rich and the poor, by the so-called developed and less-developed countries. Indeed, in the same way that geography can no longer determine "mission" from "nonmission" lands, so development or underdevelopment cannot be determined solely by geography nor by technological or material advancement. People can become slaves to technology and wealth as well as to poverty and hopelessness. It is all too evident from recent history that so-called advanced peoples can become barbarians and slaves in their use and abuse of technology and power. A small group of rich and powerful elite, or a racial or sexist minority, in an otherwise poor country maintaining control over the majority against its will, can hardly be developed from the integral human point of view. The same is true of a rich nation that has pockets of poor in its midst. A theology of development can provide that much-needed basis of critique and dialogue between the technologically and materially advanced peoples and the poor, be they within a rich nation itself or in the Third World.

PRESENT REVELATION AND IDEOLOGIES:
RESPONSE TO LIBERATION THEOLOGIANS

The objection which Latin-American liberation theologians would raise at this point is, of course, that no dialogue is possible before liberation of the oppressed from the oppressors. What is needed is not dialogue but a scientific analysis of the root causes of underdevelopment, or, as they would insist, domination. By use of a Marxist or Marxist-like critique, they identify capitalism as the root problem. The "original sin" of this economic ideology is the private ownership of the means of production; its "church" is the marketplace and its "kingdom" is the profit. Because the capitalists, the "oppressors," are not about to admit this, the only posture for the Christian and the Church is one of opposition, struggle and class conflict. The "oppressed" people and nations do not choose this necessarily; it is forced upon them by the very institutional violence of the capitalist system. The only hope is a transformation of society to a scientific socialism.[19]

The danger here is that by adopting the class struggle model too uncritically, the proponents for scientific socialism run the same risk of identifying their Church with a particular faction which is as capable as the capitalists and imperialists of earlier ages of using it for its own ends. Moreover, as Peter Berger has pointed out, the term "scientific socialism" designates the common ambition "to have one's cake and eat it too." He states:

> Its 'unity of theory and praxis' guarantees that no questions may be raised in this harmony of dreams, theories, and actions. And in the end, everybody will have everything--the fruits of progress without the price of alienation, redemption and technocratic control, community and individual choice.[20]

I would agree with Berger when he suggests that the basic Marxist error in analyzing under-development is that of ascribing to capitalism alone certain conditions that are endemic to any relations between richer and poorer economic entities. The Marxist-Leninist theory of imperialism has correctly shown how Third World countries are economically exploited by powerful capitalist nations. Indeed, under conditions of capitalism such exploitation takes a distinctively capitalist form. But relations between economically unequal partners are almost invariably exploitative, and this has nothing to do with capitalism as such. A socialist power is just as capable of exploitative relations with Third World dependencies, as the economic policy of the Soviet Union makes sufficiently clear.[21] Third World countries seem to be coming to this realization, as evidenced in the UNCTAD IV conference in Nairobi. The less-developed countries pressed the Eastern Bloc socialist nations for more aid and better access to their markets. The socialist governments of Eastern Europe have hidden behind the argument that the Third World's poverty was caused by colonialism and capitalist imperialism, and they had no obligation to make "reparations." Although unsuccessful in their attempt, it appears that Third World countries have broadened their view of exploitation.[22]

There can be no question but that development in Third World countries, or anywhere else, hinges on at least a relative independence from domination from outside powers. Similarly domestic structures of exploitation make true development impossible. There often are links between foreign and domestic exploiters through internatonal networks of economic and political power. But the Marxist "scientific analysis" does not provide tools for a critique of socialist exploitation. What is needed is a critical theory that can include within itself a critique of all available models of development. The liberation theologians have become blinded by the labels "capitalism" or "socialism." As Berger suggests, both are likely to continue existing. The deeper question is, therefore, "What kind of capitalism?" and "What kind of socialism?" Can we not think of development in categories that go beyond the capitalist/socialist dichotomy?[23]

DEVELOPMENT GOALS: A QUESTION OF ESCHATOLOGY

The availability of God in the strivings of men and women for a more just and human world gives us reason to hope that the theology of development can formulate some broadly religious guidelines and goals for development. We speak of religious goals because theology is theology only if it recognizes and attempts to deal with the transcendent dimensions of reality, that is, revelation. Moreover, in attempting to formulate goals of development—the good, the more fully human future—we are speaking in theological terms about eschatology. As Berger has stated so well, development has a religious or theological dimension:

> Development is not just a goal of rational actions in the economic, political, and social spheres. It is also, and very deeply, the focus of redemptive hopes and expectations. In an important sense, development is a religious category. Even for those living on the most precarious margins of existence, development is not just a matter of improved material conditions; it is at least also a vision of redemptive transformation.[24]

We have consistently argued that development cannot merely be identified with economic growth or well-being. Nor can it be defined by non-economic social factors such as gains in literacy, schooling, health conditions and services, provisions for housing and the like. Not that these are not part of it, but development must also include, as Berger says, "redemptive hopes and expectations." Development designates some type of terminal condition or goal, a realistic utopia, if you will, as well as the process by which successive approximations to this goal are made. The terminal condition, the realistic utopia or goal of development cannot, however, be understood as any static state; in theological terms, development concerns the signs and activities whereby we can approach, catch a glimpse of, and facilitate the inbreaking of the Kingdom of God even now. But the absolute future, the final Reign of God, is not something that humankind can establish or bring about on its own. It is God's Kingdom; it is giftlike. This does not mean that the strivings of the human community are not integrally related to the final Kingdom, but it does mean, contrary to Segundo, that humankind cannot cause the Reign of God to be effected. Rather, the Christian belief in the inbreaking of the Kingdom in the event of Jesus Christ causes them to see liberating events and movements toward human development as previews of the Kingdom.

This eschatological stance is fortified by the understanding of revelation which proclaims the transcendent immanent in creation itself. It should be a continual guard against any closed humanism or worship of anything less than the transcendent. Indeed, Christians have in Jesus the supreme example of one who overcame idolatry. As Metz and Moltmann insist in their political theology, the memory of the passion and resurrection of Jesus is at the same time both dangerous and liberating.[25] This memory is dangerous because it is a reminder that Jesus was put to death as a political criminal. But this crucified man has been raised from the dead and exalted to be the Christ of God. What society and the state had determined to be the most disgraceful of deaths--crucifixion

--is turned into the supreme moment of grace. Utter weakness became overwhelming power. The authority of God is no longer represented directly by those in high positions--the powerful and the rich--but by the outcast Son of Man. Christ's death and resurrection are the ultimate critique of any worship of political rule or worldly kingdoms.

The memory of the death and resurrection of Christ is liberating, in that it protects the state from the political service of idols and the people from political alienation and loss of rights. Christians, mindful of the passion and resurrection of the Crucified One, must work continuously to demythologize the state, society, or any institution or movement which claims one's ultimate loyalty. This "protestant principle"[26] is a prophetic warning against idolatry: "No, this is not the Kingdom; nor is that!" It is one of the peculiar contributions which the Christian tradition can make to the theology of development. The state, society, national sovereignty, the Church, liberation and development--all these must continually be mythologized and desacralized; they must never be allowed to become the object of our ultimate concern. Among liberation theologians, there exists the real temptation of allowing economic and political liberation to become the object of their ultimate concern.

DEVELOPMENT GOALS:
A QUESTION OF HUMANIZATION

1. RESISTANCE TO ABSTRACT ETHICAL PRINCIPLES: BERGER AND MOLTMANN

Denis Goulet, in his book, THE CRUEL CHOICE--which could be conceived as a theology of development in nontheological terms--says that development "covers that entire gamut of changes by which a social system, with optimal regard for the wishes of individuals and sub-systemic components of that system, moves away from a condition of life widely perceived as unsatisfactory in some way toward some condition regarded as 'humanly better.'"[27] The question arises, of course, how do we understand and determine what is "humanly better," or even more basically, how do we understand the human person in his or her relationship to others as together they strive to achieve the "good?" I agree with Berger when he says, "People who speak of development should frankly admit that they are engaged in the business of ethics and, at least potentially, of politics."[28]

In searching for a method by which ethical principles can be systematically brought to bear on public policy options, Berger says he is suspicious of abstract ethical principles, especially when they are applied to particular policy options. Either they are so general that they are of no practical use, or they produce a blindness to any alternatives to the one course prescribed "on principle." He favors instead a "case approach" to the problem of development ethics.[29] But, whether Berger wants to admit it or not, he does in fact presuppose some general universal principles in his critique of models of development.

Underlying Berger's critique is a basic understanding of the human person. For example, he states that in every human project the person within that world knows it better than any outsider. For this reason, development policy must respect the varieties and inner genius of traditional ways of looking at reality.[30] He urges "a humanistic approach to development policy which will be based on the insight that no social process can succeed unless it is illuminated with meaning from within."[31] Furthermore, Berger claims that every human project must be measured in terms of its contributions to, or destruction of the order of "meaning" (people have a right to live in a meaningful world) and in terms of the amount of human pain involved.[32] Finally, with no explanation or elaboration, Berger states that in working out his own system of ethics he accepts "a Christian understanding of man."[33] That, we may presume, would be a biblical understanding of man, which, strange as it may seem, puts Berger, in this instance, in the Barthian tradition.

With the particular understanding of revelation which has been proposed in our discussion, I am convinced that some broad ethical principles can be based on the evolving understanding of the nature of the human person. Into this understanding can be fitted Berger's preference for the "case approach," as well as his Christian understanding of the human person. Even as I have "gone against the stream" in proposing the continued use of the concept of development for discussing the urgent problems confronting the Church and all humankind in general, so once more I go against the stream and suggest that a reinterpretation of the concept of natural law can provide the most nearly adequate basis for an ethics of development. I will attempt to show that such a reinterpretation can provide a broad basis for dialogue for those holding various ideologies, and at the same time harmonize on the theological level with our understanding of revelation and eschatology.

In 1948 the United Nations accepted the "General Declaration on the Rights of Man." Underlying that declaration is an assumption that there is a "nature of the human person" with binding natural rights. Indeed, there must be some agreement about what life is worthy of the human person; otherwise there could be no basis for our legal systems. The question is, what is used to justify the good or worthy vision of life of individuals and communities? Moltmann has said, "The idea of natural and human rights and of an objective moral law is fascinating, and will remain so as long as men are corporately concerned for a true and common humanity." The difficulty he finds in such an idea is its lack of connection with the real, historical situation of men and women. With Berger, he points out that as attempts are made to derive decisions in specific cases from the general principles of natural law, "the more dimly the light of knowledge burns."[34]

Moltmann suggests that the idea of natural law and of the rights of human persons can be better mediated through legal systems in the historical process of socialization of men and women than in the earlier ideas people had of natural law. Rather than speaking of natural rights, we should speak of the "future rights". In Moltmann's words:

> So it is not the invocation of a supposedly objective moral law, but the unavoidable task of altering the world, of healing it, of bettering it, of making it more worthy of man and more worth living in, that can be regarded as the norm of justice. One then moves on from the mythology of an abstract moral law to the concrete Utopia of the rights of man and to a legal system which is intended for citizens of the world.[35]

What justification does Moltmann provide for his "concrete Utopia of the rights of man?" In an interesting Barthian turn, Moltmann appeals not to the "law of the ideal man" which, he claims, can easily change into inhuman demands, but to the Old and New Testament--the God of Exodus and the Covenant, the God of deliverance and guaranteed freedom. "The Old Testament covenant righteousness," he says, "is already open to serve as the law of all nations and as the law of the grace of God to all." For Christians, practical action in the legal ordering of society should be under the aspect of love. "Love, translated into the language of law, means the rights of one's neighbor and the acknowledgement of the other man."[36]

Moltmann's understanding of the human person is, in the end, biblical and, in this case, a Barthian understanding. Because of this, it is limited as a basis for a development ethics. It can, however, be accommodated within the natural law understanding of the human person, and indeed give that understanding a depth and clarity that it would not have otherwise.

Berger says he is suspicious of abstract ethical principles; Moltmann suggests that his way of explaining "future rights" of human persons is more successful than mediating justice through the earlier ideas people had of natural law. I suggest that the main resistance to a natural law theory has been in reaction to its overly rationalistic formulation as evidenced in Roman Catholic moral theology.

2.   A RATIONALISTIC AND STATIC CONCEPT
OF NATURAL LAW:
THE ROMAN CATHOLIC MODEL

Rationalism, rather than empiricism, has been the philosophical framework within which the natural law interpretation of ethics, politics, and law has come down to us. Moreover, the particular understanding of nature was a static one. As such, the natural law theory has rightly been accused of favoring the status quo rather than change, of stressing order and passivity even in the face of injustice. But Paul Ramsey points out that if there are inflexibilities and claims of absolute certainty and finality in a theory of natural law, they flow not from the account actually given of the meaning of natural law, but from the position of Roman Catholic moral theology which claims that natural law has been "republished" in revelation, and both are guarded and interpreted by the positive teachings of the Church.[37] It should be clear that Ramsey is referring to a doctrinal understanding of revelation and not revelation as it has been explained here. However, even in the "progressive" CONSTITUTION ON THE CHURCH IN THE MODERN WORLD of Vatican II, there is a tinge of the attitude to which Ramsey is referring:

> In her pursuit of her divine mission, the Church preaches the gospel to all men and dispenses the treasures of grace. Thus by _imparting knowledge of divine and natural law_ [emphasis mine], she everywhere contributes to strengthening peace and to placing brotherly relations between individuals and peoples on solid ground (Art. 89).

Generally the Catholic position on natural law was that it is a source of ethical wisdom and knowledge that exist apart from the explicit revelation of God in Christ through Scripture, and this wisdom is common to all mankind. Pope John XXIII, in PACEM IN TERRIS, laid out this position as the primary basis for Christian social teaching:

> But the Creator of the world has imprinted in man's heart an order which his conscience reveals to him and enjoins him to obey: 'They show the work of the law written in their hearts. Their conscience bears witness to them.'[38]

Pope John says that by these laws humans are most admirably taught how to conduct their mutual dealings, how to structure relationships between the individual and the state, how states should deal with each other, how persons and political communities should be related to the world community. It is all so neat and optimistic; some would call it naive for the very reason that it views nature, or the natural, in complete isolation from the all-too-obvious reality of sin. Neither is the natural affected nor transformed by the supernatural. The latter is merely added on top of an already constituted natural order. Moreover, the natural is not relativized by the transforming aspect of the eschatological, which acts as a negative critique of all existing structures and institutions.

There has been an attempt on the part of Catholic ethicists and moral theologians, especially since Vatican II, to integrate natural law more fully into the whole schema of creation, redemption, revelation and eschatology. In the Council documents themselves, the term natural law is generally avoided. In the CONSTITUTION ON THE CHURCH IN THE MODERN WORLD, a new phrase is used when the discussion turns to a consideration of particular contemporary problems: "To a consideration of these contemporary problems in the light of the gospel and human experience [emphasis mine] the Council would now direct the attention of all" (Art. 46).

There does not seem to be the same dichotomy between gospel and human experience as there is between gospel and natural law. Human experience is not merely natural; it includes nature as affected by grace and sin, or revelation and the refusal of revelation. Thus the rigid natural/supernatural distinction is avoided. We know humankind only as confronted with God's redemptive presence. Any "natural" state is purely speculative. Karl Rahner has pointed out that we should not waste our time speculating about some imaginary human beings who might have existed without being called to grace. These "pure nature" people do not, did not, and will not exist, and therefore are of no help in enlightening us about our existence.[39]

It was because of the identification of natural law with such an understanding of the "natural" person that the Council Fathers avoided the term. It occurs only three times in the CONSTITUTION ON THE CHURCH IN THE MODERN WORLD. One of them comes in the context of blind obedience to authority:

> ...The Council wishes to recall first of all the permanent binding force of universal natural law and its all embracing principles....Therefore, actions which deliberately conflict with these same principles, as well as orders commanding such actions, are criminal (Art. 79).

The Council points out specifically the crime of genocide and ends this same paragraph by praising "the courage of those who openly and fearlessly resist men who issue such commands."

A second reference to natural law concerns resistance to oppression and the right of revolution:

> When public authority oversteps its competence and oppresses the people, these people should nevertheless obey to the extent that objective good demands. Still it is lawful for them to defend their own rights and those of their fellow citizens against any abuse of this authority, provided that in so doing they observe the limits imposed by natural law and the gospel (Art. 74).

In spite of these few references to natural law, that the Council deliberately avoided the term is verified by Canon Charles Moeller, one of the drafters of the CHURCH IN THE MODERN WORLD. In a speech before the Geneva Conference on Church and Society in 1966, Moeller explained that the terms nature and supernature were not used in the document specifically because of ecumenical considerations.[40] In Pope Paul's encyclical ON THE DEVELOPMENT OF PEOPLES, this same policy is followed; the term natural law occurs only once, and then it is in a citation from Leo XIII. The attempt, again, is to avoid the controversy over nature/supernature, reason/revelation, natural law/gospel.

There is, however, something more significant and deeper involved here than merely avoiding a controversial term. The Council Fathers, considering current moral problems in the light of human experience and the gospel, shift to a more dynamic method of approach—the method of correlation. In doing so, they felt they must avoid as much as possible the term natural law, identified as it was with a static understanding of human nature and rationalistic approach to law. Some Catholic ethicists, following this perspective, argue that the natural law approach has lost its effectiveness. Charles Curran, admitting that he personally agrees with the recognition that all humans, because of their shared humanity, share a common ethical wisdom and knowledge, still insists that the natural law approach, from a theological perspective, embodies certain theological presuppositions which argue against its continued use in contemporary moral theology.[41] These presuppositions are basically the ones stemming from the natural/supernatural dichotomy discussed above. I, on the contrary, will attempt to show that a dynamic understanding of human persons, of their nature and their laws, has replaced the older paradigm, and the term natural law can be employed profitably within this new paradigm. Before pursuing this reinterpretation of natural law, we must look briefly at some of the Protestant positions on natural law.

3. DEPRAVED HUMAN NATURE AND SCRIPTURE ALONE: A PROTESTANT VIEW

Often Protestant theologians have rejected the natural law theory because they claim it does not take sin seriously enough; that through the fall, nature has been so damaged and the structures of "good" creation so destroyed, that nature is incapable of directing or inclining us toward the good. Others, because of their exclusive reliance on Scripture, reject all other sources of moral knowledge. This is the basic Barthian position which we have seen with varying degrees of nuance in the works of Shaull, Alves and Cone, and even in Berger and Moltmann. Often accompanying this view is a fear that natural law would somehow infringe upon the uniqueness of the Christian ethic which they maintain must be distinctive.[42]

Certainly there is not a unanimity among Protestant theologians on the distinctiveness of Christian ethics. H. Richard Niebuhr states, "The insistence on the absolute uniqueness of the Christian ethos has never been able to meet either the theoretical or practical tests."[43] Indeed, Reinhold Niebuhr declared that Karl Barth, in denying natural law and natural justice, preached "eschatological irresponsibility."[44] Macquarrie maintains that those who insist on a christocentric position in ethics involve themselves in a hermeneutic circle:

> Christ interprets for the Christian the meaning of authentic humanity or mature manhood, but he is acknowledged as the Christ or the paradigm of humanity because men have interpreted him as such in light of an idea of authentic humanity that they already bring to him and that they have derived from their own participation in human existence. No doubt the Christian finds that his idea of authentic humanity is enlarged, corrected and perhaps even revolutionized by the concrete humanity of Christ, yet unless he had some such idea, it is hard to see how Christ could ever become Christ for him.[45]

It is in the doctrine of creation rather than redemption that Christians find common cause with non-Christians in facing moral problems. That is to say, what is already present in the whole of creation is gathered up in Christ. This is not to deny that there are differences between Christian and non-Christian ethics, but these differences have to do with the ways and means that various groups or traditions perceive the goals that are implicit in all moral striving. These differences manifest themselves in the ways in which different peoples understand and engage in moral obligations which are common to all. They have to do with the different degrees of explicitness to which the idea of authentic humanity has emerged in the several traditions. Macquarrie sees natural law as that "inner drive toward authentic personhood," and as such a bridge between Christian ethics and general or secular ethics.[46]

In the understanding of revelation as I have proposed it, the teaching of Jesus as interpreted by the early Christian community and recorded in the New Testament does not add anything completely new to our understanding of the integrally developed person or of humankind in community. Rather, his life and teaching underline or, more emphatically, place in bold print those qualities and practices in human life which from the beginning have foreshadowed and facilitated the coming of God's Kingdom. In this sense, I would agree with the Catholic moralist Charles Curran that there is no specifically or distinctively Christian ethics--personal or social. Moreover, I have insisted that limiting one's understanding to the biblical paradigm of the person impedes the kind of broad dialogue needed today concerning the future of the human community. James M. Gustafson makes a similar point:

> I find a great deal of continental theology, and World Council of Churches' theology, is deeply concerned to develop a

way to engage in discourse and action with those outside of the Christian community and yet, almost ironically, its concern to have a biblical foundation for this authorization makes discourse difficult. The question of the meaning of the human, for example, does not arise in theological terms when one is discussing with genetic experimenters, or with so-social planners. Because of this, the theologian has to enter into a conversation in which questions are asked in their terms, and answers must be given in terms meaningful to them without violating theological integrity.[47]

Although traditional moral theology was tied to the notion of a static, fixed human nature set in the midst of a hierarchically ordered universe, still its basic approach to the problem of ethics was correct. Its starting place was the study of the person rather than some special Christian concept such as love. Macquarrie states emphatically:

Indeed, I shall go further and claim that natural law is foundational to morality. It is the inner drive toward authentic personhood and is presupposed in all particular ethical traditions, including the Christian one.[48]

4.   THE ONTOLOGICAL FOUNDATIONS OF NATURAL LAW:
A BASIS FOR DIALOGUE

It is the ontological foundation of natural law that provides a common ground for different ethical traditions--religious and secular. Religion and morals have been closely associated with each other in the course of history. Religion, with its system of ultimate rewards and punishments, often provided the buttress for morality; indeed, it was at times reduced to a mere incentive for moral life. Religious teachings frequently implied that human beings would not be moral, apart from such sanctions or motivations. Such a point of view can no longer be sustained, as secular moralists have amply shown. Some way of interpreting the connection between religion and morals must be found that will respect the integrity of both. I suggest, following Macquarrie, that natural law can provide the link. Natural law, like religious faith, claims to be founded in "the way things are," in some vision of the whole that can be contrasted with mere human conventions. This ontological ground, common to various forms of morality, is implicit wherever an unconditional moral obligation is recognized.[49]

The value of natural law is that it can, but need not, be given a theological or religious interpretation. It does not necessarily commit one to a theistic belief and yet the idea of "higher law" can fit into the theory. To explain natural law in terms of a divine lawgiver is perhaps the most primitive and mythological way of expressing the idea. This understanding is not uncommon in many non-Western societies which maintain what Kraemer has called the "primitive apprehension" of life.[50] Goulet points out that in so-called non-developed societies there is a connection between normative and significative values. That is, what "ought" to be done in any domain (normative values) is intimately related to the symbols the society uses to explain and mediate the meaning of life and death (significant values).[51] The separation of normative from significative values is the uniqueness of the Judeo-Christian tradition—the phenomenon of desacralization or secularization. But as Berger has pointed out, even if secularization, or as he calls it, modernity, seems to be an inevitable trend in the world today, still those who "resist development" and cling to their traditional world views must be respected for the logic of their arguments from within their own perspective.[52] A natural law approach should facilitate this respect and open the way for a more humane approach to development. The particular role of the Church in this regard will be examined later.

Explaining natural law in terms of a divine lawgiver or appealing to the "will of God" can have and has had many unfortunate results. It is not surprising that many unbelieving people are suspicious of any attempt to relate morality to any transcendent reality. Certainly it is illegitimate to suppose that God's arbitrary decree determines what is morally right or wrong. Macquarrie quotes E. L. Mascall to the effect that

> ...moral law is neither an antecedent prescription to which God is bound by some external necessity to conform, nor a set of precepts promulgated by him in an entirely arbitrary and capricious manner, but something inherently rooted in the nature of man as reflecting in himself, in however limited and finite a mode, the character of the sovereign God from whom his being is derived.[53]

If natural law is to be more than human convention which can be explained psychologically, sociologically, and anthropologically, it must have a depth, a basis in "the way things are" which in turn can place upon men and women moral demands of an ultimate character. As Macquarrie states, "The notion of human responsibility and answerability, when explored in its many dimensions implies an order which man does not create but which, rather, lays a demand on him."[54] This ontological foundation, which can form a basis for dialogue with those who accept no belief in God, can at the same time be given a theological interpretation according to the understanding of revelation which I have proposed.

5. A DYNAMIC UNDERSTANDING OF "LAW" AND "NATURE": A REINTERPRETATION

A reinterpretation of the natural law must take into consideration and be compatible with the thinking of an age whose concepts are dynamic rather than static, where change, flexibility and growth form the context of all discussions of values and goals, of the meaning of the more human future. Two statements from Vatican II reflect this new thinking: "Thus the human race has passed from a rather static concept of reality to a more dynamic, evolutionary one," and "...political authority...must be exercised within the limits of morality and on behalf of the dynamically conceived common good...."[55] Natural law, therefore, cannot be conceived as some extended system of fixed rules. As Macquarrie says:

> Just as the substance of faith can never be adequately or precisely formulated in dogmatic propositions, and just as all such propositions have time-conditioned elements that need to be expressed in new and different ways in new historical situations, so the content of the moral life is never exhaustively or adequately formulated in rules and precepts.[56]

In effect, this means that the word "law" in the case of natural law must not be understood as a system or code of laws that exists alongside the system of positive laws, but as our way of referring to those most general moral principles against which particular rules or codes have to be measured. Natural law, in this context, becomes the touchstone for determining the justice or morality of actual laws, and in the case of human development, its directives, projects and goals.

The natural law cannot be particularized beyond a few general duties such as promise-keeping

and truth-telling, gratitude and respect for nature justice, helping those in need, self-improve-
ment, and the duty not to injure others. Even
these general duties must allow for the situation-
al element. With various claims placed upon the
person and the community, one duty has to take
precedence over the others.

Not only are there changes in the formulation
of natural law directives because of the time-
conditioned elements in each and the changes in
particular situations, but also, and more deeply,
the human person's nature itself is open and the
cosmos in which people find themselves is characterized by an evolving rather than static order.
This means that the classic description of natural
law as "everlasting" and "unchanging," tied as it
was to a former understanding of nature, both of
man and the cosmos, can no longer be maintained.
The new paradigm of the nature of the human person
and the world in which he or she lives, makes it
impossible to try to measure human actions by appeal to some original human nature in some kind of
pure state. Rather, the interpretation of natural
law must be kept in balance with men's and women's
continually evolving self-understanding. Karl
Rahner has stated this shift in the self-understanding of the human person:

> Whereas man in the pre-technological age
> knew only realizable aims set up by him-
> self inasmuch as they were pre-given by
> the structure of his own physical being
> and the reality surrounding it--whereas,
> in other words, he lived previously out
> of concrete 'nature,' pre-given to him
> and supporting him biologically and as a
> human being, he can now set himself aims
> (though not without limits) that he
> chooses arbitrarily, and in relation to
> them construct...a world that did not
> previously exist in order to reach them.
> He not only interprets the world about

him and its effects in terms of his human
life, but he creates this world himself.[57]

6. THE CHARACTERISTICS OF THE HUMAN PERSON: A NEW PARADIGM

In order to describe the characteristics of
the human person according to the new paradigm, we
can profitably employ the terms which I have used
to describe the mission of the Church--dialogue,
demonstration and development. This should not be
surprising, because the mission of the Church ultimately has as its objective aiding men and women
in the community to reach their full potential,
that is, salvation. Furthermore, describing men
and women within this dynamically conceived paradigm of the human person as "dialoguers," "demonstrators" and "developers" corresponds on the
theological level to the key concepts of revelation (dialogue), ecclesiology (demonstration), and
eschatology (development). Once again, our terminology should lend itself to broad dialogue and
still be able to be given a theological interpretation.

To describe a human being as a "person in dialogue" implies that the person's nature is open--a
being-on-the-way. Dialogue further implies a partner or partners--a being-with-others. A person
becomes what he or she will be in relationship
with other people. From the point of view of human
development, it must be emphasized that both sides
in a dialogue have something to give as well as
receive. And this stems from the very nature of
the human person. Dickinson expresses this mutual
aspect of dialogue:

It is only by listening to the voices of
the disinherited and giving them a voice
in the decision-making centers of the

> world that we will become sensitive not
> only to their needs, but our own as
> well.... We...have much more to gain and
> learn by joining in the struggle against
> underdevelopment, injustice and exploita-
> tion than we have to give. For it is by
> participation, involvement and sacrifice
> that we progressively discover our own
> real identity, our meaning, our own
> humanity....[58]

To describe human persons as "demonstrators"
means that by their very nature they must act out
what they are, what they remember, what they hope
for. The human person is an embodied spirit, a
being-in-the-world who must act or demonstrate in
order to be. Human persons must order and organize their existence with others, forming structures and institutions within which they can act
out, demonstrate and celebrate what they are and
what they hope to be. Persons in dialogue must
demonstrate what they are.

Finally, to describe the human person as a
"developer" implies that human beings have come of
age and are taking responsibility not only for
themselves but for the whole human family. More
and more, people are realizing their human solidarity. Their common occupancy of this shrinking
planet and the shrinking resources of the earth
call them to responsibility for the present, but
also for future generations. As Rahner has
pointed out, men and women today not only interpret the world around them and its effects in
terms of their human lives, but they actually
create this world themselves.

To say that the human person is called by his
or her nature to be a developer is to say that he
or she is called to responsibility. In the same
way that I have argued that development can contain within itself the concepts of dialogue and
demonstration, so responsibility implies a will-

ingness to dialogue and a freedom to demonstrate the inner spirit of the human person. The Catholic Bernard Haring and the Protestant Fritz Buri have both built their theology of the Christian life on the notion of responsibility. Yet, both theologians insist that ultimately responsibility means an answerability in the face of a transcendence which lays an unconditioned claim on the human conscience.[59] In Christian terms, this transcendent reality is God. It seems that even here, however, there should be some basis of dialogue between believers and nonbelievers. Macquarrie suggests that when the idea of responsbility is explored, even in the terms of a secular ethic, "we seem to enter that area of man's being in which we strike against something of his mystery and transcendence...."[60] Both of these latter terms are employed by nonreligious and religious writers alike. Roger Garaudy has called transcendence "a fundamental dimension of reality." He claims that the transcendent dimension of reality "cannot but appear when man's presence and creative activity are included in our definition of reality."[61] It seems that as long as nonbelievers, humanists, and Marxists are willing to admit that the human person is not totally defined, that is, that the human person is open and therefore his or her responsibility is open, there should be room for meaningful dialogue.

In the same way that we can no longer speak of a fixed human nature out of which people operate, neither can we conceive the future as a static place of "rest." Rather, the end or, perhaps better, the future of the human person is fuller humanity. Macquarrie aptly states:

> ...Man really is (that is to say, really attains his end) when he ventures forward in hope, as one on his way and not bound to an unchanged and unchangeable order; when he accepts his life in this world and lays hold on the rich possibilities

that it offers; when he acknowledges his being-with-others and joins with them in building a community of concern and love; when he enlarges his freedom of action; when he exercises his power in responsibility.[62]

The human person as a responsible developer grows out of the new understanding of human nature. Christians would insist, of course, that the description of the human person given above points toward a destiny that transcends the limits of this world. But this does not mean that the human person does not have the responsibility for this world. Men and women are called by their very nature to humane world development.

7. NATURAL LAW AND PARTICULAR CASES: AN ANSWER TO AN OBJECTION

We have examined the new paradigm of the human person upon which a dynamic understanding of the natural law is based. Now we must face the objection that natural law is inapplicable in particular cases. Moltmann and Berger, as was pointed out earlier, both say that, even if some general norms of natural law were admitted, they are practically useless in trying to solve concrete problems.

It is necessary, first of all, to understand how human persons come to know the natural law. Jacques Maritain, the great champion of the natural law theory in the recent past, notes that when we speak of "a law written on the heart" it can easily be misinterpreted as some type of "ready-made code rolled up within the conscience of each of us." On the contrary, he insists, written on the heart can only mean "in the hidden depths, as hidden from us as our own heart." It is not, therefore, from the beginning a content of consciousness; nor is it known as such to every

person.[63]   For Maritain, human beings know the
natural law through the guidance and pressure of
the "inclination" of human nature.[64] He speaks of
moral judgments proceeding primarily from "connaturality or congeniality through which what is con-
sonant with the essential inclinations of human
reason is grasped by the intellect as good; what
is dissonant, as bad."[65] "These essential inclinations of human nature either developed or were
released in the course of time: as a result, man's
knowledge of natural law progressively developed,
and continues to develop."[66]

Paul Ramsey has argued that Maritain, with his
knowledge of the natural law through inclination
of human nature, is in basic agreement with Edmond
Cahn. In his jurisprudential writings, Cahn speaks
about concrete cases serving as a prism through
which natural justice is mediated.   Neither
Maritain nor Cahn will accept the idea that theoretical principles can be deductively applied to
cases. As Ramsey explains it:

> ...What Cahn says about a case at law
> operating as a 'prism' through which mo-
> ral judgments can   become clear, about
> the importance of 'enacting' the transac-
> tions we meet with and thus coming to
> 'care with' the persons involved, and the
> confidence he expresses in ordinary con-
> science when put on its mettle and disci-
> plined to the concrete case, bear remark-
> able similarity to what Maritain means by
> 'knowledge through inclination.' For both
> ...decision making...is at once natural
> and contextual or positive....[67]

I suggest that natural law (as I have attempted to reinterpret above) known through a connaturality or inclination of human nature, will be
discernible in individual cases as long as open
and honest dialogue is present and those involved

in the case are willing to open their position to the Freudian/Marxist critique which I discussed in Chapter Three. Such a procedure is of vital importance in attempting to establish the policy and goals of development projects, as well as evaluating those in process.

8. VALUES TO BE FOSTERED IN DEVELOPMENT: ESTEEM, FREEDOM AND LIFE-SUSTENANCE

With the reinterpretation of natural law based on the dynamic nature of the human person as a "dialoguer," "demonstrator" and "developer," it should be possible to formulate some development values which are universal components of a humanly better life. Stemming from the human person characterized as one in dialogue, any development project should foster the value of esteem.[68] Esteem, for both the individual and the community, is intimately related to the question of meaning, and, as Berger has pointed out, the human person has a right to live in a meaningful world. Development projects must never blatantly destroy the esteem which individuals and peoples have for their own culture, their history, their perspective on reality. In development, these factors may be deepened or transformed, but the value of esteem must always be protected. Indeed, Berger has suggested that no social process can succeed unless it is illuminated with meaning from within.

A second value that should be fostered in any thrust for development is freedom. It finds its origin in the human person characterized as a "demonstrator." The individual cannot show forth and act out the spirit that is within him if he is not free of oppression. Any development project should foster liberation for men and women from every form of enslavement, be it slavery to nature, ignorance, other people and their systems or beliefs. The human person as a demonstrator or an actor must be free to create and celebrate. Freedom heightens the opportunities for self-actualization and allows men and women to participate fully in decisions affecting their own future. No development is possible if freedom is completely absent.

Finally, related to the characteristic of the human person as a developer is the value of life-sustenance. As Pope Paul has pointed out, a person must have in order to be. Any development project must attempt to provide more or better life-sustaining goods to individuals and communities. Even as development is intimately related to dialogue and demonstration in my schema of the mission of the Church, so here life-sustenance is intimately related to freedom and esteem. Any development project must not only promote life-sustaining goods of some sort, but those for whom the project is intended must have the freedom to participate in it in such a way that their own esteem is maintained and heightened. While people have a right to food, they also have a right, as Alves has insisted, to eat bread sacramentally, that is, with meaning. Men and women as developers have rights, but also responsibilities. The value of life-sustenance in any development project should be fostered so that people may be true developers. There is no true development in any project aimed at life-sustenance in which a generation is "written off" or the calculus of human pain is disregarded.

As we turn now to examine what specific role the Church should have in the integral development of persons and communities, these general development values must be kept in mind.

THE CHURCH AND WORLDWIDE HUMAN DEVELOPMENT: ITS DISTINCTIVE MISSION

Having outlined a broad basis upon which all men and women of good will can dialogue and decide upon development goals and the means of attaining those goals, and having described the Church as that segment of the human family that sees in Jesus of Nazareth the goal, the focal point and the meaning of all human history, we must now inquire into what distinctive contribution the Christian community can and must make to that more fully human future which, from their point of view, anticipates and previews the absolute future of God--the Kingdom. At various junctures in our discussion, we have indicated how the universal aspirations of men and women of good will are compatible with the Christian perspective and, at least from our point of view, can be given a depth, a clarity and a fervor in light of the Gospel of Jesus Christ. Drawing together those earlier indicators, I should suggest that the Church can and must fulfill its mission by serving as a mediator when development projects are a source of tension or conflict, by critiquing these projects, and in certain situations by carrying out development projects of its own. We shall examine each of these tasks and see how they are closely related to the threefold mission of the Church which I have described under the aegis of dialogue, demonstration and development.

1. THE CHURCH AS A MEDIATOR IN DEVELOPMENT:
   INTERPRETATION AND DIALOGUE

Men and women have a right to live in a meaningful world. Industrialization and technology --modernity--have forced their way into the non-Western world in the form of an "irresistible bulldozer," as van Leeuwen has expressed it.[69] When traditional societies are so invaded, their normative values--the way they plant crops, raise and educate children, practice hygiene, work without the idea of earning profit--are challenged. Because of the connection between these normative values and the significative values (the symbols which the society uses to explain and mediate the meaning of life and death), a challenge in the former causes a crisis in the latter. The deep-seated understanding of the whole meaning of existence is placed in a crisis situation. Tradition which had been the overriding force for ordering individual, family and societal activities, is challenged by new ways of doing things, by a plurality of choices. The Church must, as van Leeuwen says, "interpret" until such time as this invading phenomenon is no longer suffered as blind process, but as a series of continual human decisions.[70] Often local churches have considerable credibility on the local level; they should use this in an attempt to cushion the shock of development, but also to show that such societies need not accept all of the values of modernity as a package. Compromises and adjustments between tradition and modernity are possible. Traditional customs can at times even be converted to become vehicles of modernity.[71] With the gospel values of simplicity of life and the sacredness of the family, churches should be able on the local level to encourage peoples to maintain the best in their traditions and hopefully form communities where true human values can be fostered and celebrated.

On another level, the Church can serve as a mediator in development by making its influence felt among "teams of developers"[72] who, in a sense, are replacing that group formerly known as missionaries. Through dialogue and active participation in planning, whether on the part of international organizations, particular governments or special task groups, Christians can temper the rashness and insensitivity of some development plans. They can continually remind developers that there is a deeper meaning to life than meets the eye. They can, through dialogue with representatives of world religions, help men and women in those faiths to clarify and purify their significative values and thereby help them through the crisis that results from modernization and secularization. As members of teams of developers, they can visit particular areas for limited periods of time and engage in direct dialogue with those experiencing the crisis of development, and encourage and assist the formation of action groups which can, in turn, interpret the force of modernity among the people. Through its international structure, the Christian Church can foster an informal network of such groups for sharing of experiences and encouraging one another.

2. THE CHURCH AS A CRITIQUE OF DEVELOPMENT
DENUNCIATION AND DEMONSTRATION

The Church itself, existing under an eschatological proviso, that is, realizing that it is never an end in itself but is a herald, a sign and a facilitator of the coming Kingdom, can and must denounce every institution, movement or project that attempts to identify itself with the absolute. As discussed earlier, the dangerous and liberating memory of Jesus as one who was put to death as a political criminal yet conquered even the powers of death in his resurrection, is the ultimate critique of any political rule or worldly power that would seek self-absolutization. As Moltmann has pointed out, the freedom opened up to the Church in the cross of Christ enables it to enter into permanent iconoclasm against political personality cults and national religions as well as against economic fetishism.[73]

Because at the very heart of the Christian perspective is an unwavering reverence for the life of every person—"as long as you did it for one of my least brothers..." (Mt. 25, 40); "every hair of your head has been counted." (Mt. 10, 30); "You have been purchased, and at a price." (1 Cor. 6, 20)—the Church must denounce any development project that sacrifices human beings in the present in order to achieve a better world in the future. The calculus of human pain about which

Berger has written, must be passionately pursued by the Church in its participation in human development. Moreover, this respect for life must be shown not only by prophetic denunciation of projects that disregard it, but the Church must demonstrate by its own communal life that another alternative is possible.[74] Because of the Christian community's faith in the reconciling accomplishment of Christ, it must show forth to the rest of the world a model of community life wherein wealth, power, health or usefulness is never the measure of a person's worth. This means that in its worship and prayer, and especially in its celebration of the great reconciling Supper of the Lord, rich and poor, powerful and weak, workers and those unable to work, must at least momentarily lay aside their real and imagined differences and celebrate their common hope that commitment to a more just and human world is not in vain and that the reconciling Spirit of Christ can help them accomplish that which seems impossible.

This demonstration and celebration of reconciliation and hope are, of course, always liable to abuse, even as Paul pointed out to the Corinthians. He suggested, because of their factions, because of their inconsideration of the poor-- "one person goes hungry while another is getting drunk"--it is not the Lord's Supper that they eat (1 Cor. 11, 17-23). For Paul, the doctrine of worship and Christian "ethics" necessarily converge. Not only does worship of God become ethical, but ethics becomes the festival of life. This means, of course, that the Church itself is always open to critique and in need of continual reform. But the Eucharist is not only a sign of reconciliation and unity, it is also a means of achieving them. Therefore, following the Lord's command, we must continue to celebrate the Lord's Supper in spite of divisions and conflicts within the Church, realizing that the Holy Spirit can heal in ways incalculable to humans. As long as some openness is present, these celebrations are not, as Gutierrez suggests many people feel, "an exercise in make-believe,"[75] but a distinctive characteristic of the Christian community which should be a sign of hope for all interested in the task of healing and building up the family of humanity. The Church must offer itself as a model of human liberation and development; to the extent that it does this, it makes a distinctive contribution to worldwide development.

3. THE CHURCH'S OWN DEVELOPMENT PROJECTS: PROPHETIC SUBSTITUTION

The Church must not only act as a mediator in development, it must not only critique development goals and operations and offer itself as a model of humane development, but it must under certain circumstances sponsor and support specific development projects. It is in this area that there is the most disagreement concerning the proper mission of the Church. The proponents of political theology, especially Moltmann and Metz, argue that the Church should limit itself to criticism and denunciation of injustice, and not attempt to advocate alternative solutions, let alone sponsor them. The Church does not have the competence to offer constructive alternatives; it should limit itself to prophetic denunciation.[76] Edward Schillebeeckx has argued, however, that the Church must "give lead in those moral decisions that are opening up the future."[77] The Church must take an active responsibility for devising and supporting concrete proposals and programs designed to achieve the more human future.

If one accepts this position, and I do, the question arises, what is distinctive about the Christian approach to such projects? For those who propose a broad understanding of Church, such as Baum and Stackhouse, any good work in which the Spirit is active would be part of the Church's mission, and therefore the Church's contribution would not be distinctive. Even for those who propose a more restricted and specific understanding of Church--those who proclaim Jesus as Lord, who consciously try to live in a way that makes that proclamation believable to others and who actively celebrate their faith in word and sacrament--it often appears that Church development projects, whether in the field of relief, health or education, are mere parallels of those of other agencies. I suggest that the distinctively Christian characteristic of development projects is that they can and should be specifically prophetic and substitutive. We must examine this more in detail.

Concerning the Church's substitutive role in development projects or specific action for justice, Richard McBrien has said:

> There are those, especially Wolfhart Pannenberg, Juan Luis Segundo, and I include myself, who argue that whereas formal institutional action in the matter of specific social services, in addition to proclamation, is both justifiable and necessary, such action is to be initiated and maintained only where it is clearly a matter of supplying for the deficiencies of other responsible agencies, governmental or otherwise, or, as Segundo puts it, 'only when there is a lack of personnel or institutions to handle imperative needs.'[78]

The Church's development projects must be, by their very nature, of a temporary kind. Again, the eschatological proviso must continually free the Church so that it can move toward those most in need, in areas being neglected by other institutions. It must be the leaven, the seed which opens up in a prophetic way more creative possibilities for others. The Church loses its prophetic contribution to development projects when it becomes tied to maintenance of programs or institutions which could as well be operated by other segments of the community. Pannenberg states:

> The specifically social activities of the Church (its welfare organizations, child care centers, nursing and hospital establishments, schools, etc.) are subsidiary and temporary.... The Church's effort should be directed toward making the state ready and able to assume these responsibilities which are appropriate to the political structures of society. It is strange twisting of its sense of mission when the Church becomes jealous of the state and wants to monopolize certain welfare activities. The Church's satisfaction is in stimulating the political community to accept its responsibilities.[79]

Besides the prophetic and substitutive character which I have suggested is the distinctive characteristic of Church development projects, Richard Dickinson has proposed certain priorities which should be considered in any direct Church sponsorship of development projects.[80] Some of the questions that should be put to any development plans sponsored or supported by the Church as formulated by Dickinson are:

1.   "Does this Church effort enhance the capacity of persons involved to analyze their present situation, and define and act upon their own goals?" That is to say, Church-sponsored development efforts should not settle for action without reflection, nor reflection without action. Humans not only need bread, but bread eaten as sacrament.

2.   "Does the proposed effort concentrate on enhancing the liberation of marginated and oppressed peoples?" The clear Gospel imperative is to aid those most in need.

3.   "Does the proposed effort focus on values and perceptual questions?" The point here is that other agencies often are more willing and capable of solving problems resulting from natural calamities--that is, relief, whereas the Church should be especially concerned about problems stemming from human decisions--social dislocation and the destruction of a meaningful world resulting from industrialization and the like.

4.   "Does the proposed effort concentrate on groups more than individuals?" The Church has a special vocation because of its own communal life, to foster the notion of community and corporate action.

5.   "Does the effort enhance the role of women in the social development process?" The Church cannot ignore the world-wide movement for women's rights, even though in its own internal life it has a great distance to go in overcoming its masculine image. Beyond this, enhancing the position of women is one of the chief ways of hastening development.

6.   "Does the proposed effort strengthen the capacity of national or international agencies to effect changes, especially those which are beneficial to the poorest 25% of the populace, or the poorest nations (taking the United Nations' list of 25 poorest countries)?" There must be the spirit of cooperation in all Church projects and especially an effort not to foster the mentality that governmental and intergovernmental agencies are suspect, always manipulated by leaders eager for their own power and affluence, always inefficient and/or corrupt, always oppressive of the poor.   "Some of the most important work that churches can do to promote development and justice will be the way they, with limited resources, enable those with more resources to move ahead with the job."

7.   "Does the proposed effort influence the thinking of people in rich countries as well as the poor?" This is the question of development education, or, as I have suggested, making it possible for the rich to experience the shock of underdevelopment.

8.   "Finally, does the proposed effort correspond to a local initiative and concern, preferably a Christian base?" Dickinson realizes that this criterion is open to question, but he suggests that in his analysis of many development projects in the past several years, the enthusiasm of the local Christian group was almost indispensable to the success of the effort.

To this list I should like to add a criterion which McBrien has suggested. Does "the form of ecclesiastical action...unnecessarily or unduly polarize the Church itself?"[81] Certainly a diversity of viewpoints is to be expected and tolerated. However, one of the serious issues that arises in this respect is whether the Church should support a project that employs or entails violence. A case in point is the support that the World Council of Churches gave certain African liberation groups in 1970. Although the groups were involved in education and health activities, and although the World Council designated that their aid was to be used for medical care of the sick or injured, still the main thrust of these liberation organizations was political emancipation by means of force. Unquestionably the support given by the World Council of Churches to these groups caused great strain among certain member churches. Some threatened to withdraw from the World Council. But in light of the long history of racial oppression on the part of the colonial powers involved, as well as the stalling tactics they employed in avoiding the United Nations mandate to free the colonies, it would be difficult to say that the action by the World Council of Churches unnecessarily polarized the

Church. Furthermore, because of the compromises which allowed member churches to designate which projects they wanted to support, we could say that <u>undue</u> polarization was avoided. Decisions in such cases are unquestionably difficult, but in retrospect it does appear that the World Council was justified in its action.

I suggest that there are times when the Church may find no choice but to support such liberation groups. When it does this, however, it should endeavor to specify that its aid is purely for humanitarian purposes. Moreover, the Church's involvement should parallel on an institutional level the posture that Jacques Ellul outlines for a Christian who finds himself drawn by necessity to a violent movement to defend the oppressed: He must appear as a foreign body in their midst, a kind of permanent bad conscience; a reminder of something else, a witness of the Wholly Other. His presence will imply that the undertaking is of a relative character and, moreover, that he might change camps, that indeed he must change camps once his friends have won, for in the aftermath of victory the revolutionary party assumes power and begins to oppress the former oppressors.[82]

If the Church should find itself in this position, it must never cease denouncing violence as a countersign of God's Kingdom and using all its resources to find ways of reconciliation and peace.

The Church does have a distinctive contribution to make, both in the overall field of integral development of people and the world and in specific development projects as outlined above.

SUMMARY OF CHAPTER SIX

Chapter Six is a positive attempt to outline a theology of development on the ground cleared by the critique offered in the previous chapter. The understanding of revelation formulated in this study provides a theological basis for discerning God's presence in the struggle for development as well as a prophetic denunciation of the dehumanizing aspects of underdevelopment. The revelatory "shock of underdevelopment" cuts across individuals and societies, rich and poor, and provides a basis for constructive dialogue. Contrary to the liberationists, dialogue among those of different ideologies is possible and necessary, especially since the Marxist "scientific analysis" is incapable of providing tools for its own critique.

The eschatological stance formulated in this study provides the basis for discussing development goals. It is suggested that a new dynamic paradigm of the nature and purpose of the human person has moved onto the scene, and from this it is possible to reformulate the natural law theory upon which an ethics of development may be based. This natural law basis, while not dependent upon the Christian understanding, can be given a deeper, clearer theological dimension by reference to what we accept as God's ultimate revelation in Jesus.

Once a reformulated natural law, based on the dynamic understanding of the human person, has provided the basis for development goals, particular values which must accompany the movement toward these goals can be determined: personal and societal esteem, freedom, and life-sustenance.

The Church's distinctive mission in the worldwide quest for development is outlined: Because of its unwavering concern for the life of every human being, it must (1) mediate when tensions arise from development and critique those development projects which are insensitive to the cost of human pain; (2) provide the impetus and opportunity for reconciliation among all peoples and, by its own example, urge them at least momentarily to lay aside their differences and celebrate their common hope and commitment to a more just and human world; and (3) engage in development projects of its own as long as they are substitutive and prophetic in nature. Finally, a series of criteria is suggested for determining the wisdom of undertaking and sustaining the Church's own development projects.

****

The reformulation of missionary theology as a theology of development has thus been completed. What follows in Chapter Seven, although intimately related to, and flowing logically from, the six preceding chapters, is, as the title indicates, a prospectus. It has been argued throughout that the basic perspective on revelation and eschatology will affect the theologian's understanding of the Church's mission. After criticizing the position of several theologians of liberation and revolution on these issues, I have formulated and presented my own understanding of the mission of the Church. What follows is a "look ahead" at what I suggest are the ecclesial structures that are being forged and that will facilitate the Church's mission as I have presented it. The prospectus is necessarily sketched in broad outline, and many of the questions it raises cannot be dealt with in depth. But it is based on a reading of the signs of the times and, I believe, is a necessary postscript to the preceding work.

NOTES ON CHAPTER SIX

[1]See earlier discussion in Chapter Four, pp. 146-47. Further evidence of the profound shift in the posture of Third World churches is evidenced in the Third General Conference of Latin American

Bishops, convened in Puebla, Mexico, January, 1979. For documentation and commentary see PUEBLA AND BEYOND, John Eagleson and Philip Scharper, eds. (Maryknoll, New York: Orbis Books, 1979). Contrary to the fears of many, the Latin American bishops did not turn their backs on the Church's commitment to liberation.

[2]"The Theological Problems Entailed in the Idea of 'the New Earth,'" THEOLOGICAL INVESTIGATIONS Vol. 10, p. 267.

[3]"Man in Process," CONCILIUM 75 (1972): 47.

[4]THE CRUCIFIED GOD, p. 22. Karl Rahner has developed this same thought in several essays. See, for example, "Reflection on the Unity of Love of Neighbor and Love of God," THEOLOGICAL INVESTIGATIONS Vol. 6, pp. 231-49.

[5]THE CRUCIFIED GOD, p. 23. That there continues to be considerable opposition to such a view from certain Protestant evangelicals and even among some Orthodox cannot be overlooked. In the Frankfurt Declaration of 1971, evangelicals declared that humanization is not the primary goal of mission and labeled as false teaching the idea that Christ is anonymously so evident in world religions, historical changes, and revolutions that man can encounter him and find salvation in him without the direct news of the Gospel. The full text of this Declaration was quoted in CHRISTIANITY TODAY (June 19, 1970): 5ff.

The 1974 Lausanne World Conference on Evangelism struck a much healthier balance: "We affirm that evangelism and sociopolitical involvement are both part of our Christian duty....The salvation we claim should be transforming us in the totality of our personal and social responsibilities." Quoted in ECUMENICAL PRESS SERVICE, WCC, No. 23 (August 15, 1974): 4. This same balance prevailed at the 1975 Nairobi Assembly of the World Council

of Churches, where the expected confrontation between the evangelicals and the social activists
did not materialize. See Arthur J. Moore, "Nairobi: Consolidation and Catching Up," CHRISTIANITY
AND CRISIS 36 (February 2, 1976): 2ff.

6"The Normative Anthropology of the Gospel,"
CONCILIUM 75 (1972): 57.

7THE POLITICS OF HOPE, Dennis Pardee, trans.
(Grand Rapids, Michigan: Wm. B. Eerdmans Publishing Co., 1974), p. 17.

8THE CRUEL CHOICE, p. 23. This phrase is similar in meaning to what Schillebeeckx has called
"contrast experiences." These experiences cause
people to say, "This should not go on!" From it
develops protest against war, hunger, social injustice, racial discrimination, the ownership of
vast properties, and the like. According to
Schillebeeckx, these contrast experiences show
that the moral imperative is first discovered in
its immediate, concrete, inner meaning, before it
can be made the object of a science and then reduced to a generally valid principle. See "The
Magisterium and the World of Politics," CONCILIUM
36 (1968): 29, 31.

9See earlier discussion in Chapter Five, pp.
235-37. Berger's criticism of conscientization as
developed in the work of Paulo Freire has not gone
unchallenged. Denis Goulet himself, in a review of
Berger's PYRAMIDS OF SACRIFICE, CHRISTIANITY AND
CRISIS 35 (October 13, 1975), states that Berger's
portrait of Freire and the assumptions he imputes
to champions of "consciousness-raising" are dia-
metrically opposed to Freire's spirit and work.
He does admit, however, that certain groups may
invoke Freire's name, the term consciousness-raising, or his method to inflict the kind of elitist
belittlement described by Berger (p. 236).

[10]ON THE DEVELOPMENT OF PEOPLES, para. 49. For Pope John Paul II's address to the United Nations see ORIGINS 9 (October 11, 1979).

[11]WORLD DEVELOPMENT: CHALLENGE TO THE CHURCHES, p. 9.

[12]Donella Meadows, Dennis Meadows, et al, THE LIMITS TO GROWTH (Washington, D.C.: Potomac Associates, 1972). For a critical assessment of the basic thesis of this study, see Nick Eberstadt, "Myths About Starvation," NEW YORK REVIEW OF BOOKS 23/2 (February 19, 1976): 32-37. In spite of criticisms of the LIMITS OF GROWTH study, and there are many, it did serve as a "shock of underdevelopment."

[13]TO SET AT LIBERTY THE OPPRESSED, p. 10.

[14]Actually, this exchange took place at a press conference after Dr. Birch's address as reported by James W. Kennedy, NAIROBI 1975 (Cincinnati: Forward Movement Publications, 1976), p. 77.

[15]IBID, p. 76. The official documents of the Nairobi Assembly were not yet available when this chapter was being written.

[16]For a brief report on UNCTAD IV, see "Compromise in Nairobi," TIME (June 7, 1976): 69.

[17]Erich Fromm has judged the alienation of affluence to be no less dehumanizing than the alienation of misery. Cited in Denis Goulet, "World Hunger: Putting Development Ethics to the Test," CHRISTIANITY AND CRISIS 35 (May 26, 1975): 128.

[18]Dickinson, TO SET AT LIBERTY, points out that development education has taken on the task of devising ways to help people in affluent countries understand their own implication in underdevelopment, their own need to change social structures if they genuinely want to do something about

poverty (p. 123). For a challenging presentation of this question see Marie Augusta Neal's A SOCIO-THEOLOGY OF LETTING GO (New York, N.Y.: Paulist Press, 1977).

[19]One of the most unambiguous statements of such a position is found in the final document of the First Convention of Christians for Socialism held in Santiago, Chile, in April, 1972. For this and related documents surrounding the convention, see CHRISTIANS AND SOCIALISM, edited by John Eagleson. Avery Dulles cautions that the over-influence of the Marxist critique of religion in the rhetoric of liberation theology sometimes seems to suggest that social or political revolution, with a corresponding redistribution of wealth and power, are an essential means of bringing the poor and oppressed the salvation promised by the Gospel. Any direct evangelization is treated as though it were a mere cloak for oppression. See "The Meaning of Faith Considered in Relationship to Justice," in THE FAITH THAT DOES JUSTICE: EXAMINING THE CHRISTIAN SOURCES FOR SOCIAL CHANGE, John C. Haughey, ed. (New York: Paulist Press, 1977), p. 41.

[20]PYRAMIDS OF SACRIFICE, p. 27.

[21]IBID., p. 93.

[22]"Compromise in Nairobi," TIME, p. 69.

[23]Berger, PYRAMIDS, pp. 101-02. Berger critiques the capitalist model of development exemplified by Brazil and the socialist represented by China, and rejects both as morally unacceptable because of the amount of human pain which is willfully inflicted on their people without justification. On the other hand, he points out that neither can be cited either in defense of or as a final argument against, respectively, capitalism or socialism. Neither exhausts the possibilities of capitalism or socialism.

[24]IBID., p. 18.

[25]Moltmann, THE CRUCIFIED GOD, p. 326; Metz, "The Future in the Memory of Suffering," CONCILIUM 76 (1972): 9-25. An adapted version of the Metz article appears as Chapter Seven of his FAITH IN HISTORY AND SOCIETY.

[26]See Paul Tillich, "Protestantism as a Critical and Creative Principle," in POLITICAL EXPECTATIONS, James Luther Adams, ed. (New York: Harper and Row, 1971), pp. 10-39.

[27]Goulet, THE CRUEL CHOICE, P. 333.

[28]PYRAMIDS, p. 35.

[29]IBID., p. 222.

[30]IBID., p. 171.

[31]IBID., p. 187.

[32]Berger discusses these two criteria in Chap. VII, "Policy and the Calculus of Meaning," pp. 166-89, and Chap. VI, "Policy and the Calculus of Pain," pp. 137-65.

[33]IBID., p. 227.

[34]MAN: CHRISTIAN ANTHROPOLOGY IN THE CONFLICTS OF THE PRESENT, John Sturdy, trans. (Philadelphia: Fortress Press, 1974), p. 73.

[35]IBID., p. 75.

[36]IBID., p. 76.

[37]NINE MODERN MORALISTS (New York: New American Library, 1970, c. 1962), p. 28.

[38]See THE ENCYCLICALS AND OTHER MESSAGES OF JOHN XIII, ed. by the staff of THE POPE SPEAKS

Magazine (Washington, D.C.: TPS Press, 1964), p. 328. It had been the custom that papal documents on social issues based their arguments on the "twin sources of natural law and revelation." Perhaps because Pope John addressed his letter to "all men of good will," he used the single natural law source.

39"Concerning the Relationship between Nature and Grace," THEOLOGICAL INVESTIGATIONS Vol. 1, pp. 315-16.

40"Conference sur L'Eglise dans le monde d'aujourd'hui," LAS DOCUMENTATION CATHOLIQUE LXII (1965), cited in Charles Curran, CATHOLIC MORAL THEOLOGY IN DIALOGUE (Notre Dame: Fides Publishers, 1972, pp. 128-29.

41Curran, CATHOLIC MORAL THEOLOGY, p. 10.

42Ramsey, BASIC CHRISTIAN ETHICS (London: SCM Press, 1953), p. 86, sees nothing threatening in the possibility that the foundations of Christian morality may be the same as the foundations of a generally valid natural morality. Approaching it from the opposite direction, Douglas Sturm, "Naturalism, Historicism, and Christian Ethics: Toward a Christian Doctrine of Natural Law," JOURNAL OF RELIGION 44 (1964): 40, claims that "there is a form of natural law that is a necessary implicate of Christian faith."

43THE RESPONSIBLE SELF (New York: Harper and Row, 1963), p. 168.

44LOVE AND JUSTICE, D. B. Robertson, ed. (Cleveland and New York: World Publishing - Meridian Books, 1967), pp. 33-34.

45THREE ISSUES IN ETHICS (New York: Harper and Row, 1970), p. 85.

46IBID., p. 91.

[47]This statement occurs in a review of Charles C. West, THE POWER TO BE HUMAN (New York: Macmillan, 1971), which appeared in THEOLOGY TODAY 28 (January, 1972): 504-06.

[48]THREE ISSUES, p. 91.

[49]IBID., p. 97-98.

[50]THE CHRISTIAN MESSAGE IN A NON-CATHOLIC WORLD, pp. 148-58; 230-34; 336-40.

[51]THE CRUEL CHOICE, p. 81.

[52]PYRAMIDS, pp. 180ff. Berger describes modernization as a gigantic steel hammer, smashing both traditional institutions and structures of meaning. It deprives the individual of the security which traditional institutions provided for him and tends to deprive him of the cosmological security provided by traditional religious world views (p. 23).

[53]HE WHO IS (London: Darton, Longman and Todd, new ed., 1966), p. 122, quoted in THREE ISSUES, pp. 100-01.

[54]THREE ISSUES, p. 103.

[55]CONSTITUTION ON THE CHURCH IN THE MODERN WORLD, Art. 5 and Art. 74.

[56]THREE ISSUES, p. 104.

[57]HANDBUCH DER PASTORALTHEOLOGIE Vol. II (Freiburg, 1966), p. 189, quoted in Metz, THEOLOGY OF THE WORLD, p. 144.

[58]"Why International Development: A Christian Perspective," ENCOUNTER 31 (Spring, 1970): 176.

[59]FREE AND FAITHFUL IN CHRIST, 2 vols. (New York: Seabury Press, 1978, 1979).

[60]THREE ISSUES, p. 76.

[61]"Faith and Revolution." CROSS CURRENTS 23 (Spring, 1973): 35. This article was published in the BULLETIN DU CENTRE PROTESTANT D"ETUDES, Geneva (1973) and also in THE ECUMENICAL REVIEW (January, 1973).

[62]THREE ISSUES, p. 79.

[63]THE RIGHTS OF MAN AND NATURAL LAW (New York: Charles Scribner's Sons, 1943), p. 62.

[64]MAN AND THE STATE (Chicago: University of Chicago Press, 1951), p. 98, n. 13.

[65]"On Knowledge through Connaturality," in THE RANGE OF REASON (New York: Charles Scribner's Sons, 1952), Chap. 3, pp. 22-29. Cited in Ramsey, NINE MODERN MORALISTS, p. 275.

[66]NINE MODERN MORALISTS, pp. 275-76.

[67]IBID., p. 277.

[68]These values to be fostered in development are discussed in slightly different manner in Goulet, THE CRUEL CHOICE, Chap. 6, "Three Strategic Principles," pp. 123-52.

[69]CHRISTIANITY IN WORLD HISTORY, p. 317.

[70]IBID., p. 409. Van Leeuwen sees this, in effect, as the mission of the Church today.

[71]PYRAMIDS, p. 175. Gunnar Myrdal, THE CHALLENGE OF WORLD POVERTY, p. 26ff, notes that "...when the traditional valuations are brought up on a 'higher' more articulate level, they are often found not to be in conflict with modernization ideals. Indeed, for the most part they either support these ideals, or, at least, remain neutral."

[72]Goulet discusses a "new brotherhood of developers"--qualified specialists with a specific code of ethics. Such a code might be: "Whatever community I visit, there I will work on behalf of those in greatest need, with them and on their terms, not as a dispenser of superior wisdom but as a cooperator in the common task of creating wisdom to match our sciences. I will refrain from all condescension, paternalism, exploitation and manipulation...and the regimen I adopt shall be for the benefit of man's universal needs, not for any particular interests." THE CRUEL CHOICE, p. 181.

[73]See THE CRUCIFIED GOD, esp. Chap. 8, "Ways towards the Political Liberation of Man."

[74]The document JUSTICE IN THE WORLD, issued by the Third International Synod of Bishops which met in Rome in 1971, mentions that the Church's specific responsibility is to defend the dignity of the human person by denouncing injustice and witnessing to justice through its own structures and manner of life. (Washington: United States Catholic Conference, 1971), para. 23, 52.

[75]A THEOLOGY OF LIBERATION, p. 137. Camilo Torres was one who adopted this position. He stated in his "Message to Christians," "I have ceased to say Mass to practice love for my fellow man in the temporal, economic, and social spheres. When my fellow man has...carried out the revolution, then I will return to offering Mass, God permitting." See Camilo Torres, REVOLUTIONARY WRITINGS, R. Olsen and L. Day, trans. (New York: Herder and Herder, 1969), p. 173.

[76]This has been the consistent position of Metz, but it appears that Moltmann is moving more toward activism. In THE CRUCIFIED GOD, he states, "...The Church...must take sides in the concrete social and political conflicts going on about... and must be prepared to join and form parties. It

must not ally itself with the existing parties, but in a partisan fashion intervene on behalf of betrayed humanity and suppressed freedom" (p. 53).

[77]GOD THE FUTURE OF MAN, N. D. Smith, trans. (New York: Sheed and Ward, 1968), p. 159.

[78]"The Church and Social Change: An Ecclesiological Critique," in THEOLOGY CONFRONTS A CHANGING WORLD, Thomas M. McFadden, ed. (West Mystic, Conn.: Twenty-Third Publications, 1977), p. 52. This position is both more specific and more realistic than, for example, Hans Kung's in ON BEING A CHRISTIAN. Kung states, "The Church and its representatives may, should and must take a stand publicly even on controversial social questions where, but only where, it is empowered to do so by its special mandate: wherever and as far as the Gospel of Jesus Christ itself (and not just any sort of theory) unambiguously (and not only obscurely) demands this" (p. 568). The question, of course, is who decides and upon what basis? Kung seems overconfident in his assessment of the ability of men and women today to discern exactly and unambiguously what the Gospel of Jesus Christ demands in particular situations. Either that, or he would admit to very few instances when the community as community should take a public stand on a controversial social question. The latter is, in fact, in keeping with the persistent Lutheran strain of "patient expectation" evident in his theology.

[79]THE THEOLOGY OF THE KINGDOM OF GOD, pp. 90-91.

[80]TO SET AT LIBERTY THE OPPRESSED. The following is a summary of Chap. 5, "Priorities: One Perspective," pp. 111-24. Because the summary follows very closely the order presented in the chapter--I have omitted and combined certain parts --individual page references will not be given. These priorities parallel, to a large extent, the

criteria offered by Segundo, THE COMMUNITY CALLED CHURCH, pp. 96-97, for testing the authenticity of the Church's participation in development projects. It also includes most of the criteria that McBrien proposes for the Church's involvement directly in the political process. "The Church and Social Change," pp. 52-54.

[81]"The Church and Social Change," p. 54.

[82]VIOLENCE, pp. 49-50. John Bennett comments that the group appointed by the World Council of Churches to discuss the issue of revolutionary violence was not able to agree on the general question of violence; some of its members felt compelled to say that "nonviolence does not present itself as an option unless they would withdraw totally from the struggle for justice." The group was able, however, to agree that there are some forms of violence in which Christians may not participate and which churches must condemn. They state:

> There are violent means of struggle --torture in all forms, the holding of innocent hostages and the deliberate or indiscriminate killing of innocent non-combatants for example--which destroy the soul of the perpetrator as surely as the life and health of the victim.

See "Violence, Nonviolence and the Struggle for Social Justice," THE ECUMENICAL REVIEW 25 (October, 1973): 443. Quoted by Bennett in "Love and Justice," in Theology and Change, R. H. Preston, ed., p. 141.

CHAPTER SEVEN

AN ECCLESIOLOGY FOR THE THEOLOGY OF DEVELOPMENT: A PROSPECTUS

DENOMINATIONAL DIFFERENCES: A HINDRANCE TO THE CHURCH'S CONTRIBUTION TO DEVELOPMENT

Although specific examples of Protestant or Catholic thought have been given throughout our discussion, the word Church has been used without any denominational distinction. This has been a deliberate attempt to underline the fact that the Christian community, that is, the Church, can no longer turn toward the rest of the world and effectively dialogue with it, critique and serve it, and especially be an example or model for it, through the divisive prism of denominational differences. Without glossing over existing divisions and imagining that a unity exists where in fact it doesn't, still we must constantly remind ourselves that as Christians we profess the same Lord, share the same faith, and seek and serve the same coming Kingdom.

Certainly it is true that the ecumenical movement has had its impact. As pointed out by the former General Secretary to the World Council of Churches, Willem Visser't Hooft, there is no comparison between the present situation in which numerous opportunities exist for contact, cooperation and fellowship, and the isolation and ignorance among the various churches even fifty years ago.[1]

This opening to ecumenical dialogue and cooperation has been made possible by the recognition of what Visser't Hooft has called "a sense of proportion," or, as the Second Vatican Council has expressed it, "a hierarchy of truths."[2] Christians have been moved to focus attention on their common faith, the weight of which is so great that those who hold it belong together even if they disagree on some of the consequences which flow from that faith. Visser't Hooft's says, "Polarization loses its sharpness and ceases to be dangerous when we remain clearly aware that no discord in the less weighty matters of faith can divide us as long as we hold on together to the central truth."[3]

Ecumenical dialogue and cooperation have been made possible not only by recognition of this "sense of proportion" or "hierarchy of truths," but also by the growing acceptance that pluralism within unity is a trait which stems from the New Testament Church itself. In the New Testament the variety of doctrinal statements, theologies and ecclesial structures makes it impossible for any church to raise exclusive or absolute claims for its particular organizational structure. No church structure, whether papal, episcopal, presbyterial or congregational, can claim exclusive apostolic origins.[4] This forces the Christian Church today to remain open in principle both to all the possibilities of ecclesial order which existed in the New Testament Church and to the continual need of institutional reform.

A church characterized by pluralism must have, in addition to a common bond of faith, a consensus on the operational level if it is to be effective in carrying out its mission. It must have, as Stackhouse insists, good social organization—"a symbol system or language system, a polity, an economy, a pattern of mores, and constituent members—all of which interact whenever the ecclesia functions."[5]

In this chapter an attempt is made to outline in general terms an ecclesiology that will provide for diversity and pluralism but also be functional for carrying out the mission of the Church as it has been presented under the aegis of development. It is, as the chapter title indicates, a prospectus. It is based not merely on projection, however, but on current trends. It is being forged and implemented, at least to a certain extent, on the "cutting edge" of the Church's activities--in local, national and international conferences and councils, but also, and perhaps more importantly, in struggling Christian communities in the Third World, especially among the young. Walbert Buhlmann, in THE COMING OF THE THIRD CHURCH, says:

> Many young people in the Third Church are even less concerned about the divisions between the confessional camps. Even if their roots are in the anti-ecumenical past, still they are less sensitive to the weight of the ancient structural divisions. What counts for them are the larger religious groupings, Christianity, Islam, Hinduism; they consider the distinctions within Christianity insignificant. Besides, all the young states find themselves confronted by the central problem of creating national unity. Wise heads of state have often exhorted Christians not to be focal points for division but rather ferment of unity. After all, the Christians of those countries can no longer afford, as a minority, to present themselves before the non-Christian block as an array of between five and fifty different Churches. They ought therefore to take the lead with far-reaching imaginative plans for fraternal collaboration....[6]

CHURCH POLITY:
THE KEY TO ECUMENICAL ECCLESIOLOGY

More and more it becomes clear that the fundamental issue dividing Christians, especially the

large divisions among Catholics, Anglicans, Orthodox and Protestants, is that of ecclesial polity.
In other words, the problem centers on the question of leadership and authority in the Church,
that is, the function of ecclesiastical office and
especially the authority held and exercised in the
Roman Catholic tradition by the college of bishops
with the pope at its center and head. Indeed, as
Pope Paul VI often said, he was the main obstacle
to Church union.

The question here is much deeper than that of
mere external organization. The conception that
one has of ecclesiastical office or leadership
determines the way one understands the process by
which Christians come to know the meaning of the
Gospel, as well as the way they seek to express it
in words and actions. As McBrien points out, when
trying to make up their minds about matters that
touch upon their understanding and living of the
Gospel, Catholics will always give serious consideration to the guidelines proposed from the
official, collegial source.[7] This does not mean,
however, that they will follow these guidelines
blindly, nor that they will never disagree with
such guidelines. But, unlike other Christians,
Catholics accord antecedent attention and respect
to the stated positions, past and present, of the
Church's college of bishops, whether expressed
collectively or through its spokesman, the bishop
of Rome. For Catholics, the college of bishops
has an irreplaceable function of holding in creative tension Scripture, tradition and contemporary
Christian experience.

In his ETHICS AND THE URBAN ETHOS, Max
Stackhouse underlines the importance of the question of ecclesial polity:

> Especially important in ecclesiology
> is the question of polity, of how such
> groups structure themselves, for how they

organize themselves and pattern their distribution of power and authority gives evidence both of what they conceive the shape of the future to be, and how they think it ought to be under the vision of the future.[8]

Stackhouse suggests, however, that the Church, in ecclesiological terms, has already begun to enter a new period. The new paradigm of Church, as we might call it, was anticipated in several nineteenth century motifs, and is deeply influenced today by both the insights of social science and the fresh perspective on the conciliar Catholic tradition stimulated by the Second Vatican Council. Based on this ecclesiological shift, Stackhouse outlines a polity for an ecumenical ecclesiology which offers many valuable insights for structuring the united Christian effort in implementing a theology of development.

According to Stackhouse, denominationalism has become the major pattern of ecclesiological organization in modern society. The concept of denomination differs from the "church/sect" typology developed in the thought of Max Weber and Ernst Troeltsch, although it may derive from either.[9] Denomination is derived from "church" when "church" is forced into the position where it is no longer part of, nor protected by, the government. Denomination is a derivation of "sect" when "sect" extends its organization and influence into larger groups and beyond a first generation of converts. Denomination, as Stackhouse describes it:

(a) may be coterminous with political boundaries but includes only some of the population in its voluntary membership, (b) admits that it does not have a corner on the truth by encouraging, or at least not undercutting, pluralism, and (c) develops an independent economic structure by which it attempts to mobilize sentiment and material resources to serve mankind.[10]

Three traditions--the Catholic, the Calvinist and the sectarian--have attempted to establish an ecclesiology fundamental to the question of the destiny of individuals and society. Stackhouse points to a convergence of these three prototypical forms of denominational social organization into a fourth, synthetic possibility which he designates "conciliar denominationalism." The result is a consensus theology of Church polity.

The peculiar Catholic polity is characterized by a corporate structure governed by a hierarchical pattern of authority. It includes not only Roman Catholic but Anglican and American Methodist religious traditions. Stackhouse denies that this structure needs to be monolithic. Its policies and polity are worked out by votes of elders meeting in council, but communication and feedback with lower echelons are not unusual. Indeed, the principle of subsidiarity is practiced in operational matters, and only in points of conflict at a particular level is appeal made to the next higher level of authority. A non-ecclesial counterpart would be a modern corporation.

McBrien insists that the leadership in the Catholic Church must try to reflect the actual consensus of the Church. If the Pope and bishops are convinced that the consensus of the Church is moving in the wrong direction, they have the obligation to attempt to create a new, countervailing consensus. According to McBrien:

If the spirit is with them, the new consensus will eventually win the day. But the Pope and bishops never have the right to impose their views on the Church without such an organic process. If, by chance, they do attempt to impose such a position, the Church itself will, and must, reject it.[11]

The vision of the future in this Catholic type of ecclesial polity is predominantly that of ful-fillment. Natural patterns of creation are seen as organically striving for fuller and richer development as they move into higher and higher states of existence. This is made possible by bringing "natural" resources into "supernatural" relationship according to rightly understood "natural law" through divinely ordained manage-ment—that is, the hierarchy. The danger is, of course, totalitarianism and of identifying the institutional structures with the Kingdom of God. The benefits of such a polity are the sense of order, security and efficiency of operation which it presents. Stackhouse claims that conciliar decisions and executive leadership from this Catholic polity are compatible with the new consensus.[12]

The second ecclesial polity which has attempt-ed to give an overall social organization to its institution and members is the Calvinist or cove-nantal type. The fundamental characteristics of this mode of organization are "oligarchical ap-pointment or election to authority, based on com-petent definition of and obedient behavior to that which is of ultimate power and worth as recognized by certified peers." Its structure is charac-terized by pluralistic centers of power which are created not by differentiation of previous centers and subordinate to a dominant authority pattern as in the Catholic corporate polity, but through the contracting of like-minded persons who coordinate their interests and bind themselves to a disci-pline and a given aim. Unity is gained in this polity through inter-group alliances and federa-tions. Representatives are designated to inter-pret or specify the rules for the interaction or to consolidate coalition action on specific issues. Here governing bodies are structurally derivative and decision-making is based upon a combination of technical competence, consensus formation, and codes of discipline. A non-ecclesial parallel is a contemporary university.

This Calvinistic polity affirms democracy among the elite, the competent, and those within the fold. But the danger is in identifying the covenant with divisions of class, race or interest group, and of resisting the formation of new covenantal groups that make similar exclusive claims. On the positive side, the covenantal mode of organization holds up the ideal of a pluralistic, open and competent polity with centralized leadership derivative and therefore accountable. It ensures a plurality of responsible local communities seeking to work within a broad ecumenical consensus.

The third traditional type of ecclesial polity is the sectarian or "movement" mode of organization. Stackhouse calls this form of ecclesial polity "the minority report of the theological tradition through Catholic and Protestant denomination perspectives." Some sectarians withdraw in order to avoid the evils of the world and develop an intensively personal and small group pietism. Others are aggressive activists who confront the evils of the world and attempt to transform them. The sectarian polity is evident in Unitarian-Universalist, Quaker, and some Baptist traditions. It appears in evangelical, populist, and some pentecostal movements, as well as in revolutionary cadres of the Third World. Running through these groups is a basic conviction that every individual has the innate capacity to decide where his or her loyalty will rest and where he or she will stand. Responsibility for what results from this voluntary decision is up to the individual. One's decision may be emotional or rational, mystical or moral, but it must be personal and involve the voluntary assumption of a new style of life according to a transformed vision of the future.

Such a polity is suspicious of the Catholic corporative or Calvinist covenantal forms of social organization. Structural centers of loyalty are considered of little or no importance. The danger in this mode of organization is that it is prone to produce messianic figures and demagogic leaders who demand total commitment. In its best moments, the sectarian movement opens the way for dynamic charismatic leadership, it spearheads unpopular but just causes, and it is a continual critique of the other two types of polity. In the Catholic tradition, religious Orders have played an analogous, although not identical, role as the sectarian movements have in the Protestant tradition.

The convergence of the traditional ecclesial polities into an ecumenical ecclesiology is noted in two important shifts. They are the modification of the covenantal type of organization toward the corporate and the corporate toward the covenantal. Put in another way, a Catholicized Protestantism and and Protestantized Catholicism are converging in a new denominationalism centered in a council. It will have executive leadership according to the corporate model, but authority will be dependent on ratification, approval and consent of the council which, in turn, will appeal to subsidiary covenantal groups. Added to this are certain movements, congregations of "freewheeling action" Stackhouse calls them, in a certain way paralleling the sects, but formed and suported by the larger community. Here, it appears a third shift has taken place which allows these groups and movements enough room within the larger Christian community so that they are not marginalized and forced to withdraw. On their part, they seem willing to remain within the Church while at the same time criticizing much of its structure and practice. More will be said about these groups later. But under such an ecumenical ecclesiology, conciliar denominationalism seems to point the way to new structures that will display both stability and change, consensus and dissent, order and freedom, theory and action.[13]

Such a prospectus involves, of course, numerous problems both theological and practical; I do not minimize them. But conciliar denominationalism is based both on a reading of the signs of the times--the ecumenical movement is a fact--and the theological shift in the understanding of revelation and eschatology. It is based on the "coming of age" of the churches in the former "missionary territories" with their demand for a theology of the local church,[14] and at the same time an awareness in all churches that share in the ecumenical movement that the present state of division is an intolerable anomaly. I agree with Lukas Vischer, when he states that whatever convictions local churches may have of themselves, "they all recognize that this task of being a sign of Christ's presence can be fulfilled only in a common effort on which all are agreed. No church can cure this obscuring of the sign on its own."[15]

It has been suggested that conciliar denominationalism flows logically from the understanding of revelation formulated in this study. God has always been available to the human family in diverse ways--indeed, in creation itself. In a unique and definitive way, God was present in Jesus of Nazareth. But God did not cease to be available after this event of ultimate significance. Through the life-giving Spirit of Christ, God continues to be available in the ordinary affairs of men and women. God's presence in power and truth is always mediated and therefore in need of discernment and interpretation. The Church, confident that the Holy Spirit abides within it, yet also aware that the Spirit cannot be confined within its bounds, must be open to the lure of the Spirit, mediated through the signs of the times, to ever-new actualization. The redemptive presence of God within creation--transcending it, but not extrinsic to it--results in the conflation of the natural/supernatural dichotomy and thereby desacralizes the concept of "divine right" in church organization and leadership.

In keeping with our understanding of revelation, conciliar denominationalism does, however, give privileged place to the constitutive writings of the early Christian community (the New Testament) in clarifying and purifying its present ecclesiology. This allows the Church to be comfortable with a unity without a uniformity. It also forces all Christians to take seriously, as denominational conciliarism does, the special role of Peter in the Church. More will be said about this factor later.

The understanding of eschatology developed in this study provides the parameters for a conciliar denominationalism. First of all, our eschatology insists upon the distinction between the Church and the Kingdom of God. The Church is subordinate to the Kingdom and joins with all men and women of good will in laboring for it. Even as it finds in the life, death and resurrection of Jesus, meaning for the present and hope for the future, it must declare this good news through dialogue, it must demonstrate to others through its life and celebration in community a glimpse of the coming Kingdom, and it must dedicate itself to human development so that the obstacles to God's Kingdom may be removed. This understanding places the Church, too, under the eschatological proviso. It conceives election to membership in the Church not a call to privilege but responsibility, and therefore opens its members--especially leaders--and its structures to the Freudian-Marxist critique discussed in Chapter Three. The definition of denominationalism as outlined by Stackhouse and the concept of conciliar leadership appear to be open to such a critique.

Finally, our eschatological stance insists that while the shalom of God's ultimate future cannot be established by us, neither can it arrive without the cooperation of the human family. Therefore, the Church must be passionately dedicated to integral human development. Conciliar denominationalism, especially because it recognizes from the beginning the inevitability of and need for various action groups that can spearhead development projects and prod the Church at large to take more seriously its mandate to work for justice, seems to point the way toward a united Christian effort in development. Stackhouse has pointed out that denomination is by nature reformist rather than revolutionary or acquiescing.[16] The presence and acceptance of various action groups or parties--the built-in provision for a "loyal opposition" within the Church--the realization that diversity within unity is bound to create tensions but that these can be creative as long as dialogue and openness are present, are all qualifications that should provide encouragement for those who want radical change; this should allow them to be effective within the evolving structure. Such qualifications should hasten reform and should prevent, to a great extent, acquiescence of the Church to unworthy powers. A further note on these action groups or parties seems worthwhile.

ACTION GROUPS, MOVEMENTS AND PARTIES
IN THE CHURCH:
DIVERSITY IN UNITY

The attempt to incorporate the best from the polity of the sectarians into an ecumenical ecclesiology is bound to raise certain questions. The history of most sects shows that they either withdrew from the "church of sinners" to form the true "community of saints," or they agitated the larger church to such a degree that they were either marginated or driven out. Indeed, recently Metz has been warning that the great pastoral and theological task for the Church today is to preserve church consciousness from an increasing "sect mentality." This is displayed, he claims, by those who are continually proclaiming their own "orthodoxy" and loyalty to the Church and warning that unless the Church shields itself from the challenges of the world it cannot remain faithful.[17] This is in line with Metz's criticism of the privatization of faith; I agree with it and certainly it is not that aspect of sectarian polity that is being appealed to here. Rather it is that mode of organization which arises among highly motivated individuals in spontaneously formed groups, movements, or parties dedicated to some specific aspect of the Church's mission or determined to pressure the Church at large to do its job better.

As indicated earlier, religious Orders in the Catholic Church performed this function to a certain extent. Their spontaneity was brought under control, however, by the requirement of having to obtain a legitimizing charter or commission from the Pope. It is interesting that, with the first of the social encyclicals of the popes in modern times, RERUM NOVARUM (1891) of Leo XIII, the Church recognized the right of workers to organize in order to achieve certain goals. At Vatican II the Church recognized that what it had been teaching concerning "voluntary associations" ad extra--that is, outside the Church, applied as well to free association ad intra--within the Church. In the CONSTITUTION ON THE CHURCH IN THE MODERN WORLD, we find:

> In our era, for various reasons, reciprocal ties and mutual dependencies increase day by day and give rise to a variety of associations and organizations, both public and private. This development, which is called socialization, while certainly not without its dangers, brings with it many advantages with re-

spect to consolidating and increasing the qualities of the human person, and safeguarding his rights (Art. 25).

Even more importantly, in the DECREE ON THE APOSTOLATE OF THE LAITY, which, overall, could not be described as progressive, we read:

For in the Church there are many apostolic undertakings which are established by the free choice of the laity and regulated by their prudent judgment. The mission of the Church can be better accomplished in certain circumstances by undertakings of this kind, and therefore they are frequently praised or recommended by the hierarchy (Art. 24).

Even though the next sentence warns that no project can claim the name "Catholic" unless it has obtained the consent of the lawful Church authority (shades of the copyright mentality!), still the recognition has been given to voluntary and spontaneous groups within the Church itself. Since the Second Vatican Council, numerous associations, ad hoc groups, and movements have arisen among the clergy and laity within the Catholic Church without specific sanction by the Church's leadership.

Other organizations and movements have arisen with special vigor in recent times. Many of them cut across denominational distinctions without drawing their participants away from membership in their own denomination. The most significant among these is the pentecostal or charismatic movement. It can serve as an interesting "test case" at one extreme for our proposed conciliar denominationalism. Many see pentecostalism as a dangerous movement toward disengagement of the Church from its diaconal mission within the world. There can be no dispute that often such a movement inculcates individualism, or passivity, thus constituting an opiate for social justice, development, and necessary ecclesial structural reform. On the other side, however, those involved in the pentecostal movement argue that they exert a profound but indirect influence on development. The pentecostal movement has made great strides in Third World countries such as Brazil, Chile, Zaire, and Indonesia. By generating among the people, especially the poor, a sense of their importance and dignity in the sight of God, and by urging participants to lead sober, thrifty and pious lives, the pentecostal movement can be a great boost to development in an indirect way. As Dickinson has stated:

> If...the chief obstacle to development is ...that years of colonization, poverty and feudal social structures have alienated the masses from a belief in their own capacity to contribute to, and change history, the pentecostal movements often are capable of contributing a great deal to personal and social development.[18]

Walter Hollenweger, one of the chief proponents and commentators on the pentecostal movement, underlines this same idea:

> What is decisive is not deprivation, but the feeling of deprivation.... The function of sects, from the sociological point of view, lies in the overcoming of this feeling of deprivation (status contradiction, loneliness, poverty, sickness, racial discrimination, speech and language difficulties, handicaps of character, etc.).[19]

Conciliar denominationalism can and must provide a place for such a movement. Admitting the dangers of individualism and withdrawal, conscious of the implicit problems of authority based on spontaneous, charismatic leadership, still the Church must be open to such movements because it cannot determine on some preconceived ideological basis where God may be available or where the Holy Spirit may be active. Such determination has been the error among many of the liberation theologians. It does seem that certain minimal requirements can and should be asked of the pentecostals or any other group or party in the Church. In keeping with the overall mission of the Church, which has been discussed earlier, I suggest the following guidelines for such groups: (1) That they remain open to dialogue with the larger Church, willing to participate in conciliar debate and abide by their consensus decisions. (2) That they remain open in their membership and willing to worship with other Christians. (3) That they admit that their special concern or project does not constitute the whole of the mission of the Church. (4) That they recognize that integral human development has some relationship to the coming Kingdom of God.

It must be admitted, of course, that many of the fundamentalist sects would not agree to any of the above guidelines. The problems are formidable, but even here there are signs of hope. In Latin American, where 80% to 90% of the Protestant missionaries belong to radical evangelical groups distinguished by fierce anti-Catholicism, Buhlmann says that contacts are being multiplied and a certain degree of cooperation is developing.[20]

If the pentecostal movement represents a "test case" at one extreme of these voluntary groups within the Church, groups of revolutionary Christians represent the other extreme. Richard Shaull describes such Christians as "small groups of dissenters who are in but not of the established

order." Juan Luis Segundo speaks of "elite communities of historical engagement." Gustavo
Gutierrez speaks of a divided Church, a Church
that cannot expect reconciliation until the present capitalistic society is destroyed and a new
society, qualitatively different, is established.
The implication seems to be that only those committed to revolutionary transformation in the manner which Gutierrez outlines, are in the "true"
Church.

In each of these examples the criteria outlined above should be applied. I shall limit myself
here to a number of general observations. The
first concerns dialogue. There has been a tendency among Latin-American liberation theologians
to change dialogue into declaration. In other
words, they claim a priori that any theology done
outside of the Latin-American context is so dependent on capitalistic and imperialistic ideology
that it has nothing more to say to them. No
longer will they listen to European and North
American theologians; from now on they will tell
them. Hugo Assmann, one of the radical Latin-
American theologians, announced at the 1973 Geneva
Conference, for example, that "incommunication"
was to take the place of dialogue with European
theologians because they are Europeans.[21] Others,
such as Jose Miguez Bonino, call for dialogue and
suggest that liberation's "new way of doing
theology" opens the possibility for "a fruitful--
though conflictive--dialogue between Northern- and
Southern-based theology.[22] Conciliar denominationalism should provide room and support for the
liberation theology movement, if one may speak of
it as a movement, but it must guard against its
provincial tendencies.

The second criterion concerns common worship
and fellowship. There is a tendency among some
Latin-American theologians to say that because the
Church is in fact divided between oppressors and
oppressed, no common celebration, especially of

the Eucharist, is possible. Once again Assmann
has said that Christians committed to liberation:

> ...find themselves obliged to denounce
> the ideology of a false unity-without-
> conflict in the Church, which is a major
> point of difference between them and
> others in viewing the whole historical
> existence of the Church. They can no
> longer accept that eucharistic conditions
> can automatically obtain in a Church that
> includes oppressors and oppressed.[23]

Gutierrez, as was pointed out earlier, suggests
that many revolutionary Christians share this
view. I submit that the Eucharist, as not only a
sign of unity but a means of achieving unity, must
be celebrated with the humble conviction that what
is impossible for men and women may not be impossible for the Lord. Conciliar denominationalism
presumes--and I am aware of the magnitude of the
presumption--that there would be a mutual recognition of the ordained or official ministry among
the various Christian traditions.

Finally, revolutionary Christians, if they are
to participate in conciliar denominationalism,
should admit that their particular perspective and
goals are neither the only nor the total mission
of the Church. One cannot help but be disturbed
by a statement such as Segundo's which claims that
liberation theology is "theology seen not from one
of the various possible standpoints, but from the
one standpoint indicated by Christian sources as
the authentic, privileged one for the right understanding of divine revelation in Jesus Christ."[24]
Liberation theology claims, of course, to be reflection on revolutionary practice. The implication of Segundo's statement, therefore, is that
the action of these revolutionary groups is the
one, authentic, and privileged way of working for
the Kingdom. There is no question about the obligation of the Church to be on the side of the poor

and the oppressed, but there is a danger if they are identified exclusively by a particular "scientific social analysis."

These comments are not meant to imply that revolutionary groups would be excluded from conciliar denominationalism, but they do point out the need for such groups to submit their views and actions to the test. As the Orthodox theologian Nikos Nissiotis has said:

> There must...be...groups engaged in contestation, shaking the mass of Christians out of their apathy and urging them to accept their responsibilities in the world, reacting against the inertia of the Church authorities and making the members of the hierarchy conscious of the fact that external appearance, prestige and established order are not enough.

He insists, however, as we have, that "they must do it in the Church in the fullest sense of the term and not in any way which tends towards an individualistic, sectarian or anthropocentric extremism which takes its norms from an absolutist political ideology."[25]

A question remains about how to deal with spontaneous groups which arise to meet some special need or champion some specific cause. Theodore Hesburgh suggests employing the "Gamaliel principle" in these cases; it seems worthwhile:

> If this enterprise, this movement of theirs, is of human origin it will break up of its own accord; but if it does in fact come from God, you will not only not be able to destroy them, but you might even find yourself fighting against God (Acts 5, 39).

Hesburgh states further that it is the Holy Spirit who is at the heart of the Church's life, progress and change:

> No one has to be responsible for everyone everywhere and all the time--except God, and he, for all of us in these troubled times, is the Holy Spirit, sent by Our Lord to inspire, guide, strengthen and comfort us.[26]

CONCILIAR AUTHORITY AND INDIVIDUAL DENOMINATIONS: THE PETRINE PROBLEM AND CONSTITUTIONALISM

It was mentioned in the previous section that action groups and movements must be willing to take part in conciliar debate and abide by conciliar decisions. It is presumed, of course, that these decisions would respect the diversity of the various traditions in all but bare essentials. Indeed, what the Second Vatican Council said about lawful diversity within the Roman Catholic communion should be applied to the entire Body of Christ:

> Such a mission requires in the first place that we foster within the Church herself mutual esteem, reverence, and harmony, through the full recognition of lawful diversity. Thus all those who compose the one People of God...can engage in dialogue with ever abounding fruitfulness. For the bonds which unite the faithful are mightier than anything which divides them. Hence, let there be unity in what is necessary, freedom in what is unsettled, and charity in every case.[27]

Lukas Vischer points out the problem with current church councils which are composed of various denominations:

> A Christian Council can only influence the churches in the direction of unity when it is allowed to do so and when the individual churches take joint decisions seriously. Many Christian Councils, however, are debarred in principle from exercising any influence on the life of the churches. All questions relating to unity have been expressly reserved by the constitution of the Council to the churches themselves. The Council is to deal exclusively with external matters which raise no awkward questions about the character, order and self-understanding of the individual churches themselves.[28]

The Roman Catholic theologian Heribert Muhlen has made a bold proposal for an ecumenical council of all Christian churches with genuine binding authority on all. His basic argument is "what must be, can be." It is the same position that I have taken in this chapter. Muhlen states:

> If there is to be a council at all, it must have <u>authority</u>. 'The Holy Spirit and we' must 'decide' (Acts 15, 28). The Great Council will not just declare or plead. In order to mediate among <u>all</u> participants, it must address its binding command to all.[29]

Muhlen admits that it will be especially laborious to find an acceptable formula for the position of the pope in such a council. Without getting into the lively debate which has been going on in recent years on the whole question of papal infallibility and the authority of the magisterium, I shall merely suggest several observations which could at least provide the basis for a solution: (1) In its definition of papal infallibility, the First Vatican Council (1870) declared that this infallibility is the same "with which the divine Redeemer willed his Church to be endowed." As McBrien points out, it is the Church as a community which has been given the Spirit of truth and which cannot fundamentally err in its understanding of the heart of the Gospel. "The Pope is infallible only insofar as he enunciates and proclaims the infallible faith of the whole Church, Catholic and non-Catholic."[30] (2) The Second Vatican Council declared that the college of bishops is the possessor of supreme and full authority over the whole Church.[31] This authority is never independent of the pope, who occupies a position as first among the bishops, but neither is this authority bestowed upon the college by the pope. Once mutual recognition is given the ministry of leadership in the various traditions--this presupposes that apostolic succession is something broader than the so-called "pipeline theory"-- leaders of the various denominations are seen as sharing in this supreme and full authority over the whole Church.

My third observation considers the role of the pope himself. Avery Dulles has suggested that even now the pope could describe his role and function in the Church within parameters that would make his position acceptable to many Christian denominations.[32] Dulles envisions the possibility of a constitutional papacy, one not even vested in a single person or even in the bishop of Rome. He speaks of the possibility of a "primacy of jurisdiction" being replaced by a "primacy of honor." In such an arrangement the pope would preside over "the assembly of charity" and foster collegial relationships among the regional bishops and particular churches.

Yves Congar, who argues that supreme authority in the Church is always collegial, suggests that the Petrine function of the pope might be theologically described as a symbolic or "sacramental" representation--in the pope's official person--of the authority vested in the whole college of ministers.[33] Finally, McBrien, insisting that the Church must willingly demythologize its understanding of the papacy to bring it into greater conformity with New Testament and historical scholarship and contemporary theological reflection, describes the pope's position in this way:

> While he remains the symbol of faith and unity for all the churches of the world, and while his office retains, in principle, the greatest authority for moral and doctrinal utterance, the Pope himself can no longer function as an absolute monarch, embodying in his single person all executive legislative, and judicial power--without limitation, without accountability, without the possibility of correction.[34]

In his book, THE REMAKING OF THE CHURCH, McBrien offers "an agenda for reform" for the Christian community. Although this agenda is aimed primarily at the Roman Catholic communion, many of its propositions could and should become part and parcel of our envisioned conciliar denominationalism. Like Dulles, McBrien calls for the reintroduction of the principles of constitutionalism into the Church--limitation of power, accountability, and openness to correction. He proposes the decentralization of power based on the "time-honored principles of subsidiarity," and he outlines a procedure for the selection of Church leaders based on the ancient canonical principle that "he who governs all should be elected by all." Full and equal participation of women at every level in the Church's life, including ordination to the diaconate, priesthood and the episcopacy, should be instituted. Finally, and perhaps most importantly, McBrien proposes a bill of rights for those within the Church so that the freedom demanded for the Church outside would be insured for those inside.[35] Concerning this last point, the general tendency of liberation theologians to discount internal Church reform as narcissistic ignores that aspect of the mission of the Church which calls it to demonstrate clearly by its own inner life that which it proclaims and for which it works.

The task of the pilgrim Church, as Gabriel Fackre rightly points out, is "to work to shape new, present structures of mission commensurate with persons, powers, and problems that plead for ministration."[36] The task of integral human development of persons and peoples, the task of liberating men and women from oppresive structures and powers, the task of removing those obstacles that stand in the way of a more fully human future, seem to be pleading for ministration. The Church's mission in these areas must be coordinated and structured. "The challenge of the modern world to the Church, and serious reflection on our missionary task, impose on us," according to Buhlmann, "the grave duty...to abandon our introspective and retrospective outlook for a more forward looking and open one...."[37]

Conciliar denominationalism seems to be the sign of the times as far as Church polity is concerned; I suggest the Spirit is luring the Church toward this new ecumenical ecclesiology that will enable it to fulfill its mission as outlined in this theology of development--this new missionary theology.

SUMMARY OF CHAPTER SEVEN

Chapter Seven is an outline for an ecumenical ecclesiology that will facilitate the mission of the Church as reformulated under the aegis of development. It is based on the common faith which Christians share and the realization that the Church today cannot fulfill its mission in the world and be a hopeful sign of the future Kingdom if it continues in its own disunity. Further, it is based on the confidence that the Holy Spirit is calling Christian churches to recognize a "sense of proportion" or a "hierarchy of truths" among their formulated beliefs and teachings.

It recognizes denominationalism as the major pattern of ecclesiastical organization in today's society and pinpoints church polity as the key element which divides the churches. An attempt is made to pull together the best elements of the three major church polities evidenced in the history of the Christian Church: the Catholic corporate, the Calvinist covenantal, and the sectarian spontaneous.

Noting a convergence that is taking place between the corporate and covenantal traditions toward a new denominationalism centered in a council, this new conciliar denominationalism is found compatible with the understanding of revelation and eschatology developed in the previous chapters. Then the legitimacy and value of the sect-like action groups, parties or movements within the Church are explored, and guidelines are suggested for their association with, and participation in, the broader life of the Church.

Finally, the question of the authority and power of such a council, as has been suggested, is briefly examined with special emphasis on the key question of the Petrine ministry. It is suggested that even this problem is not an insurmountable obstacle to an ecumenical ecclesiology--an ecclesiology which would actualize missionary theology as the theology of development.

NOTES ON CHAPTER SEVEN

[1]"What Can We Do to Overcome Unnecessary Polarization in the Church?" CONCILIUM 88 (1973): 122.

[2]DECREE ON ECUMENISM, art. 11. Avery Dulles has said that because of the hierarchy of truths, the Dogma of the Assumption of Mary should not be an insurmountable obstacle to church unity. See Dulles, "Ministry and Intercommunion: Recent Ecumenical Statements and Debates," THEOLOGICAL STUDIES 34 (December, 1973): 643-78.

[3]"What Can We Do?" p. 122.

[4]Ronald Modras, "The Elimination of Pluralism between Churches through Pluralism within Churches," CONCILIUM 88 (1973): 84.

[5]ETHICS AND THE URBAN ETHOS, p. 149.

[6]Walbert Buhlmann, THE COMING OF THE THIRD CHURCH (Maryknoll, New York: Orbis Books, 1977), p. 220.

[7]WHO IS A CATHOLIC? (Denville, New Jersey: Dimension Books, 1971), p. 31.

[8]ETHICS AND THE URBAN ETHOS, p. 143.

[9]See Max Weber, ECONOMY AND SOCIETY, Roth and Wittich, eds. (Totowa, New Jersey: Bedminster Press, 1968), pp. 1164-66, 1207-10; and Ernst Troeltsch, THE SOCIAL TEACHINGS OF THE CHRISTIAN CHURCHES, 2 vols., O. Wyon, trans. (New York: Harper and Row, 1960), 2: 993ff, 997-1002.

[10]ETHICS AND THE URBAN ETHOS, p. 156. The following discussion is based on Stackhouse, pp. 156-58.

[11]DO WE NEED THE CHURCH? p. 227.

REFORMULATION AND ITS IMPLICATIONS :377

12ETHICS AND THE URBAN ETHOS, pp. 158-59. The following discussion is based on Stackhouse, pp. 160-64.

13IBID., p. 171.

14See the comments of Archbishop Picachy at the recent Roman Synod on Evangelization in Chap. Two of the present study, p. 36. Also, Lukas Vischer, "Christian Councils - Instruments of Ecclesial Communion," THE ECUMENICAL REVIEW 24 (January, 1972): 86, comments on the agreement in recent ecclesiological debate on this matter: "Almost all the churches today stress with renewed emphasis the importance of the local Church. The Church always means primarily the congregation in a particular place or in a particular situation, the baptized who come together for the eucharist and maintain fellowship with Christ together.... At the same time, however, they belong to a uni- versal fellowship." Also see McBrien, WHO IS A CATHOLIC? pp. 14-15.

15"Christian Councils," p. 80.

16ETHICS AND THE URBAN ETHOS, p. 156.

17"Prophetic Authority," in RELIGION AND POLITICAL SOCIETY, pp. 202-03.

18TO SET AT LIBERTY THE OPPRESSED, p. 45.

19THE PENTECOSTALS (London: SCM Press, 1972), pp. 465-66.

20THE COMING OF THE THIRD CHURCH, pp. 217-18.

21Referred to by Moltmann in his "An Open Let- ter to Jose Miguez Bonino," p. 57.

22DOING THEOLOGY IN A REVOLUTIONARY SITUATION, p. 62. Enrique Dussel, on the other hand, accuses the Europeans of not listening to the "barbarians' theology" of the Third World. "The voice of Latin America is no longer a mere echo of European theology," Dussel declares. "...We have taken up our stand on the further side of the modern, oppressive, European closed system." "Domination-- Liberation: A New Approach," CONCILIUM 96 (1974): 56. Needless to say, such language does not enhance the possibility of fruitful dialogue.

[23]THEOLOGY FOR A NOMAD CHURCH, p. 139.

[24]"Capitalism--Socialism," p. 105.

[25]"Should there be Parties in the Church in the Future? (A) An Orthodox Answer," CONCILIUM 88 (1973): 93.

[26]"What Can We Do to Overcome Unnecessary Polarizations in the Church?" CONCILIUM 88 (1973): 132.

[27]THE CONSTITUTION ON THE CHURCH IN THE MODERN WORLD, Art. 92. In the CONSTITUTION ON THE CHURCH, Art. 13, the Chair of Peter is said to preside over "the whole assembly of charity and protects legitimate differences, while at the same time it sees that such differences do not hinder unity but rather contribute toward it."

[28]"Christian Councils," p. 77.

[29]"Steps toward a Universal Council of Christians," THEOLOGY DIGEST 21 (Autumn, 1973): 200. Muhlen has made a much more substantial contribution to this discussion in his MORGEN WIRD EINHEIT SEIN: DAS KOMMENDE KONZIL ALLER CHRISTEN: ZIEL DER GETRENNTEN KIRCHEN (Paderborn: Ferdinand Schoningh, 1974). Muhlen hopes for a cleansing and vivifying influence of the charismatic movement on traditional Catholic structures. He states that we may be forced to admit that no such worldwide council can be called now, but he cautions that we must ask ourselves, "Can Christianity continue to

exist without such a binding, authoritative council?"

[30]WHO IS A CATHOLIC? pp. 141-42.

[31]CONSTITUTION ON THE CHURCH, Art. 25.

[32]See the essay by Dulles in A POPE FOR ALL CHRISTIANS - AN INQUIRY INTO THE ROLE OF PETER IN THE MODERN CHURCH, Peter J. McCord, ed. (New York: Paulist Press, 1976), pp. 48-70. This entire volume is valuable as an indication of the present state of the question as far as the papacy in ecumenical perspective is concerned.

[33]MINISTERES ET COMMUNION ECCLESIALE (Paris: Cerf, 1971), pp. 179, 202 (with references to Rahner, Schillebeeckx, Semmelroth, Dejaifve, Rusch, and B. C. Butler). For a brief discussion of this question with ample bibliographical references, see "Papal Primary in a Pluriform Polity," by Paul Misner, JOURNAL OF ECUMENICAL STUDIES 11 (Spring, 1974): 239-61. See also Congar's "Le probleme ecclesiologique de la papaute apres Vatican II," MINISTERES, p. 181.

[34]THE REMAKING OF THE CHURCH (New York: Harper and Row, 1973), p. 92.

[35]IBID., pp. 68-108.

[36]HUMILIATION AND CELEBRATION, p. 282.

[37]THE COMING OF THE THIRD CHURCH, p. 220.

INDEX OF PERSONAL NAMES

ABOUT THE AUTHOR

Edmond J. Dunn, a former Papal Volunteer in Lima, Peru, is chairperson of the Theology Department at St. Ambrose College, Davenport, Iowa, Rector of the College Seminary and Associate Director of the Permanent Diaconate Program in the Diocese of Davenport. Ordained a priest in 1972, Dunn earned his doctorate in Systematic Theology from Boston College, having participated in the Andover Newton--Boston College Joint Doctoral Program. Dunn has a Master of Divinity from both Andover Newton Theological School and Pope John the XXIII National Seminary and a Master in Music from the University of Iowa. Born in the rural Iowa farm community of Oxford, he did his undergraduate studies at St. Ambrose College. Edmond Dunn brings to this study both practical experience of a missionary and the critical thought of an ecumenically trained theologian.

395

ABOUT THE AUTHOR